Eduardo de Filippo
Four Plays

The Local Authority, Grand Magic,
Filumena Marturano, Napoli Milionaria

Eduardo de Filippo was one of Italy's leading popular dramatists, a fearless social critic, a supreme man of the theatre, and a humane and compassionate writer. The four plays in this volume present different facets of his prolific output, which focused on the lives of the Neapolitan people, their dubious cunning nourished by centuries of hunger, their fantasies and their love of life.

Grand Magic: 'De Filippo spins a weird and wonderful play about theatrical illusion and obsessional delusion . . . a compelling mixture of playful comedy, robust humanity and painful emotion, while the final twist raises the hairs on the back of the neck . . . There is a marvellous richness to the play . . . entrancing and constantly surprising.' *Daily Telegraph*

'*Napoli Milionaria* is a leisurely but cunningly organised and deeply felt story of small people caught in a large conflict. The play has an irresistible sense of warm, beastly and unscrupulous life . . . Peter Tinniswood's version is in a Liverpool accent, which proves to be a masterstroke: the dialogue acquires a cocksure swagger and a sense of vigorous, endearing vulgarity.' *Sunday Times*

Eduardo de Filippo was born in Naples in 1900 into a theatrical family and was connected with the stage, as a performer and writer, from his early years. His plays, which have been perf . . . . . y countries throughout the world, include *Nabo . . .* l Theatre, London, 1991), *Too M . . .* 46; Lyric Theatre, London, 1 . . . Theatre, 1995), *Inner Voices* (194 . . . *Monday* (1959; National Theat . . . (1960). He also wrote poetry, . . . ons. He died in 1984.

EDUARDO DE FILIPPO

Four Plays

The Local Authority
Grand Magic
Filumena Marturano
translated by Carlo Ardito

Napoli Milionaria
adapted by Peter Tinniswood

with an introduction by Carlo Ardito

Methuen Drama

METHUEN WORLD CLASSICS

3 5 7 9 10 8 6 4

This edition first published in Great Britain
by Methuen in 1992
Reissued with a new cover in 1998 by Methuen Drama
Random House, 20 Vauxhall Bridge Road, London SW1V 2SA
and Australia, New Zealand and South Africa

The Local Authority (Il Sindaco del Rione Sanita),
Grand Magic (La Grande Magica), and
Filumena Marturano first published in Great Britain in 1976
by Hamish Hamilton Ltd and St George's Press
translation copyright © 1976 by Carlo Ardito
Napoli Milionaria adaptation copyright © 1992 by Peter Tinniswood
Introduction copyright © 1992 by Methuen Drama
This collection copyright © 1992 by Methuen Drama

The translators have asserted their moral rights

A CIP catalogue record for this book
is available from the British Library

ISBN 0 413 66620 4

Random House UK Limited Reg. No. 954009

Printed and bound in Great Britain
by Cox & Wyman Ltd, Reading, Berkshire

Caution

Contents

Chronology	vii
Introduction	ix
THE LOCAL AUTHORITY	1
GRAND MAGIC	95
FILUMENA MARTURANO	173
NAPOLI MILIONARIA	247
Note on adaptation	248

Eduardo de Filippo:
A Chronology

Plays

Farmacia di turno	1920
Uomo e galantuomo	1922
Ditegli sempre di si'	1927
Filosoficamente	1928
Sik-Sik, l'artefice magico	1929
Chi é echiú felice'e me!	1929
Quei figuri di trent'anni fa	1929
Natale a casa Cupiello	1931
Gennareniello	1932
Quinto piano ti saluto!	1934
Uno coi capelli bianchi	1935
L'abito nuovo (with Luigi Pirandello)	1936
Pericolosamente	1938
La parte di Amleto	1940
Non ti pago!	1940
Io, l'erede	1942
Napoli Milionaria	1945
Occhiali neri	1945
Too many ghosts	1946
Filumena Marturano	1946
Le bugie con le gambe lunghe	1947
Grand Magic	1948
Inner Voices	1948
La paura numero uno	1950
I morti non fanno paura	1952
Amicizia	1952
Mia famiglia	1955
Bene mio core mio	1955
De Pretore Vincenzo	1957

Il figlio di Pulcinella   1958
Dolore sotto chiave   1958
Saturday Sunday Monday   1959
The Local Authority   1960
Tommaso d'Amalfi   1963
L'arte della commedia   1964
Il cilindro   1965
Il contratto   1967
Il Monumento   1970
Ogni anno punto e da capo   1971
Gli esami non finiscono mai   1973

Note: English titles are given for those plays which have been translated into English.

Introduction

Eduardo de Filippo was born in Naples on 24 May 1900, and although not actually born in a theatre, he first appeared on stage at the age of four. Playwright, actor-manager and director, he dominated the Italian stage until shortly before his death in 1984, when he had just completed a translation into seventeenth-century Neapolitan of Shakespeare's *Tempest*.

Eduardo, as he has always been known in Italy, was the child of an extra-marital relationship between the noted playwright Eduardo Scarpetta and Luisa de Filippo, a niece of Scarpetta's wife. At the age of fourteen he became a full-time professional actor in Scarpetta's company. From then on his career was only interrupted by military service in 1920, during which he still managed to act, partly through organising and directing entertainments for the troops.

It was in 1920 that his first play, *Farmacia di turno*, had its première, and in 1923 he and his brother Peppino returned to Scarpetta's company. In 1931 Eduardo, together with Peppino and his sister Titina, both distinguished actors, set up La Compagnia il Teatro Umoristico i de Filippo, and opened with Eduardo's play *Natale a casa Cupiello* at the Kursaal Theatre in Naples. Contracted to appear there for nine days only, their stay was extended to nine months, something of a record for an Italian theatre, where long runs are rare. Soon the de Filippos began to tackle more challenging work and their fame spread beyond Naples to the entire country. The three toured extensively throughout Italy for the next twelve years.

Busy as he kept throughout his life, writing, acting and

directing, Eduardo often complained that he seldom had the opportunity to see other writers' plays. He did, however, succeed in snatching enough time off to see performances of some of the plays of Luigi Pirandello, an author he much admired. Pirandello had himself a high regard for Eduardo's work. In 1936, after Eduardo had appeared in leading roles in many of Pirandello's plays, Pirandello proposed that they should write a play together. *L'abito nuovo* was the result of their collaboration. Sadly Pirandello died during the early rehearsals of the play, which eventually opened successfully under Eduardo's direction.

Napoli Milionaria, staged in 1945 with this sister Titina and himself in the cast, saw Eduardo's emergence as an important and mature playwright. There followed *Filumena Marturano*, one of his most successful plays, in 1946. Then came *Grand Magic*, *Inner Voices*, *Saturday Sunday Monday* and *The Local Authority*. There was evidence now in his work of greater social commitment. 'At the centre of all my plays,' Eduardo maintained, 'lies a conflict between the individual and society. That is to say, my plays stem from an emotional stimulus: reaction to injustice, disgust at hypocrisy, compassion for a person or group of people, a revolt against outmoded laws. On the whole, if an idea has no social meaning or application, I am not interested in developing it.'

Eduardo was often questioned on the use of Neapolitan dialect in his plays. His answer was always direct and uncompromising: 'I use dialect as a means of expression, and nothing more. Just as I use standard Italian. The content of the play is what matters, not the words. Devoid of content all we're left with is a mass of inanimate sounds, and if they happen to be in dialect it would just be so much folklore, which I detest.' Though there is still in some Italian theatrical circles a lingering prejudice against the Neapolitan dialect, it is as used by Eduardo quite as comprehensible as the Venetian of Goldoni's best comedies. As Harold Acton pointed out in an appreciation of Eduardo's work: '. . . basically the language is Italian, but it contains a multitude of words and expressions which, if less elegant than the Tuscan, are more highly coloured and to some ears more melodious. It is scarcely surprising that Eduardo prefers to write in his native dialect.' In fact Eduardo offers a natural mix of Italian and easily accessible Neapolitan in most of his plays. Their success in Italy and indeed in translation and performance throughout the world is a measure of the universality of his means of expression.

The Local Authority is on the surface a study of 'alternative justice', but as drama it achieves the stature of tragedy through its unflinching involvement with, and fear for, humanity. Antonio Barracano is an elderly leader of the 'camorra', the Neapolitan mafia. It is to him that the local peasants, artisans and shopkeepers turn when they want advice on how to solve their problems, settle their disputes, borrow money or occasionally, just occasionally, destroy their enemies. Antonio is, in short, the 'Don', the local authority, the man no one can buy, the man who is more reliable than an expensive, possibly fruitless appeal to a corrupt legal system. But the family-loving, impressively fair-minded Antonio is a man of dark shadows himself. When he has to deal with some severity with a wealthy local baker, Arturo Santaniello, a man as proud and violent as himself, he tempts providence once too often. From the opening scene, where a living-room is transformed into a first-aid post in the dead of night by a silent cast, to Antonio Barracano's last supper, Eduardo grips his audience with innate theatricality, fully engaging the emotions as he forces us to consider the nature of justice.

In *Grand Magic* Eduardo's tone is sombre and the subject he tackles more of a puzzler. Calogero di Spelta is a man so jealous that he will hardly let his wife out of his sight. Her lover enlists the help of a seedy magician, and during a performance at a seaside hotel 'Professor' Otto Marvuglia conjures away Calogero's wife, enabling her to elope with her lover and accidentally activating a theatrical box of tricks of rich complexity. Some of the earlier part of the play is devoted to the unmasking of the Professor's grand magic: witnesses to his astonishing feats turn out to be planted colleagues, and his pretensions to occult powers so much make-believe. In the second act the play takes on a more intriguing form. Calogero, accompanied by a police inspector whose aid he has sought, calls on Otto demanding the return of his wife. Otto manages to persuade him that the passing of time, four days in this case, is an illusion, that the performance is still in progress, and that Calogero's wife is in a small portable box which has been in Calogero's possession since the evening of her disappearance. Otto tells him that his wife will reappear only if Calogero opens the box 'in good faith'. At the same time behind Calogero's back Otto quietly informs the police inspector that Calogero's wife has eloped with her lover, whereupon the policeman with true Mediterranean courtesy discreetly withdraws, unwilling to hurt the feelings of a cuckolded husband. Calogero is left alone with Otto, who persuades him that the supernatural performance is far from over. Years elapse, and with Otto feeding his self-deception, Calogero is more than ever determined to play the game out to the end. When finally Otto takes pity on Calogero and urges him to open the box, arranging at the same time for the return and reappearance of his wife who is now seeking a reconciliation, Calogero refuses to comply. He cannot reconcile himself to the fact that his wife has been unfaithful to him. He clutches the box, still unopened, determined to leave it shut for ever. When the play was first staged in 1948 the critics shouted: 'Pirandello!' But while Eduardo himself acknowledged that no contemporary playwright could help being influenced by the Sicilian master, he insisted that *Grand Magic* was not attempting to convey the message of many Pirandellian characters. *Grand Magic*, Eduardo maintained, was not about illusion and reality or the nature of reality itself, it was about faith in one's wife. Like Pirandello, Eduardo admitted that a measure of illusion may be necessary to people to make life tolerable, since the truth is often more than we can bear, but nevertheless he maintained that in this play he was exploring a process of self-deception and of human frailty in a single individual. Unlike Pirandello's Henry IV, who thinks he has found a universal answer, Calogero, the deceived husband, in his pathetic and moving yet determined self-deception has only found an answer for himself.

Filumena Marturano, which he wrote with his sister Titina in mind for the title role, is one of Eduardo's most popular plays and is familiar to audiences the world over. It is being constantly revived in its original form and in various adaptations for stage, radio and television. Wealthy Domenico Soriano took a woman from a brothel to share his home. For twenty-five years she has loved and slaved for him as mistress and housekeeper, with little appreciation from her master and without complaint on her part. Indeed, so great is her pride as measured against her treatment at Domenico's hands that she reminds him she has never once cried or shown her distress during her years with him. When they are both getting on in years and he wants to marry a younger, more attractive and more socially acceptable girl, Filumena takes to her bed and pretends to be dying. She begs Domenico to arrange a death-bed marriage, and he agrees. The ceremony over, Filumena jumps lightheartedly out of bed and Domenico realises he has been tricked – and it is at this point that the curtain rises on the first act. Revelations come thick and fast. Filumena tells Domenico that unknown to him she has three grown-up sons. He threatens to have the marriage annulled and embarks on ludicrously funny legal proceedings. Filumena for her part strengthens the chains with which she binds him by adding another revelation: that he, Domenico, is the father of one of the three sons. She refuses to tell him which one. She will have no discrimination against the other two. Act three sees a transformation in Domenico's character that confers on him a greater human and moral stature. He finally accepts Filumena and her sons and will not insist on being told which of the three is his. They will be treated alike. In the final moments of the play Filumena quietly celebrates her victory by shedding tears of happiness for the first time, as Domenico hastens to comfort her. Eduardo's humanity and moral optimism shine through the entire play. His is not a hollow world, it is a world in which old-fashioned notions are important, where life has meaning and love will prevail.

In *Napoli Milionaria* Eduardo shows us how ordinary people are corrupted, how families are torn apart by black marketeering and mindless self-interest. Amalia, a practical woman of the people, keeps her family afloat during the second world war by her activities on the black market, much to the disapproval of her law-abiding husband Gennaro. 'If it was left to you, we'd all be starving,' says his elder daughter Maria. 'Wrong,' counters Gennaro. 'If it was left to me we'd all be living like honest people.' But despite his misgivings Gennaro goes along with the family and aids and abets them in their activities: in a riotously farcical scene in the first act Gennaro lies on a bed used as storage space for black market goods and pretends to be dead, to hoodwink the police busy searching the house. Following the Allied landings in Naples in 1943, Amalia prospers on the black market. Gennaro himself has vanished, possibly captured by the Germans, missing and presumed dead. Amalia redecorates and modernises their once modest apartment, and a euphoric post-liberation atmosphere predominates in Naples. Her daughter Maria and her girl friends consort with American soldiers. Amalia herself is courted by Errico, her handsome associate in black marketeering for whom she is planning a birthday party. On the night of the party two important events occur. First Maria tells her mother that she is pregnant, and then Gennaro, whom everybody has given up for dead, returns. In ragged clothes he wanders into the room and at first thinks he's mistaken the house, as he hardly recognises the people or the furniture. The party originally meant for Errico turns into one of welcome for Gennaro. But Gennaro is ill at ease with the people around him. They don't want to listen to the story of his vicissitudes in the war. They are bored. They tell him not to brood on past misfortunes. Gennaro leaves the festive table to sit at his sick little daughter's bedside and reflects on his situation. He has been carted off by the Germans and on getting back has found that his son has become a thief, his wife has been unfaithful and made money unlawfully, his daughter has been having an affair with an American soldier, and his younger daughter is critically ill. The war has been responsible for all this. The play ends on a note of redemptive compromise. Perhaps a kind of war is still in progress, but life must go on, as Gennaro concludes in his closing speech: 'All we can do now is wait. We must see the night through.'

The texts of Eduardo's plays have been carefully edited and published over the years thanks in great part to the efforts of his wife, Isabella Quarantotti de Filippo, who has seen many editions of Eduardo's work through the press. Furthermore she has been active in helping and collaborating with translators of her husband's work in many countries, and I for one was not the first or the last to benefit from her generous help. This has ensured that such of Eduardo's work as has been performed and published abroad has preserved the spirit and intention of the original, however much may inevitably be lost in the process of translation or adaptation. Harold Acton once wrote that 'Eduardo's best plays defy the translator's exertions.' Peter Tinniswood in his excellent version of *Napoli Milionaria* refutes this as well as anyone could, as does the continuing success of Eduardo's plays outside Italy.

I particularly wish to thank Sir Richard Eyre for directing a superb production of *Grand Magic* in 1995 at the Royal National Theatre, where it enjoyed a highly acclaimed five months' run.

In contrast to the meaningless and pessimistic world of many contemporary dramatists, Eduardo's message is one of usually undisguised optimism. Given the awfulness of the world he describes in much of his work, his optimism is valid because it is sustained in the face of overwhelming odds, for above all the function of theatre, says Eduardo, 'is the desperate attempt on man's part to put some meaning into life'.

Carlo Ardito
London, 1998

The Local Authority

(*Il Sindaco del Rione Sanità*)

translated by Carlo Ardito

CHARACTERS

Antonio Barracano
Armida *his wife*
Geraldina
Gennarino ⎱ *his children*
Amedeo ⎰
Dr Fabio Della Ragione
Arturo Santaniello
Rafiluccio Santaniello *his son*
Rita *engaged to Rafiluccio*
Immacolata
Vicienzo Cuozzo
Palummiello
Nait
Catiello
Pasquale Nasone
His wife
Peppe'
Zibacchiello
Luigi
Vicenzella

This version was first produced in Great Britain on the BBC
World Service on 9 June 1979 with the following cast:

Antonio Barracano	*Paul Scofield*
Dr Fabio Della Ragione	*Gordon Gostelow*
Arturo Santaniello	*Malcolm Hayes*
Armida Barracano	*Petra Davies*
Rafiluccio	*Paul Gregory*
Rita	*Tammy Ustinov*
Vicienzo	*Sean Barrett*
Pasquale	*Leonard Fenton*
Geraldina	*Frances Jeater*
Amedeo	*Adrian Egan*
Immacolata	*Margot Boyd*
Catiello	*John Gabriel*
Peppe'	*Michael McStay*
Zibacchiello	*Adrian Egan*
Luigi	*Michael McStay*
Vicenziella	*Tammy Ustinov*
Pasquale's Wife	*Frances Jeater*

Directed by *Gordon House*

ACT ONE

(*A light, pleasant living-room on the ground floor of a large house at the foot of Mount Vesuvius, near Terzigno or Somma Vesuviana. The furnishings are expensive and the furniture massively heavy. Through large french windows can be seen lush olive groves and row upon row of vines clinging to chestnut posts, the last in sight being set off against the silvery blue of the Gulf of Naples. It's nearly dawn after a clear early September night.* IMMACOLATA CAMPESE, *in her nightdress, is slipping into a dressing-gown as she enters and walks towards the upstage wall, just as the muffled sound of a bell is heard. The bell rings again and becomes more irritatingly strident as she removes a painting from the wall. In the small niche hidden by the painting is a push-button and an old-fashioned speaking-tube.* IMMACOLATA *presses the button, then puts her ear close to the speaking-tube*)

IMMACOLATA (*listens, then replies*) Very well. (*Walks to a different part of the room, takes another painting off the wall, presses another button. A second bell rings. She talks into another speaking-tube*) Open the gates. (*She lights a candle and hurriedly goes into an adjacent room. After a while she comes back, opens a door leading to yet another room and vanishes. She comes back and goes out through another door*)

(GERALDINA *enters through the door used by*

IMMACOLATA *when she first appeared.* GERALDINA *is the youngest of* ANTONIO BARRACANO'S *children. Temperamentally she is very much like her father; impulsive, generous, proud and resolute, the sort of person who would sooner face a firing-squad than condone injustice. She is attractive, tall and dark. Her well-shaped hands and feet show that she comes of good stock. The look in her dark eyes is disconcerting because of its impenetrability. She has just been woken up and is still sleepy, though in control of herself. Like* IMMACOLATA, *she is wearing a dressing-gown. She piles up her dishevelled hair and puts in a hairpin to keep it in place as she approaches a cupboard. She opens the cupboard and takes out a large square of white muslin and a surgical smock; the former she spreads out on the central table, as if she were laying it for dinner, and places the latter on the back of a chair.* GENNARINO *enters. He is about twenty-three. His hair is tousled and he is wearing pyjamas. A trifle more indolently than his sister, he opens another cupboard and takes out a large rectangular tin box containing surgical instruments, then a chromium-plated steriliser, two large bottles, one containing iodine and the other sublimate of mercury, and a spirit burner.* IMMACOLATA *returns with two white enamel basins, a supply of rolled bandages, a large pack of cotton wool and a pile of white linen towels. From this moment on the three, in complete silence, their movements recalling the precision of parade-ground drill, set about turning the room into an operating theatre. Four sturdy kitchen chairs are used as trestles on which two boards are placed; these are in turn covered with a sheet by the women, while* GENNARINO *places a standard lamp by the side to provide suitable lighting for the makeshift operating table.*

FABIO DELLA RAGIONE, *the doctor, enters. He is about sixty-five. A pleasant man, with an expressive face and very intelligent eyes, though he is cold and fatalistic by nature. He is wearing a pyjama jacket over his trousers. He approaches the table and casts a rapid glance around to see if anything is missing.* IMMACOLATA *helps him into the white smock.* GERALDINA *pours surgical spirit into the basin.*

GENNARINO *collects the instruments from the box and drops them into the basin.* IMMACOLATA *lights a match and sets fire to the spirit, which flares up and floods the four characters with light, casting their elongated shadows against the walls, where they seem to engage in a spectral dance.*

Offstage, from some distance, the muted voices of three men and a heavy, dragging shuffling of feet are heard. The three are PALUMMIELLO, NAIT *and* CATIELLO. CATIELLO *is the Barracanos' porter, utterly devoted to the family)*

PALUMMIELLO (*off*) Holy Mother of God ... Holy Mother of God! (*Puts a hand over his mouth to stop himself from crying out in pain. He has been shot in the right leg*)

CATIELLO (*off*) Quiet ... quiet! We're nearly there.

PALUMMIELLO (*off*) It hurts like hell ... I can't walk!

NAIT (*off*) C'mon, mate ... you'll be all right.

CATIELLO (*off*) Are you a man or a mouse?

PALUMMIELLO (*off*) Let me rest a bit.

(The three stop)

CATIELLO (*off*) Come on, get a move on!

NAIT (*off*) The wound'll go septic.

CATIELLO (*off*) And the doc's waiting.

PALUMMIELLO *(off)* Holy Mother of God, help me! Help me ...

(They start walking again)

CATIELLO *(off)* Don't think about it. Better not think about it.

NAIT *(off)* Think of something else. Sing something ...

PALUMMIELLO *(off)* I daren't sing. Holy Mother of God!

(They enter. The wounded man is placed on the operating table and the expertise displayed is worthy of the most efficient casualty ward. Each attends to his task with quiet competence. IMMACOLATA closes the shutters to the french windows. GENNARINO switches on the standard lamp which provides illumination for the operating table; a shaft of dazzling light falls on PALUMMIELLO, now stretched out on it. GERALDINA hands rubber gloves to the doctor. IMMACOLATA gingerly makes for the kitchen)

FABIO *(to NAIT)* Who are you?

NAIT I did the shooting. They call me Nait.

FABIO *(to GERALDINA)* Syringe.

(GERALDINA picks up a syringe and fills it with the drug indicated by FABIO)

PALUMMIELLO *(cries out in sudden pain)* Holy Mother of God!

FABIO Don't shout. Don Antonio is asleep. *(to NAIT)* So you shot him, you were saying.

NAIT Yes doctor, sir.

FABIO *(taking the syringe from GERALDINA)* What are you doing here?

NAIT Well, you see, it all happened round a quarter to two at the bottom of Via Marina, you know, near the crossing that takes you to San Giovanni a Teduccio if you turn right, and if you turn left to the Pompei motorway ...

PALUMMIELLO (*in pain*) Help me!

FABIO (*phlegmatically*) I told you not to shout. (*To* GENNARINO) Undo his trousers. (GENNARINO *complies and* FABIO *expertly administers the injection*) The pain will soon get better. Geraldina, scissors please.

(GERALDINA *picks up a pair of scissors and begins to cut the wounded man's right trouser leg from the foot upwards. In the basin the flame produced by the surgical spirit begins to die down.* FABIO, *using forceps, selects and picks up from the basin the instruments he needs for the operation*)

FABIO (*to* NAIT) You were saying ...

NAIT Well ... Then we took a shot at each other ... He fired first and missed, you know ... (*Takes a pistol out of his pocket*) This is his gun. (*Shows it around as if to hand it to somebody*)

FABIO (*quickly*) Don't touch it, anyone. Did you pick it up by his side?

NAIT Yessir.

FABIO Then put it back in your pocket. Who do you want to give it to, anyway? Go on ...

(NAIT *puts the pistol back in his pocket*)

PALUMMIELLO (*clenching his teeth in an endeavour to overcome pain*) I was losing blood and was looking for help, but there was no one about. When he realised he'd hit me and I'd fallen ... he just buggered off.

NAIT Was I supposed to wait for the law to come and pick me up? I turned into an alley leading to the railway depot and walked away normally. But the farther I got the louder he seemed to be shouting: Help me! Help me! Then I said to myself: What if I've really hit him bad? What if he bleeds away and dies on me? And he kept screaming: Help me! Help me! That sort of thing, in the middle of the night, gives you quite a turn. And what the hell, when all's said and done we're mates. I tell you, doc, I ran so fast my ticker's still working overtime this minute. I found a cab and went back to find him. I loaded him on the cab and brought him straight here.

PALUMMIELLO I didn't recognise him at first. I just thought he was a stranger passing by. If I'd known it was him I'd have shot him good and proper.

NAIT I couldn't have left you lying there, not knowing how bad you were.

PALUMMIELLO (putting out his hand with an effort) Thanks.

NAIT (shakes hands effusively) Don't mention it, mate. I had to do it. Now all you've got to think about is getting better.

PALUMMIELLO When I'm well again I'll shoot you, and I won't miss next time.

NAIT But why? Are you short of target practice?

FABIO Shut up, both of you. I've an idea the shooting is due to the most stupid reasons.

NAIT No, sir. No. The reason's very important. Now get this, he ...

FABIO (curtly) You're getting on my nerves. I don't want to know anything. (By way of comment on the incident, and extending it to the whole lawless class to which NAIT and PALUMMIELLO belong, adds) What a splendid system: I'm going to shoot you. Right. I'll shoot back. I don't suppose it's your fault. You're just poor ignorant fools.

(IMMACOLATA *enters carrying a tray with a steaming coffee pot, cups, and so on. She serves first the doctor, then the others*)

PALUMMIELLO (*plaintively*) Give me a drop of water...

FABIO   You're not to drink.

PALUMMIELLO (*cries out in pain*) Holy Mother of God!

FABIO   I asked you to be quiet. It's no use feeling sorry for yourself. Why not think about it before the shoot-up?

PALUMMIELLO (*referring to* NAIT) He's a bloody sod.

NAIT   And the same to you.

FABIO (*sipping his coffee*) All right. You're both sods.

NAIT   Do you want to hear why it happened?

FABIO   I'm not interested. Basin, please.

(GERALDINA *has been busy stripping* PALUMMIELLO'S *leg, folding the trouser leg back up to his thigh, and baring the wound. The operation begins.* GERALDINA, IMMACOLATA *and* GENNARINO *act as assistants. They plunge their hands into a container full of disinfectant, then lift them out and let them dry.* FABIO *puts his coffee cup aside, puts on the rubber gloves and plunges his hands in the disinfectant. One of the assistants prepares the cotton wool, another gauze tampons, a third paints the area surrounding the wound with iodine. Then another assistant begins to hand* FABIO *the instruments he requires. Everything proceeds with smooth efficiency. The silent operation will last barely five minutes.*

PALUMMIELLO *twists about but is held down by* GENNARINO'S *strong arms. Whenever* PALUM-

MIELLO *groans or is about to cry out,* IMMACOLATA *promptly places a hand on his mouth*)

FABIO (*operates calmly. He is now about to insert into the wound the instrument which will remove the bullet*) Now the handkerchief.

(IMMACOLATA *produces a spotless white handkerchief, shakes it open and quickly stuffs it into* PALUMMIELLO's *mouth.* FABIO *proceeds with the operation. Absolute silence within. From the nearby main road can be heard the sound of horse bells round the collars of undernourished horses struggling to pull carts overladen with produce to market, and the hoarse voices of sleepy drivers monotonously chanting ancient folk songs handed down from father to son.* FABIO *has now extracted the bullet. After medication,* IMMACOLATA *opens the shutters and then helps* GERALDINA *bandage* PALUMMIELLO's *leg. It's getting lighter out of doors.* PALUMMIELLO *has fainted, but his pulse is strong.* GENNARINO *relaxes his grip on the patient and takes advantage of the respite to sip his coffee*)

NAIT (*anxiously*) How is he?

FABIO (*shows* NAIT *the bullet*) Point twenty-five.

NAIT Mm ... (*As if divine intervention had saved his friend's life*) He should lay it at the feet of Our Lady of Pompei ...

FABIO No. He shouldn't take it to the shrine. I don't think Our Lady of Pompei would like to add yet another specimen to her vast collection of bullets. (*Ironically*) He should put it among the excavations, to show what gigantic strides civilisation has made. Let's take him outside ... a bit of fresh air will do him good. Immacolata, put a chair out. (IMMACOLATA *complies*) Cover him up with a blanket. The moment he comes to, he can go.

PALUMMIELLO *(feebly)* But ... I'd like to talk to Don Antonio.

NAIT So would I.

IMMACOLATA *(firmly, implying that* ANTONIO's *sleep is sacred)* Don Antonio is still asleep!

GENNARINO And the later he wakes up the better.

FABIO *(to* IMMACOLATA*)* Did he go straight to sleep last night?

IMMACOLATA Yes. He didn't say much, but I can always tell the way he's feeling by his gestures. The fireworks started at half past eleven.

GENNARINO There were three competitors: Turrese, Pachialone and the Siberian Dwarf.

GERALDINA *(admiringly)* Turrese was marvellous.

GENNARINO So was Pachialone.

GERALDINA Oh, come, there's no comparison. Turrese was much better. First of all his rockets went up so high that you had to crane your neck till it hurt to follow them, then they burst into fan-like shapes, and then, just as you thought it was all over, there was another burst and then another ... Towards the end he released a few more which exploded five or six times. The three final bangs nearly shattered the windows: I thought the house was going to come crashing down.

IMMACOLATA And Don Antonio just looked on. When a rocket burst everybody looked at him to see the expression on his face, and he moved his head like this— *(She nods, aping one of* ANTONIO's *gestures of approval)* As if to say: Good, that's very good.

CATIELLO But when it came to Pachialone's turn, Don Antonio began to look very cross. And after two or three of the Siberian Dwarf's rockets, he just said: Goodnight! ... as if he thought he wasn't any bloody good.

Just said goodnight to his friends and went to bed.

IMMACOLATA Of course, to show their respect everybody left as well. Must have been around half past twelve. Ten minutes later I went and peeped into his bedroom, as I usually do. He was fast asleep.

FABIO Does that mean he doesn't know about his wife's accident?

IMMACOLATA No. Don Antonio had been in bed for some time when it happened.

FABIO How is she? Have you had any news?

IMMACOLATA They looked after her at the hospital in Naples. They say she had to have twelve stitches.

FABIO Damnation! It would happen the night I came back late from town. I could easily have taken care of her.

GENNARINO Amedeo and I drove her to the hospital.

FABIO Did they keep her in?

GENNARINO No. When they'd finished with her she wasn't really well enough to stand the car journey back here, so Amedeo took her to his place. He said that the moment she felt better, tomorrow possibly, he'd bring her home. Just as well she stayed there, because she wasn't at all well when we left the hospital, then father would have woken up and heaven help us ...

IMMACOLATA At three this morning Mr Amedeo telephoned and said she was feeling better and was having a rest.

FABIO To think that I've warned Don Antonio hundreds of times ... Of course he's so keen on those dogs. He dotes on the wretched things, spends all his time looking after them. He doesn't seem to realise they're dangerous. They're a menace to everybody in the house. Take my word for it, Malavita did it, and he isn't a dog. He's a wild beast.

IMMACOLATA When he opens his jaws wide it's like looking into the mouth of hell ... God, how ugly he is!

GENNARINO I'll shoot the one who did it. Either
Munaciello or Malavita will have to reckon with me.

GERALDINA God help you if father hears you say
that.

GENNARINO When he finds out what one of them did
to mother, he'll dispose of it himself.

FABIO He'll do that all right ...

IMMACOLATA Don Antonio worships his wife. I don't
think the dog responsible is going to get off scot-free.

(*During this dialogue the three men have lifted* PALUM-
MIELLO *and placed him in a chair outside on the
veranda. Having done this, they all strip down the
operating table and generally tidy up the room*)

GENNARINO I think I'll have a shower and get dressed.
I'll drive to Naples the moment I've had some breakfast,
as I'm needed at the shop.

IMMACOLATA I'll see to your breakfast straightaway.

GENNARINO If you'll excuse me, doctor.

FABIO By all means.

(GENNARINO *leaves*)

GERALDINA I'd like some more coffee. (*Goes back to
her room*)

IMMACOLATA What about you, doctor? Can I get you
anything?

FABIO I've just had some coffee.

IMMACOLATA A little later then.

FABIO I'll tell you what, when Don Antonio gets up,
bring me a glass of cold milk when you serve his breakfast. That way I'll keep him company.

IMMACOLATA And a few biscuits...?

FABIO Just as you like.

CATIELLO   I'm off now. I feel peckish, too. My stomach's rumbling. I've got some pasta left over from yesterday. All right for me to go?

FABIO   Go along.

CATIELLO   (*pointing to the painting on the right wall*) If you need me, just ring.

FABIO   Are we expecting many people this morning?

CATIELLO   Not many. There were going to be about ten, but yesterday Don Antonio asked me to put off seven of the ones on the list. He said he comes out here to Terzigno to rest.

FABIO   He's quite right. When I think that in just under three weeks we'll be going back to Naples, I begin to quake. Always at it ...

CATIELLO   It's only to be expected. Don Antonio is a power to be reckoned with in the Sanità district up in town.

FABIO   So he is. There are days when there's a queue outside.

CATIELLO   This morning we're only expecting three. There's Pasquale Nasone ...

FABIO   Who is he?

CATIELLO   Just rubbish. But his case won't take long. The moment he heard that Don Antonio had taken an interest in the matter we couldn't keep him away. There'll be no complications. Vicienzo Cuozzo, the plaintiff, is coming with him. In the end they'll just shake hands in Don Antonio's presence and all will be settled. The third is Rafiluccio Santaniello, the baker's son. His old man, Arturo Santaniello, has the shop in Via Giacinto Albino. Rafiluccio came yesterday and the day before yesterday, and Don Antonio agreed to see him this morning. As you see, it's not going to be one of those full days.

FABIO   Thank heaven for that.

CATIELLO (*pointing at* NAIT *and* PALUMMIELLO) What shall we do about those two?

FABIO Shut the french windows on your way out. Tell them that if they want to hang on for Don Antonio they'd better wait outside.

CATIELLO Right. (*On his way out, to* NAIT) If you give me a hand we'll put our friend out there. (*Points to somewhere in the distance*) He'll get the early sun over there. (*With* NAIT'*s help moves the chair on which* PALUMMIELLO *is resting to the appointed spot, which is hidden from view. A little later he comes back through the veranda and turns to* FABIO) Done. I'm off.

FABIO Shut the windows. (CATIELLO *closes the windows and leaves*)

IMMACOLATA (*enters*) Don Antonio's woken up.

FABIO So early? It's only a quarter to six.

IMMACOLATA He rang three times, and that usually means he's been awake for some time. Oh dear, he's up and about! (*Rushes towards* DON ANTONIO'*s room, but stops dead as she sees him enter*) Here he comes!

FABIO It's been a hot night.

(ANTONIO *appears at the door. He is seventy-five but looks younger, and carries himself in a straight-backed, regal manner. His bronzed skin would set off the healthy white of his eyes but for an instinctive defensiveness which compels him constantly to survey and watch all that is going on around him. The result is that his eyelids are always nearly closed, as though he were permanently in need of sleep. In the rare moments when he opens his eyes wide, the skin puckers up at the sides as he smiles with studied bonhomie; then one detects a spine-chilling inner look which closely resembles the apparently tame glance of an animal saddened by a life spent in captivity. He is wearing a well-cut dark green dressing-gown, under which he is still wearing a white night-shirt, its collar bordered with red piping, as well as old-fashioned long pants tied at the ankles, over naked feet in slippers. On seeing* ANTONIO, *the doctor jumps to his feet and greets him with the hint of a bow.* IMMACOLATA *backs a few paces and hazards a shy smile, though she is very much on the alert, awaiting a word, a gesture on* ANTONIO'*s part indicative of his mood that morning. She wishes to avoid any possible tactical error in her dealings with him.* ANTONIO *returns their greetings with a double nod, then slowly approaches the table and sits down. Long pause during which a silent exchange takes place between* IMMACO-LATA *and the doctor. At length* ANTONIO *looks at* FABIO *for a moment and with a nod points to a chair on the other side of the table.* FABIO *sits down)*

ANTONIO (*massaging one of his feet, addresses the doctor without looking at him*) Did you get up with the lark? (FABIO *and* IMMACOLATA *glance at each other. They have not quite understood which of them is being addressed.* DON ANTONIO, *still massaging his foot, has imperceptibly turned to look at them in his heavy-lidded way*) Immacolata always gets up early. I meant you, doctor.

FABIO   You meant me, of course ...

ANTONIO   Well?

FABIO   There's been a surgical emergency ...

ANTONIO   (*indifferently*) I see.

FABIO   Gunshot wound. Nait and Palummiello took pot shots at each other. (*As if beginning a report*) Towards half past four ...

IMMACOLATA   It was three forty-five ...

FABIO   Was it? Well, no matter ...

ANTONIO   (*lifts his left hand to interrupt the doctor*)

Not now, doctor. We'll talk about it later. (*The doctor puts his right hand over his mouth, and with his left makes a gesture signifying: I'll say no more*) Immacolata!

IMMACOLATA   Sir.

ANTONIO   Bring me the tactless thing.

IMMACOLATA   (*all at sea*) The ... what?

ANTONIO   The straight-talker.

IMMACOLATA   (*turning to the doctor*) What's he asking for? (FABIO *looks just as puzzled*)

ANTONIO   The only thing in this world that tells you the truth: the mirror.

IMMACOLATA   Just like me not to understand. I'll fetch it. (*Goes out*)

ANTONIO   (*after a meditative pause*) No, I'm wrong. There's something else that never lies: death. Man, who belongs to that disgusting, two-faced species called humanity, can swindle his way through life and pretend to be deaf, dumb, blind, paralysed, tubercular, mad ... he can even pretend to be at death's door. And the doctors, including you, have to waste time making the most thorough investigations to establish whether the illness is genuine or not. But when a man's dead, his heart tells the truth: it stops. That's the only time when a doctor can be sure of his diagnosis without fear of error: death has taken place due to heart failure. Am I right, doctor?

FABIO   Oh ... only too right, I'd say.

IMMACOLATA   (*comes back with a mirror*) Here's the straight-talker. (*Hands it to* ANTONIO)

ANTONIO   (*looking into and addressing the mirror*) Charming manners you've got! What are you trying to tell me? So what if I'm seventy-five? Is that a crime?— This? (*Pointing to a deep furrow between his eyebrows*) This has got nothing to do with age. This is called Giacchino; he was the watchman of the Marvizza estate.

Remember him? (*Turns to* FABIO, *his jaw jutting out and his eyelids nearly closed*) Giacchino ...

FABIO He's been pushing up daisies for a long time. Serves him right.

ANTONIO This particular mark was already there when I was eighteen. These other ones (*Pointing*) recall other incidents. Look, doctor, I'll tell you what really gives my age away. If I put my finger on my face and press, there's a hollow there when I take my finger off, as if I'd pushed my finger into a piece of dough. It takes the flesh some little time to even out again.

FABIO (*with conviction*) Let me tell you, Don Antonio, that you have an iron constitution and nerves of steel ...

ANTONIO Let's go into the metal business, then! (*Hands the mirror back to* IMMACOLATA) Here you are. Truth isn't always palatable. (IMMACOLATA *takes the mirror*) Immacolata.

IMMACOLATA Yes sir?

ANTONIO I'll get dressed now.

IMMACOLATA Very well. Won't you have your shower first?

ANTONIO I've had it.

IMMACOLATA (*disappointed*) And you didn't call me?

ANTONIO I really didn't need any help. Besides, I wanted to be on my own. I'll have breakfast first, then I'll get dressed.

IMMACOLATA I'll see to it immediately. (*Leaves the room*)

ANTONIO (*yawning*) In spite of the sleeping tablet you gave me, I hardly slept three and a half hours.

FABIO What I gave you was a tranquilliser. Sleeping tablets aren't good for you.

ANTONIO I need at least five hours' sleep. Three isn't enough.

FABIO You could always take two of my tablets. One before dinner and one after.

ANTONIO I even heard the car drive up to the gates. And Catiello's voice. And everything that went on in here. I suspected it might be a surgical job, but then I knew you'd call me if you needed me.

FABIO It wasn't necessary. It was all very straight-forward.

ANTONIO Did Geraldina help out?

FABIO Yes. Geraldina, Gennarino and Immacolata.

ANTONIO What about Amedeo?

FABIO He wasn't here.

ANTONIO Why?

FABIO He went to Naples.

ANTONIO Strange. Last night, after the fireworks, it got so late he said he was going to stay the night ...

FABIO I'm afraid there was an accident.

ANTONIO An accident?

FABIO Have your breakfast first, then I'll tell you.

ANTONIO Is it that serious?

FABIO Not serious. They'd have called you if it had been. Just rather troublesome. I wasn't here when it happened, and I'm very sorry I wasn't.

ANTONIO (*slightly worried*) Where's Armida?

IMMACOLATA (*enters carrying an oval nineteenth century tray, decorated with floral motifs, on which are a milk jug, two glasses, a kitchen knife with a razor-sharp blade and a loaf of fresh home-made bread*) Here you are sir. (*Places the tray in the centre of the table*) I'll bring the ham and figs presently.

ANTONIO Wait. (*Turns to the doctor*) Well?

FABIO Tell him what happened, Immacolata. You were at home.

IMMACOLATA What do you want me to say?

ANTONIO (*icily*) Has anything happened to my wife?

FABIO Donna Armida was bitten by one of the dogs.

ANTONIO When? (*Takes up the knife and begins to slice the loaf*)

IMMACOLATA (*pouring milk into the glasses*) About one in the morning. We'd all gone to bed. (*Hands the full glasses to the two men*) Donna Armida is always the last. She likes to tidy up the house without people fussing round her ... getting a few things ready for the following day. Anyway, I heard a scream and when I got to her she was more dead than alive. Her dress was all torn and bloodstained. (ANTONIO *listens as if the story does not directly concern him. He dips the bread into the milk and begins to eat.* FABIO *sips his milk*) Gennarino and Amedeo took her to Naples by car, to the hospital. I wanted to call you, but Donna Armida said you weren't to be disturbed, that you needed your sleep.

ANTONIO (*coldly, but obviously affected by the news*) This bread is really good. I tell you, bread and milk is the best possible breakfast one could have.

IMMACOLATA The milk's fresh in from the farm.

FABIO You should have a glass at night, too.

ANTONIO No. Not at night. (*Pause*) Where is she now?

IMMACOLATA In Naples, at Amedeo's house. He took her straight there after the hospital.

ANTONIO Did he telephone?

IMMACOLATA You bet he did. He rang at about half past two and said that Donna Armida was asleep and that the moment she was better he'd drive her back here.

ANTONIO Which one did it? Munaciello or Malavita?

IMMACOLATA She didn't say.

ANTONIO (*after a moment's reflection*) It couldn't have been Munaciello. Munaciello's a sensible dog and is quite attached to Armida. Malavita, on the other hand, is a savage beast. He'd have a go at anyone.

FABIO Those mastiffs are dangerous, you know.

(IMMACOLATA *comes and goes, busy with her chores*)

ANTONIO You had this emergency operation, you were saying ...

FABIO That's right.

ANTONIO What are the circumstances of the case?

FABIO The ones responsible are out there. (*Points to the veranda*) They're two good-for-nothings. Nait and Palummiello. It's not quite clear why they did it. I doubt whether their case will interest you.

ANTONIO Why are they still here?

FABIO They'd like to talk to you. Presumably to settle the matter.

(IMMACOLATA *returns with a portable 'valet' on castors, on which is* ANTONIO's *well-pressed suit, as well as accessories, shirt, tie, handkerchief, shoes and a jewel case containing a gold chain, watch, cufflinks and rings*)

ANTONIO (*assisted by* IMMACOLATA, *takes off his dressing-gown and his night-shirt*) Well, doctor, have you reached a decision?

FABIO Don Antonio, you know me. I'm a straightforward sort of man ...

ANTONIO I asked you whether you had reached a decision.

FABIO Look, Don Antonio, don't let's mince words. I know my departure upsets you. And no wonder. After thirty-five years and more of close collaboration and—dare I say it—of friendship, I can well understand my decision won't exactly please you. It's bound to make your task more difficult, as you've had me to help you all along. Yes, it may be presumptuous on my part, but you're bound to miss me. You needed me in your work, and I'm not forgetting you've devoted two thirds of your life to it. Am I right?

ANTONIO (*aided by* IMMACOLATA, *has put on his trousers, socks and shoes. He notices that* IMMACOLATA *is about to take the gold cufflinks from the jewel box in order to slip them into the shirt cuffs*) Immacolata, how many times have I told you that you're not to do this? Your hands are sweaty and dirty from the kitchen.

IMMACOLATA (*showing him her hands*) My hands aren't dirty!

ANTONIO (*curtly*) Call Geraldina.

IMMACOLATA (*resigned*) Very well. I'll call Geraldina. (*Goes out*)

ANTONIO Yes, you're right. Go on.

FABIO (*with deep-rooted conviction*) I'm tired, Don Antonio, tired of going round in circles.

ANTONIO When are you leaving?

FABIO The day after tomorrow.

ANTONIO By air?

FABIO Yes. I've got the ticket.

ANTONIO (*equivocally*) Hm ... The day after tomorrow is Friday. Do you think it's wise to leave on a Friday? They say it's an unlucky day for journeys. Oh, well, it's your decision. I suppose whichever plane you catch you're bound to be in New York by Saturday at the latest.

FABIO (*suspiciously*) What are you getting at?

ANTONIO Just that it's my duty to have you met at the airport by friends of mine, who will receive you with the respect you deserve.

FABIO (*suddenly sensing danger, turns pale. Pause*) Don Antonio, is that a threat ...?

ANTONIO No, not a threat. A warning. (*With sincerity and convinced of his own impartiality*) You know, doctor, when I go to bed at night and rest my head on the pillow, I can't go to sleep unless my conscience is clear. Consequently if I take certain radical measures affecting a particular person, who happens to be you in this case, I've got to be convinced that I couldn't act in any other way. And then I must warn the party concerned. Do I make myself clear?

GERALDINA *(enters followed by* IMMACOLATA*)* Good morning, daddy! *(Rushes up to* ANTONIO *and embraces him affectionately)*

ANTONIO *(tenderly)* Hullo, sweetheart ...

GERALDINA *(showering him with kisses)* Did you sleep well?

ANTONIO Not too badly.

GERALDINA *(showing him her hands)* See how clean they are? I'll put in your cufflinks. *(Begins to fit the cufflinks into the shirt cuffs)*

ANTONIO Where's Gennarino?

IMMACOLATA He's choosing a tie for you. He asked me which suit you were going to wear and when I told him he said the tie I'd picked *(Shows him the tie)* wasn't at all suitable.

ANTONIO *(pleased)* Gennarino has good taste. I bet you he'll bring four or five ties along presently and ask me to pick one. Then he'll start arguing with me and in the end I'll have to put on the one he likes best.

GENNARINO *(enters with six assorted ties)* 'Morning, dad.

ANTONIO Good morning. Give me a kiss. *(They kiss)*

GENNARINO *(displaying the ties)* Which one would you like to wear?

IMMACOLATA *(pointing to the one she had originally placed on the 'valet')* What's wrong with this one?

GENNARINO A tie is a matter of personal choice. The man who wears it has got to pick it himself, and dad

here has never needed any advice. (*Turns to* ANTONIO)
Which one would you like?

ANTONIO   Tell me the one you like best.

GENNARINO   To tell you the truth, I rather fancy this
one. (*Points to the loudest of the six*)

ANTONIO   Gennarino, I'm seventy-five years old ... when
will you get that into your head? How could I possibly
wear that sort of tie?

GENNARINO   These seventy-five years are becoming an
obsession with you. One could never tell your age by
looking at you ...

ANTONIO   Perhaps not, but I feel it.

GERALDINA   Nonsense! My daddy's still a young man!
(*Puts her arms round him and kisses him as before*)

GENNARINO   In my opinion this is the tie that goes
best with this suit.

ANTONIO   All right, all right, let's have this one and be
done with it. (*Takes the tie chosen by his son, slips it
under the shirt collar and begins to knot it*) What time
are you going off?

GENNARINO   If you hurry up we can go together.

ANTONIO   I'm not going out. I've got things to attend
to here.

GENNARINO   And I've got a lot on in Naples. I've landed
three interior decoration jobs. Newly married couples.
The contracts are signed and sealed and the prices fixed.
I've even had an advance. Shall I tell you how much I'm
making on the deal?

ANTONIO   That's none of my business.

GENNARINO   I bet you'd be pleasantly surprised if I
told you ...

ANTONIO   I'm pleased if you're happy, let's leave it at
that.

GENNARINO   And I'm delighted to see you look so fit
and well.

ANTONIO (*to* IMMACOLATA) Have the dogs been fed?

IMMACOLATA Not yet.

GERALDINA Did they tell you about mummy?

IMMACOLATA He knows.

GENNARINO Dad, with your permission I'd like to destroy the dog myself.

GERALDINA The poor brute!

IMMACOLATA Poor brute my foot! Your mother nearly died of shock!

GENNARINO Look, let me take care of it: a bullet between the eyes and we'll talk no more about it.

IMMACOLATA Amen. I'm sorry though, in a way. I got quite fond of Malavita, but we'll all be better off when he's been put to sleep. Don Antonio, the reason I haven't fed them yet is on account I'd like you to tell me whether I'm to put out two bowls or just the one.

ANTONIO (*to* GENNARINO) The dogs are my concern. You mind your own business. (*To* IMMACOLATA) Two bowls, as you've always done.

IMMACOLATA All right, all right.

(ANTONIO *is now fully dressed.* GERALDINA *hands him his gold watch, chain and various rings*)

GERALDINA (*admiringly*) Oh, daddy, you look so handsome! (*Embraces him and kisses him*) When people ask me when am I going to get married, I say to them: Where am I going to find a man like my father? (*Has picked up* ANTONIO's *slippers, folded up his dressing-gown and now takes them back to* ANTONIO's *room*)

(IMMACOLATA *clears the table, and* GENNARINO *leaves the room to put the remaining ties away*)

FABIO (*quietly*) Don Antonio, you were saying ...

ANTONIO Regarding your departure?

FABIO Yes.

ANTONIO Now, doctor, you are as free to go on living
all the years that God Almighty granted you, as you are
to put an end to your days here and now. If you decide
to leave, you have Antonio Barracano's word for it, you'll
put an end to your days rather prematurely. (FABIO
registers fear) You call this a threat? Hm ... You've been
close to me for so many years ... You know my nature ...
How can you possibly think that? Threats are useless
as a rule. A man threatens another to gain some advantage over him. If he fails to get what he wants, more
often than not he doesn't bother to act on his threat,
and everything stays the same. Or rather, not exactly
the same as before: the man who was threatened and
did not give in cuts quite a heroic figure, while the other
confirms himself as a big mouth and nothing else. I have
made my decision. It's up to you to make yours. As you
see I am not issuing a threat. Just a warning.

FABIO Haven't you had doubts on the validity of the
work we've been doing for the past thirty-five years ...
Doubts that could make you change your mind?

ANTONIO (thinks it over for a moment) Hm ... Yes, I
have. You'll have to explain to me what you meant by:
I'm tired of going round in circles ...

FABIO (looks fixedly at ANTONIO with a pained expression. Then decides to unburden himself) At long
last it's come to me, Don Antonio. I've just realised what
we both are: I am a stupid hanger-on and you are a
raving madman.

ANTONIO What did you say I was?

FABIO (exasperated by ANTONIO's apparent calm) A
raving, deluded madman! That's what you are. I was
unlucky enough to meet you at the age of thirty-two and
to believe in you. I followed you round like a dog, I
helped you, and what have I got to show for my pains?

I am sixty-four, I'm going senile and I haven't a single illusion left. Thirty years is a lifetime, you know, a whole lifetime, and we've spent it shielding a network of criminals who are a disgrace to our country. We've risked going to jail, you and me, not once but hundreds of times, and what for, I ask you? For the sake of protecting the most despicable, abject scum ... They're the sores of society ...

ANTONIO   You mean they're the victims of society. That's what you should be calling them.

FABIO   Victims?

ANTONIO   Yes. They're poor ignorant underdogs, and society knows only too well how to exploit them. My dear doctor, the whole grasping machine of what you call society revolves round and is fed by the crimes and felonies committed by these poor devils. Oh yes, the ignorant underdog is as valuable as stocks and shares. He pays dividends. Put one of the poor bastards beside you, and you're in clover for the rest of your life. But the underdog's got wise to the system. He knows that he can't get anywhere without money and connections. He says to himself: If I go to court to settle my case, even though I'm in the right, what if the other side's got money, the right connections ... and three or four paid witnesses? Because, as you know only too well, witnesses are to be had for the asking. Provided the price is right they'll testify to anything. There's scores of them touting for business outside the courthouse. 'Do not bear false witness'. That's what our Lord Jesus Christ said. If He went out of his way to urge it, you can bet your life it was big business in his day as well. And it's going on now, doctor. (*Impersonating the severe voice of a magistrate*) 'Swear now to tell the truth, the whole truth and nothing but the truth.' And the four hired witnesses merrily swear. Ah, you'll say, but our man can accuse them of perjury. Oh, yes? But where's the proof? There's never any proof or evidence, or if there had been it's long since vanished, because money works wonders ... So the poor sod is duly convicted and in addition gets summonses for defamation of the witnesses' characters. Why should he go through all that? Far better for him to go right up to the other fellow and deal with the matter himself. True, he'll go to jail all the same, but at least he'll have had the satisfaction of knowing that the other fellow's safely dead. (*Pause*) What about me, doctor, eh? Am I not a murderer? What about Giacchino, the watchman out at the Marvizzo estate? Didn't I bump him off? Do you know why I did it?

FABIO   No. And what's more I never asked you.

ANTONIO   You must believe me when I tell you I had right on my side. I was perfectly justified in doing what I did. The man had to die. I provided a watertight alibi and produced eight phoney witnesses. Self-defence, just as simple as that. I was acquitted, I've got a clean record to this day and I've even got a firearm permit.

FABIO   What are you getting at?

ANTONIO   I was just pointing out that for those with money and connections it's all plain sailing.

FABIO   And for those who haven't any? Do they perish in the storm?

ANTONIO   No. They come to me.

FABIO   And yet no matter how much we try to settle things for them, they still go on slaughtering each other.

ANTONIO   You're forgetting how many killings and crimes we've prevented.

FABIO   But what you've undertaken is on too large a scale ... Besides, I'm tired of mending broken heads, stitching up stomachs, pulling out bullets from legs, arms, shoulders ... (*Begins to lose control of himself. A nervous tremor begins to affect his right arm and slowly*

*communicates itself to the rest of his body. His voice
rises in pitch till it becomes typical of a man in the grip
of an attack of hysteria*) I've paid dearly for the doubtful
privilege of knowing you. You've kept me by your side
for thirty years like a prisoner or a hostage. It's the third
time my brother's paid for my ticket. He wants me to
join him in America, to lead a quiet, dignified life of
retirement. It's the third time you've blocked me. Why
not be done with it and have me killed right here rather
than in the States? (*Opens out his arms and thrusts out
his chest*) Go on, kill me, that'll be another problem
you've settled! (*Shouting*) I was a respectable doctor.
My father, Oreste Della Ragione held the Chair of
Medicine at the University of Naples for forty years.
(*Stamps his foot and bursts into tears like a child*) I've
brought shame on his name ... I'm a disgusting creature,
a stinking sewer ... (*Staggers and collapses, luckily on a
chair*) I'm all fucked up! That's what I am.

GERALDINA (*rushes in, alarmed*) What's happening?

(IMMACOLATA *also enters*)

GENNARINO (*enters*) What's all the commotion about?
FABIO (*his teeth chattering, finds it difficult to articulate*) I've g-got to get to b-bed. (*Feels his own pulse*) In
ab-bout f-five minutes I'll g-go down with a t-tempera-
ture ...
IMMACOLATA (*full of concern*) Oh, doctor ...
GENNARINO Would you like a glass of brandy?
FABIO J-just get my b-bed ready and a hot w-water
bottle. (IMMACOLATA *leaves the room*) Take m-me to
my r-room. (GERALDINA *and* GENNARINO *lead him
out of the room*)
ANTONIO (*has been looking on impassively and now
firmly drives his point home*) If you're going to be ill it

would be very unwise for you to set out on a long trip so soon.

FABIO   I s-suppose you're right.

ANTONIO   Still, you'll get better soon. Will you leave then?

FABIO   (after a short pause) I don't know. J-just now I've got to g-get over this attack. (Leaves the room with GERALDINA and GENNARINO)

CATIELLO   (enters unobtrusively through the french windows) Don Antonio, if it's convenient ...

ANTONIO   Who is it?

CATIELLO   We've got Pasquale Nasone, Vicienzo Cuozzo and Rafiluccio Santaniello with a girl.

ANTONIO   Rafiluccio Santaniello?

CATIELLO   The baker's son.

ANTONIO   Oh, yes. Who else?

CATIELLO   We've also got Nait and Palummiello. They'd like a word with you.

ANTONIO   (to GERALDINA, who has just come in) Geraldina ...

GERALDINA   Yes, daddy?

ANTONIO   Get me the file on the Cuozzo Nasone case.

GERALDINA   (takes a bundle of files from a cupboard, sits down at the table and looks for the appropriate folder, running through the names) Nasone, Nasone, Nasone ... Cuozzo, Cuozzo, Cuozzo ... where on earth is it?

ANTONIO   (to CATIELLO) Show them in.

CATIELLO   The whole lot of them?

ANTONIO   Yes.

CATIELLO   Right. (Goes out through the french windows)

GERALDINA   (has tracked down the file) Here it is.

ANTONIO   What's it all about?

GERALDINA   It's an IOU for three hundred thousand

lire endorsed to Pasquale Nasone and drawn on Vicienzo Cuozzo.

ANTONIO Yes, I remember now. A little matter of ten per cent interest a week, turning into forty per cent after a month.

GERALDINA That's right.

ANTONIO What's Rafiluccio Santaniello's trouble?

GERALDINA There's nothing in writing about him. He's never been to you before.

ANTONIO And ... Nait and Palummiello?

GERALDINA They're the two in this morning's shooting.

ANTONIO Yes, yes ... I see. But why come to me after the shooting?

CATIELLO Come along in ... (*Opens both french windows and shows in* VICIENZO CUOZZO, PASQUALE NASONE, NAIT, PALUMMIELLO, RAFILUCCIO SANTANIELLO *and* RITA AMOROSO. *The girl is poorly dressed, in rags in fact, which makes her obviously advanced pregnancy more pitiable. She is cadaverously pale and signs of malnutrition are evident. Luckily she can still force a smile, and smile she often does, as if to stop people feeling sorry for her. She is unsteady on her legs, but* RAFILUCCIO, *a handsome lad though in as miserable a situation as she is, supports her lovingly.* VICIENZO, *a cabinet-maker, is soberly dressed, and looks downcast and bitter. On entering he takes his hat off and turns to* ANTONIO)

VICIENZO Your servant, Don Antonio.

PASQUALE (*an utterly amoral man. Something between the owner of a gambling den and a brothel keeper. Dresses showily and displays much jewellery. He assumes a servile, cringing demeanour towards* ANTONIO) Your very humble servant, Don Antonio.

RAFILUCCIO Good morning, Don Antonio.

ANTONIO (*has acknowledged each greeting with a nod*)

You must be Rafiluccio Santaniello.

RAFILUCCIO Yes, sir. (*Pointing to* RITA) My fiancée.

ANTONIO (*after a pause, during which he takes in* RITA's *swollen stomach and suppresses an expletive*) Hm ... If you wait any longer you'll have a wedding and a christening on the same day.

RAFILUCCIO (*happily*) How right you are!

ANTONIO So you wanted to see me.

RAFILUCCIO To tell you the truth my problem is very complicated, and ...

ANTONIO I see, one of those. I tell you what: take your girl for a walk. I'll have you called in a little while.

RAFILUCCIO Just as you please, Don Antonio. (*To* RITA) Come along. (*They go out*)

ANTONIO Let's see Nait and Palummiello.

NAIT Sir!

PALUMMIELLO Here I am.

ANTONIO Sit down, both of you.

NAIT Sir! (*Sits down a little way off with* PALUMMIELLO)

ANTONIO (*to* PASQUALE NASONE) What's your news?

PASQUALE Oh, the usual things. My sister's had another baby ... making it six in all: two boys and four girls.

ANTONIO Providence will doubtless look after them all.

PASQUALE Amen. We can't complain.

ANTONIO (*pointing to* VICIENZO) Well, now, shall we see whether we can settle this little matter?

PASQUALE What exactly?

ANTONIO Vicienzo has children as well.

VICIENZO I've got six.

PASQUALE No doubt providence will look after them too.

ANTONIO Look here Pasquale, I'm a man of few words

and I won't beat about the bush. This is the way matters stand: the other day I went into town to do some shopping. I bumped into Vicienzo here. I knew his father well, a gentleman if ever there was one, and a great friend of mine. To make a long story short Vicienzo told me he was facing ruin and destitution, and all because of an IOU for three hundred thousand lire, on which he had been paying thirty thousand a week interest for the past seven months. He quite simply told me that his only way out was to shoot you dead.

PASQUALE Shoot me dead?

VICIENZO (*quivering with despair*) He's ruined me all right, Don Antonio ... me and my family. I don't even earn thirty thousand a week, believe me. I've been paying up for seven months ... and I still owe him the three hundred thousand. And my kids are starving! This swine is quite merciless. I can't tell you what we go through at the end of each month! My wife's even had to sell our mattresses. I had a suit, a new one for Sundays ... I've even had to sell that!

PASQUALE Frankly I don't understand you. When you needed the money you borrowed it gladly enough. Didn't you know that you had to pay it back? If you'd returned it within a week you'd have been laughing: a loan of three hundred thousand would only have cost you thirty thousand. I'm afraid, Don Antonio, some people don't know how to run their affairs.

VICIENZO I had to borrow the money to pay for my daughter's operation and hospital bills.

PASQUALE All right, but unless you pay me back I'll be in queer street myself. I've got a family to support as well.

VICIENZO God, what a bloody hypocrite you are! You've got yourself a new car through letting rooms by the hour, if you know what I mean, and your wife even receives her clients in the house when you're in.

PASQUALE   First return the money you owe me, then we'll have a little chat on morality.

ANTONIO   Well, shall we bring matters to a close?

PASQUALE   To a close? You say this fellow wants to kill me. Ask him if he feels like spending the next thirty years in jail.

ANTONIO   That's what he said the other day. But he changed his mind, and last night he called on me to tell me about a change of programme.

VICIENZO   (*dumbfounded*) I ... called on you yesterday?

ANTONIO   (*coldly*) You be quiet. Last night you came here and brought me the three hundred thousand lire you owe this man.

VICIENZO   (*more astonished than ever*) I...?

ANTONIO   We were saying that Vicienzo brought and lodged with me the sum of three hundred thousand lire.

PASQUALE   Forgive the interruption, Don Antonio, but why didn't he give me the money?

ANTONIO   Because he finds he cannot possibly afford to pay the interest due for the past month, consequently he asked me to put in a good word for him. If you bear in mind that in seven months your three hundred thousand brought you in eight hundred and forty thousand in interest, and if you are the charitable, humane fellow I take you to be, I feel sure you'll cut your losses and call it quits.

PASQUALE   (*pacified and pleased at the prospect of collecting the money*) How could I say no to Don Antonio Barracano? Your wish is my command.

ANTONIO   Have you brought the IOU along?

PASQUALE   I've got it right here. (*Takes it out of his wallet and displays it*)

ANTONIO   (*delicately takes it from him*) I'll referee the whole transaction.

PASQUALE I'll go along with that.

ANTONIO I hope you won't mind if it's all in ten thousand notes ...

PASQUALE Not a bit. I've got a poacher's pocket right inside here.

ANTONIO That's fine. Geraldina, my sweet little darling, open the drawer.

GERALDINA Which drawer, daddy? (*The table has no drawers*)

ANTONIO This one, my sweetheart. (*Pretends to open an imaginary drawer at the centre of the table*) Here we are, here are three bundles of one hundred thousand lire each. (*Pretends to take out the three bundles*) One, two and three. (*Places the imaginary bundles on the table and turns to* PASQUALE) I'm afraid I haven't counted it. Would you be kind enough to do so yourself, in my presence?

PASQUALE (*hasn't yet got the drift and stares at* ANTONIO, *uncertain whether to doubt his own or* ANTONIO's *sanity*) What am I supposed to count, Don Antonio?

ANTONIO This money.

PASQUALE (*as if to say: Let's cut all this out!*) But Don Antonio, really ...

ANTONIO I said count it. (*With a steely gaze at* PASQUALE)

PASQUALE (*both terrified and fascinated by* ANTONIO's *hypnotic look, realises that his only way out is to count the imaginary sum. Under* ANTONIO's *watchful eyes, and the amused looks of the others,* PASQUALE *pretends to count thirty ten-thousand lire notes*) One, two, three, four, five, six, seven, eight, nine, ten ...

ANTONIO That's one hundred. Count on.

PASQUALE One, two, three, four, five, six, seven, eight, nine, ten.

ANTONIO   Two hundred. Count on.

PASQUALE   One, two, three, four, five, six, seven, eight, nine, ten.

ANTONIO   Three hundred. All in order?

PASQUALE   Yes sir.

ANTONIO   Shake hands and let there be peace between you.

VICIENZO   It's all right by me. (*Puts out his hand to* PASQUALE)

PASQUALE   By me too. (*Shakes hands with* VICIENZO)

ANTONIO   Good.

PASQUALE   I'd better be on my way ... (*Begins to walk out*)

ANTONIO   Are you going to leave the money behind? Go on, take it, take it.

PASQUALE   Really, Don Antonio ...

ANTONIO   I said: take the money.

(PASQUALE *goes up to the table, pretends to take the three bundles of notes, then slowly leaves the room*)

ANTONIO   (*picks up the IOU from the table and shows it to* VICIENZO) Is this the IOU?

VICIENZO   Yes sir.

ANTONIO   We may as well tear it up. (*Tears it up*)

VICIENZO   (*beside himself with joy and at a loss for words to express his gratitude*) Don Antonio, may you live to be a hundred. You've saved my life ... my family ... (*Kneels in front of* ANTONIO, *takes one of his hands in his and kisses it repeatedly*) These are the hands of a saint, I tell you! (*Still not satisfied, bends his head, clutches* ANTONIO's *feet and kisses them*)

ANTONIO   Who do you take me for ... St Peter?

(GERALDINA *and* CATIELLO *tear* VICIENZO *away*)

VICIENZO (*moved to tears*) Don Antonio is our father! He's father to the whole of Naples! And we all want you to know we love you, we worship you!

CATIELLO (*escorting* VICIENZO *out of the room*) Don Antonio has got the message. Off you go now.

GERALDINA (*echoing* CATIELLO) Father's got a lot to do. Other people are waiting for him.

VICIENZO (*repeats, just before being pushed out of the room*) We worship you, Don Antonio! (*Then goes out, though he is still heard shouting with fanatical fervour once or twice in the distance*) Don Antonio is our father! He's everybody's father!

ANTONIO Let's get on. (*To* GERALDINA) Who's next?

GERALDINA (*scanning the files*) Santaniello.

NAIT We're still here.

ANTONIO Who are you?

NAIT Nait.

ANTONIO (*notices* PALUMMIELLO, *who is approaching him with a limp*) You're the one who's been shot in the leg?

PALUMMIELLO Yessir, Don Antonio. Palummiello's the name.

NAIT I hang around the port, you see. When a party of sailors lands I make myself known and if I find the right type I take him up to the 'Colorado', the nightclub in Via Marina. Now my health's not been so good ... you know what it is to be out at all hours, in the wet ... I've been laid up for three weeks with bronchitis and pneumonia. (*Points to* PALUMMIELLO) This cheating sod asked the management at the 'Colorado' to give him my job. Don Antonio, I've got to earn a living.

PALUMMIELLO I didn't ask them. They asked me.

ANTONIO (*to* PALUMMIELLO) Which district do you belong to?

PALUMMIELLO Montecalvario.

ANTONIO *(to* NAIT*)* And you?

NAIT Yours. Sanità.

ANTONIO *(to* NAIT*)* Have you got the gun on you?

NAIT Yessir.

ANTONIO Put it on the table. (NAIT *complies*) We're dealing with two separate offences in this case. One committed by Palummiello against Nait. (*To* PALUMMIELLO) The 'Colorado' is in his district. Don't you ever trespass again. He's got a living to earn. Understood?

PALUMMIELLO Yessir.

ANTONIO Shall I have you watched?

PALUMMIELLO No need to, sir.

ANTONIO But the other offence, surely that was Nait's ... and aimed at me.

NAIT *(worried)* Look, Don Antonio ...

ANTONIO Palummiello trespassed, inasmuch as he worked a territory not his own, but this transgression doesn't give you the right to take pot shots at him. You belong to the Sanità district: why didn't you come to me first? And why didn't you take him to a hospital afterwards? Were you afraid of the law?

NAIT No sir. Because if he wants satisfaction ...

ANTONIO *(interrupting)* You mean you'll let him have another go at you? Where will this madness end? Don't you know that life is sacrosanct? I shoot you, you shoot me ... then we'll have brothers, brothers-in-law, fathers, uncles ... there'll be a massacre, out and out war! Now just you listen: don't ever do this again or I'll have you jailed. You belong to the Sanità district, don't forget that. And if you should go to jail, I'll make sure you're not even given a glass of water once you're inside, not even a clean handkerchief. I'll let you rot in there. The incident between you is closed. Shake hands. (NAIT *and* PALUMMIELLO *look at each other for a moment, then shake hands affectionately*) As for you ... (*Slips off a heavy signet ring from his right hand and holds it in his left)*

NAIT Were you talking to me?

ANTONIO *(suddenly and rapidly slaps* NAIT *with sufficient force to take his breath away)* And next time you go independent and start shooting you may as well forget the name of Antonio Barracano. But if you should happen to remember it before you get it into your stupid head to use your gun, come and ask my permission first. *(Takes the pistol from the table and hands it to* NAIT) Take this gun and get out.

(Still somewhat stunned, NAIT *takes the pistol from* ANTONIO. PALUMMIELLO *notices that* NAIT *isn't steady on his legs and props him up. The others follow the scene holding their breath)*

PALUMMIELLO *(after a pause, in a whisper to* NAIT) Shall we go? *(Without waiting for* NAIT's *answer pushes him towards the exit)*

*(*NAIT *allows himself to be pushed, as if he were dreaming.* ANTONIO *seems utterly unaffected by the scene and hardly notices.* NAIT *is about to go out through the veranda when he turns towards* ANTONIO *and looks at him.* PALUMMIELLO, *on the alert, watches his friend's every move)*

NAIT *(slowly lifts his right arm as if he were about to point his pistol at* ANTONIO, *then turns the weapon towards himself as if to examine it, and appears lost in thought. Presently he pockets the pistol and turns to the assembled company with the hint of a smile)* Goodbye, everyone! *(Goes out, followed by* PALUMMIELLO)

ANTONIO Call Santaniello.

RAFILUCCIO *(comes in through the veranda, with* RITA) Here I am, Don Antonio.

ANTONIO   Sit down and tell me this complicated story of yours.

RAFILUCCIO   Thank you. (*Pulls out a chair for* RITA, *then sits down in another chair next to her*)

ANTONIO   Well?

RAFILUCCIO   You don't remember me?

GERALDINA   I do. Your father's got the bakery in Via Giacinto Albino ...

RAFILUCCIO   He's got two shops now ...

GERALDINA   He's expanded.

RAFILUCCIO   The shop in Via Giacinto Albino is still the same, but the one he opened two years ago in Via Roma is ultra-modern. It's got two entrances. He does very good business. He's got the best clientele in Naples.

GERALDINA   The school I used to go to was in Via Giacinto Albino, and in the morning I always used to buy a roll for my tea at your shop. Remember me?

RAFILUCCIO   Of course I do.

GERALDINA   What's happened to that lovely dark-haired lady who used to serve behind the main counter, the one with the pretty gold necklace?

RAFILUCCIO   That was my mother. She died when I was six. You know how bad the air raids were in the war ... She had a bad heart and couldn't stand being cooped up in the shelter. We lived on the first floor, and the block next to ours was hit by three bombs ... a splinter flew in through the window and killed her instantly.

GERALDINA   I am sorry!

ANTONIO   Shall we get to the point?

RAFILUCCIO   Don Antonio, I'd like to talk to you in private. The matter is very delicate.

IMMACOLATA   (*enters*) Madam's back. Donna Armida's back.

GERALDINA Mummy's here, how wonderful! (*Jumps to her feet and rushes towards the veranda*) Mummy!

(ARMIDA *enters with her son* AMEDEO. *She is about forty-five, still attractive. She is pale and her eyes are red with recent sleep. A woollen cardigan on her shoulders, she has fixed her hair hurriedly with tortoiseshell combs. Her chest is bandaged up to her left breast*)

ARMIDA (*visibly moved at* GERALDINA'S *greeting*) Hello darling! (GERALDINA *is about to embrace her mother but* ARMIDA *stops her with a gesture*) Please don't, darling ... (GERALDINA *understands and backs away*) It hurts terribly just at the moment. (*Points at her left breast, then notices her husband*) Antonio!

ANTONIO Armida ... What on earth have you done to yourself?

IMMACOLATA She's as white as a sheet!

AMEDEO She had to have twelve stitches. (*Goes up to his father*)

ARMIDA That's right, Antonio. (*Fights back tears and forces herself to smile to cheer him up*)

AMEDEO We've got Malavita to thank for this.

GENNARINO (*has just come in with the others*) Look, dad, with your permission I'll destroy Malavita. (*Pulls a pistol out of his pocket*)

AMEDEO If you don't mind, I'd rather claim that privilege. (*He also takes out a pistol*)

ARMIDA (*with maternal concern*) Mind you don't hurt yourselves with those guns ...

ANTONIO Just a moment. First, Armida, there's one thing I must know. As for Malavita, there's only one gun that'll deal with him, and that's mine. Now, where was it that Malavita attacked you? In your own room?

ARMIDA   No.

ANTONIO   When did it happen?

ARMIDA   It was about one in the morning. I was collecting eggs from the chicken coop.

ANTONIO   My dear, tell me how much I love you ...

ARMIDA   Very much.

ANTONIO   And do you love me?

ARMIDA   How can you ask such a question ...

ANTONIO   I know it must have hurt you terribly last night, and it's hurting still, but tell me: who do you think is in greater pain at this very moment, you or me?

ARMIDA   You.

ANTONIO   And the scar on your breast, where do you think I'll carry that?

ARMIDA   On your heart.

ANTONIO   Malavita's a watchdog. He watches over the house, the family and even over the hens. It was you who caused the accident. (*To his sons*) Put those guns away. (AMEDEO *and* GENNARINO *obey*) The dog was in the right. (*No one says a word, and* ARMIDA *appears to accept* ANTONIO's *verdict*) How are you feeling now?

ARMIDA   (*making light of the whole thing*) Better. But I think I'll go and lie down all the same.

IMMACOLATA   Come with me, I'll bring you a nice bowl of soup in bed.

(*They all escort* ARMIDA *to her room*)

ARMIDA   (*on her way out*) They told me at the hospital I'm to have anti-rabies injections.

AMEDEO   No, I don't think you'll need to. All we have

to do is produce a certificate from the vet stating that the dogs are healthy.

(They have all left the room, except ANTONIO, RAFILUCCIO *and* RITA*)*

RAFILUCCIO   Don Antonio ...

ANTONIO   Listen boy, I am sorry, but as you can see today isn't really going to be convenient. Come back tomorrow.

RAFILUCCIO   Forgive me, Don Antonio, but the matter is both urgent and serious.

ANTONIO   It'll keep for twenty-four hours, surely. *(Is about to leave)*

RAFILUCCIO   Don Antonio, tomorrow I must kill my father.

ANTONIO   *(stops within a step of the door, turns to* RAFILUCCIO *and stares at him incredulously. Pause)* I didn't quite catch that.

RAFILUCCIO   *(detached)* Tomorrow I must kill my father.

*(*RITA *bursts into tears, a mixture of muffled moans and sobs, which neither* RAFILUCCIO *nor* ANTONIO *seem to notice)*

ANTONIO   *(conscious at last of the wretchedness of the two, regards them long and carefully)* I suspect you've already made up your mind.

RAFILUCCIO   *(equably)* Yes. I have.

ANTONIO   That means we'll have to spend a long time over it. Can you come back in a couple of hours?

RAFILUCCIO   Two hours? Right. I will.

*(*RITA, *aware of* RAFILUCCIO's *arm on her shoulder, realises the audience is at an end. They leave. She tries to control her sobs but without much success,*

and her moans are heard as she crosses the veranda and beyond, as they walk out into the Barracano estate. ANTONIO *doesn't wait for the sound of* RITA*'s lamentations to vanish in the distance. He listens for a while, then, his head bent, goes to his wife's room as*

THE CURTAIN FALLS

ACT TWO

(The same. Two hours later. ARMIDA, *a woollen shawl on her shoulders, is sitting in an armchair by the veranda, taking a little sun and air.* GERALDINA *and* IMMACOLATA *are sitting by her side.* FABIO *is sitting at the table, his back to the audience, facing the three women)*

ARMIDA What's the time?

FABIO *(glancing at his watch)* A quarter to nine.

ARMIDA Why isn't Antonio back yet?

GERALDINA It takes time to get to the municipal kennels and back again.

IMMACOLATA It's quite a long way from here. They came to fetch the dog less than an hour ago.

ARMIDA Why didn't Gennarino go with them?

GERALDINA You know what Gennarino is like about getting to his shop in time. He just drove off.

ARMIDA What about Amedeo?

IMMACOLATA Don Antonio sent him to Naples on an urgent errand. I didn't quite hear what it was all about. All I caught was: Amedeo, get him into the car and bring him right over.

ARMIDA Who could that be?

IMMACOLATA I've no idea.

ARMIDA *(to* FABIO) Why didn't you go with Antonio?

FABIO   My dear Donna Armida, I was in bed with a temperature. My teeth were chattering. Isn't that so, Immacolata?

IMMACOLATA   I had to get him two hot water bottles.

FABIO   I'm better now, but I've only just got out of bed.

GERALDINA   It's funny, you know, but whenever you're about to go off on a long trip, something always seems to happen and you go down with a temperature.

FABIO   Perhaps the American climate doesn't suit me. I suppose it affects my health even from a distance.

ARMIDA   (*still worried about* ANTONIO) Are the kennels really very far?

FABIO   Don't worry too much. This isn't the first time Don Antonio's dogs have been put into quarantine.

ARMIDA   You know what he's like. He's got a heart of gold, but he tends to interpret the law in his own peculiar way. Suppose they treat the dogs badly over there, he'll lose his temper and not realise he's dealing with the authorities—in fact that'll make it even worse —and the whole thing might end badly.

FABIO   I'm afraid you don't know Don Antonio well. You may know him as a husband, but I know him as Don Antonio Barracano much better than you. You've never seen him in Court, have you, when he bows and says: I'm at your service, M'lud. (*Raises an imaginary hat and bows in the manner usually adopted by* ANTONIO *in the presence of a magistrate*)

ARMIDA   Well, that's in front of the judge ...

FABIO   Oh no ... He's like that with the meanest usher or clerk of the court, with anybody who has anything to do formally with the legal profession, however modest his position in it. Don Antonio realises that even the usher isn't to be treated like a nobody. He's an official, with all the duties and responsibilities that go with it. Don Antonio, believe me, knows how to conduct himself. He might even get away with it and come back with the dog in tow.

GERALDINA I don't think so. Last time they kept it under observation for a couple of weeks.

RAFILUCCIO (*rushes in and stops, gasping for breath*) Oh, excuse me ...

ARMIDA Who is he?

IMMACOLATA He came earlier. He's here to see Don Antonio.

GERALDINA He's Rafiluccio Santaniello, mummy.

RAFILUCCIO Your servant, ma'am.

GERALDINA Has anything happened to you?

RAFILUCCIO The young lady with me ...

IMMACOLATA The one who went for a walk with you?

RAFILUCCIO Yes. Well, Don Antonio asked me to come back in two hours. We were out there together, by the barn. We didn't know where else to wait. The two hours aren't up yet ... there's another twenty minutes or so to go. Perhaps it was the sun ... Rita's so delicate ... I'm afraid she's not very well and I'm very worried about her.

IMMACOLATA The poor thing!

GERALDINA Where is she now?

RAFILUCCIO At the back of the olive grove, at the far end.

IMMACOLATA Doctor...

FABIO Bring her in here. I'll have a look at her.

GERALDINA Come with me, Immacolata. We'll fetch her. (*Goes out*)

IMMACOLATA Come along, young man. (*She leaves the room with* RAFILUCCIO)

FABIO That must be the baker's son, the one with the shop in Via Giacinto Albino.

ARMIDA And the girl?

FABIO I don't know her. How are you feeling now?

ARMIDA   A little better, thank you.

FABIO   I'm sorry I wasn't on hand when you had the accident. A little later I'll send to the chemist's for some drops that'll make you sleep if you should be in pain in the night.

ARMIDA   Thank you, doctor.

IMMACOLATA   (off) We're nearly there.

GERALDINA   (off) Gently does it. Lean on me.

RITA   (off) Thanks. I'm much better now. I think I fainted. It must have been the heat.

IMMACOLATA   (enters propping up RITA, who is also leaning on GERALDINA's arm) Nothing to worry about. (As the two women proceed towards the centre of the room and get RITA to sit down by the table, RAFILUCCIO stops by the veranda) Just a touch of the sun, as the young man said. Have a rest in here. You'll feel better in no time at all.

ARMIDA   Hadn't the doctor better examine her? I think the poor girl's pregnant.

RITA   (proudly, with a smile) Seven months gone.

ARMIDA   (to RAFILUCCIO) Is she your wife?

RAFILUCCIO   (with masculine vanity) She's my woman.

IMMACOLATA   What are you waiting for, doctor? Go on, examine her.

FABIO   No point in examining her. The fact she's pregnant is irrelevant. She's suffering from malnutrition, that's what's the matter with her. (Goes up to RITA) Can't you see how pale she is? Look at those dark rings under her eyes. (Takes one of her hands in his) Look at this ... this poor wretch is freezing to death. (Checks her pulse) No wonder: I can hardly feel her pulse. (To RITA) When did you last eat? (RITA averts her eyes, then begins to sob and moan) You can't have had anything for quite some time.

RAFILUCCIO   (confirms bitterly) That's right doctor.

She hasn't eaten anything for quite some time.

FABIO This has built up over a long time. She can't have been eating properly for months.

RAFILUCCIO Right again, doctor.

FABIO I like that. A few minutes ago you said proudly: This is my woman ... And you haven't even bothered to feed her properly.

RAFILUCCIO (*walks up to* FABIO) Doctor, look at that girl you've just examined. Look at her. She's just a bit of skin and bone strung together, just a bit of rubbish anybody might pick up off the floor ... (*Pretends to pick something up*) and say: This is useless rubbish ... Away into the dustbin. Look at her. Is she wearing smart clothes? No, sir. What about silk stockings? Oh, no. Does she go to the hairdresser's? She doesn't. And yet that little bundle of skin and bone, just as it stands, with those lovely eyes ... that bit of rubbish is ... my woman. And look at me. Look at me. Look at my shoes. (*Lifts a foot and shows the underside of his shoe. The sole is in shreds*) Look at this suit ... (*Bends his arm and lifts it, showing a gaping tear at the elbow*) Would you care to look at my shirt? (*Takes off his jacket and shows the innumerable repairs and patches on his shirt*) What would you say I am? Another useless heap of rubbish? Yes. The sort of thing one shoves to one side in the street. (*Moves his foot forward rapidly, scraping it against the floor tiles as if pushing away a nauseating object*) Into the dustbin with you as well! And yet, do you know what this revolting sight represents for her? Her man.

RITA (*admiringly*) Isn't he just lovely?

RAFILUCCIO I occasionally do portering work at the docks ... but more often than not, as there's so many of us, they shut the gates in my face. I turn my hand to anything when there's work going, I've been a labourer,

porter, watchman, odd-job-man, lavatory attendant ...
I give her what little I earn. We share food when we
can afford it, and when we can't, we go without.

FABIO You two will die of starvation.

RAFILUCCIO Us three, you mean. There's a creature
inside her. My son.

FABIO This pride in your paternity does you credit.
But unless this girl gets something to eat here and now
she'll faint again, or worse.

ARMIDA (*concerned*) Immacolata, see to it.

IMMACOLATA (*makes for the kitchen*) The things you
see in this world ...

FABIO (*tears off a sheet from a prescription pad he has
taken out of his pocket, writes out a prescription for
RITA and hands it to RAFILUCCIO*) Run off to the
chemist's and get this made up.

RAFILUCCIO (*in some embarrassment, holding the
prescription*) Right now?

FABIO Yes. Are you afraid to leave your woman alone
here with us?

RAFILUCCIO No, but ...

RITA (*attempting to sound matter-of-fact*) He never
carries money. He says he'd only lose it. I carry it for him.
(*Produces a bulging knotted handkerchief, tries to undo
it and fails. She can't quite focus her eyes. She tries again
and again she fails*)

RAFILUCCIO Give it here. Let me. (*Undoes the knot
and looks among the few items inside*) These are the
bus tickets. We bought return ones to come here.
Mustn't lose them or we'll be stranded in Terzigno.
(*Puts back the tickets*) This is your bracelet. (*Holds up
a cheap bracelet made of multicoloured imitation coral*)

RITA The string's broken. Mind you don't lose the bits.

RAFILUCCIO Where's the money? Oh, here it is. (*Takes
the money, three one hundred lire coins, and turns to

the doctor) Will three hundred lire be enough?

FABIO How should I know?

ARMIDA Tell the chemist the Barracanos have sent you. We've got an account.

RAFILUCCIO Why should you pay for us?

ARMIDA It's such a little thing ...

RAFILUCCIO I can't accept.

GERALDINA Oh, come on. Besides, I'm in your debt.

RAFILUCCIO You? In my debt?

GERALDINA On my way to school I used to buy rolls for my tea at your shop, remember? You always gave me a doughnut behind your father's back. I used to love those doughnuts! Just add up how many doughnuts you gave me over the years and you'll find that after paying the chemist we'll still owe you some change.

ARMIDA (*to* RAFILUCCIO) Go on, and be quick about it.

RAFILUCCIO (*somewhat moved*) If you'll excuse me. (*Goes out*)

IMMACOLATA (*enters carrying a tray on which are a steaming bowl of soup, cheese, milk and fruit*) The soup's nice and hot, and there's a piece of boiled meat inside. (*Puts the tray on the table*)

ARMIDA (*to* RITA) Go on ... whatever your name is ... eat up.

(RITA *lowers her eyes and remains silent*)

FABIO Have the hot soup first.

GERALDINA Yes, have the soup, the meat, then a nice glass of milk ... there's some fresh cheese, too.

(RITA *makes no move*)

ARMIDA Aren't you hungry?

IMMACOLATA Of course she is. You'll see, by and by she'll eat all right. I think she's a bit shy.

GERALDINA Would you like us to leave you alone?

RITA I want Rafiluccio. I'd like him to have some.

GERALDINA He's gone to the chemist's. You'd better start on your own.

RITA (giving in) All right ...

GERALDINA (aside, to the others) I think we'd better leave her alone, or she won't eat a thing.

IMMACOLATA I think we'd better.

ARMIDA I think I'm going to have a bad night. My shoulder's beginning to hurt. (Goes to her room)

IMMACOLATA (following ARMIDA) I'll come and help you.

FABIO (to ARMIDA) I'll get Catiello to fetch you those drops. (Leaves the room with ARMIDA and IMMACOLATA)

(RITA, after a short pause, takes a look round, then picks up a fork and plunges it into the soup bowl to spear the piece of boiled meat. She takes the meat out and looks at it carefully, considering its size. She notices with disappointment that the meat is barely enough for one, places the meat on a plate, pours some of the soup over it, then covers it with another plate. Having done this, she tentatively begins to have some of the soup, gradually picking up speed and yielding to the all too legitimate demands of her hunger)

ANTONIO (enters as RITA is gulping down the soup and observes ironically) Slow down, girl. Nobody's running after you.

RITA (startled, lets the spoon drop into the bowl and leaves the table like a thief caught in the act) The lady said I should eat. I told her I didn't want anything.

ANTONIO Finish it then. It'll do you good.

RITA No, thanks. I've had enough soup. But I think I'd like to taste some of the cheese.

ANTONIO Go on. Good stuff, this. (*Cuts a chunk of cheese for* RITA *and gives it to her*)

RITA Thank you. (*Begins to eat*)

ANTONIO You're Rafiluccio's fiancée eh?

RITA Not quite his fiancée.

ANTONIO He told me you were.

RITA That's what he usually says when he introduces me to strangers. But when he really knows someone he tells them I'm his woman.

ANTONIO I wonder what he means by that?

RITA I know. He explained it all to me.

ANTONIO You'd better tell me, then.

RITA You don't know?

ANTONIO Perhaps I do. But I'd like to know if Rafiluccio means the same thing.

RITA You tell me first: that'll give me the time to eat the cheese.

ANTONIO Very well. 'My woman' isn't used either to refer to one's fiancée or one's wife. In both cases the woman concerned would find the term offensive. A wife's a wife, and when talking about her one should say 'My wife'. A man who knows how to weigh his words only uses 'my woman' in two circumstances. First when mentioning a mistress ... or such like. Secondly when he sets out to ... how shall I put it ... protect a certain kind of woman ... a prostitute in fact ... from a drunken gang: in other words he claims provisional ownership of the lady in question and says: Hands off. She's my woman.

RITA Perhaps that's what it meant in your day, and you're not exactly young. But not now. As Rafiluccio put it to me, it means something else now. It's like this. You see, I never knew my parents. I was brought up by the Sisters of Charity at Torre del Greco. When I was fifteen—that was eight years ago—I went into service with a respectable family who lived in Via Giacinto Albino. They were very fond of me, and I used to buy our bread at Rafiluccio's father's shop in the same street. For upwards of seven years, for all you could tell, I never looked at Rafiluccio and he never took any notice of me. I used to go in, buy a couple of loaves and go home.

ANTONIO What's this got to do with ...

RITA Let me go on. One morning, about eighteen months ago, I was buying bread as usual ... 'Can I take you to the pictures tonight?'

ANTONIO Was that Rafiluccio?

RITA No. Some young chap doing his shopping. I'm sorry, I said, but I'm not in the habit of going to the pictures with strangers. All right, he said, I'll go with Rafiluccio in that case, and asked him if he'd go with him. I'm afraid not, said Rafiluccio. Tonight—and he stared hard at me—I've got an appointment at nine on the dot in the foyer of the Santa Lucia cinema. And he went on staring at me. I understood. At nine that night just as I was going into the cinema, Rafiluccio's arm slipped into mine. I was walking on air ... I couldn't see a thing. I was waiting for him to say something. In the end he said: Do you love me? Yes I do, I answered, and I have for the past seven years. Then I asked him: When did you first notice me? Seven years ago, he said. Two people, one thought. From that evening on nothing mattered any more; not anything or anybody. When I am with him I'm happy, and everything we do together seems right. Rafiluccio explained to me that this happens when two people are made for each other. In other words, the woman is only a complete person when she meets the right man, and the same goes for him. I have found Rafiluccio and he has found me.

ANTONIO I see. A meeting of twin souls. Tell me something. Do you know anything about this decision Rafiluccio has made?

RITA (*nods quickly*) Yes. (*She breaks into tears*) He's obstinate. Once he's made up his mind there's nothing one can do. He's had this obsession for months.

ANTONIO Do you think what he's decided to do is right?

RITA (*still sobbing*) When we're together and we talk about it, he convinces me he's right, but then when I'm alone and I go over what he said, I think he's all wrong ...

ANTONIO Couldn't you get him to change his mind?

(*RAFILUCCIO enters and stops by the french windows*)

RITA What can I do? With Rafiluccio this isn't just an idea he's playing with, it's an illness. He can't think of anything else. He can't sleep at night any more. Please help him, Don Antonio. If only you could do something ...

RAFILUCCIO (*walks up to* RITA) We've come here because I, not you, had to speak to Don Antonio. (*Turns to* ANTONIO) You must forgive her, she doesn't realise what an important person you are. (*To* RITA) Haven't I told you to keep your mouth shut when I'm not with you?

ANTONIO As a matter of fact it was I who put a few questions to her.

RAFILUCCIO All she need ever answer is: I don't know a thing, ask Rafiluccio when he comes back. (*RITA begins to sob*) And stop crying, do you hear? It's not good for you. That's all she does all the time.

ANTONIO Well, young man, if you want to talk I'm ready.

RAFILUCCIO Rita, why don't you go for a walk while I have my talk with Don Antonio ...

RITA Let me stay. I'd like to hear what he has to say.

RAFILUCCIO (*firmly*) Go on. Take a walk.

RITA   Don Antonio, please ask him to let me stay.

GERALDINA   (*enters*) How did it go, daddy?

ANTONIO   Well, there seems to be nothing wrong with the dog. We can have him back next week.

GERALDINA   (*to* RITA) Did you have something to eat?

RITA   Yes, thank you.

IMMACOLATA   (*enters*) Has she had something to eat?

ANTONIO   Some soup and a bit of cheese. Take her to the kitchen with you. She'll eat some more, I'm sure.

IMMACOLATA   (*clearing the table*) Come with me, girl, come along. (*Takes the plate with the piece of boiled meat*)

RITA   No, no ... I put that on one side for Rafiluccio. Have it, Rafiluccio. It's boiled meat.

RAFILUCCIO   I'm not hungry. (*To* IMMACOLATA) You can take it away.

RITA   Eat it up ... just to make me happy.

RAFILUCCIO   I'm not hungry.

ANTONIO   Look, leave the meat here and perhaps his appetite will come back, but please leave us now. We've got things to discuss.

IMMACOLATA   (*to* RITA) Come.

RITA   I shan't be a moment. (*Goes up to* RAFILUCCIO, *squeezes his hands and gives him a long, loving look*) I'm going, just as you asked me. Have your talk with Don Antonio. I'm sure he'll give you good advice. And remember I'm your woman. (*In a whisper*) And eat up that meat! You had no breakfast this morning.

RAFILUCCIO   Yes, yes; don't fuss.

RITA   (*to* IMMACOLATA *and* GERALDINA) Where's the kitchen?

GERALDINA   This way. (*They leave the room*)

ANTONIO   She seems a good girl.

RAFILUCCIO   She's wonderful.

ANTONIO   Sit down, boy.

RAFILUCCIO Thank you. (*Sits down*)

ANTONIO Well?

RAFILUCCIO (*embarrassed*) Well, Don Antonio ... it's like this ...

ANTONIO Before you start, let me tell you that I know something of the world. I've been around, and you could say that my life has been a long series of practical decisions. Two hours ago you told me with mathematical certainty that you must kill your father. Now you're tongue-tied. You've had time to think things over. Are you trying to tell me you've changed your mind?

RAFILUCCIO No, sir. I'm a bit nervous because this is the first time I've met you. I've heard so much about you. When your name is mentioned, people stand to attention. It's because I respect you that I can't talk as freely as I'd like to. But I haven't changed my mind. What I told you two hours ago still stands.

ANTONIO Meaning that by tomorrow you'll have liquidated your own father?

RAFILUCCIO There's no other way.

ANTONIO But why? Who said so? All right, let us assume there is no other way. You've made your mind up and you mean to go through with it. But then why come to me at all? Are you just informing me as a matter of courtesy, giving me some kind of advance press release? I'm not interested. Or do you take me for some kind of father confessor? If you came to me and said you needed advice, I'd gladly try to help you. But it's no use just telling me in advance you're not going to budge. There's something you've still got to learn, and that is that a man is only truly a man when he can back down gracefully, when he's not ashamed of reversing a decision. When he can admit to himself he's made a mistake and assumes responsibility for it, even tries to make amends. When he appreciates the superiority of another man and is not afraid to admit it. When he can weigh up carefully both his courage and his fear. Rafiluccio: I am that other man. Do you want to leave now, or would you like the benefit of my advice?

RAFILUCCIO (*undecided*) Don Antonio ...

ANTONIO (*gravely*) He is your father. You understand that?

RAFILUCCIO Does he realise I'm his son? When I came into the world my father was already there, with a home of his own. But when he was born, I wasn't there. Don Antonio, Arturo Santaniello isn't a father, he's a rotten bastard.

ANTONIO If you've come to me for advice, I'll decide whether your father's a rotten bastard or not. It could well be you're the rotten bastard.

RAFILUCCIO Don Antonio ...

ANTONIO Let's go on. When did you last see him?

RAFILUCCIO Thirteen months ago.

ANTONIO How did you part?

RAFILUCCIO He said to me—these were his very words: I no longer recognise you as my son. Get yourself a job in another bakery, and don't you dare come into my home tonight or ever again.

ANTONIO And I suppose people began to tell your father you were saying this and that about him, and others told you that your father had been saying this and that about you. You haven't seen him since?

RAFILUCCIO No.

ANTONIO Have you had a good education?

RAFILUCCIO (*downcast*) I'm afraid not. I left school when I was nine. My father said it was better for me to learn a trade and took me into the shop. But I can read and write.

ANTONIO I can't. (*Laughs*) That is, I can read a bit, but not write. I can read newspapers, especially large block letters and headlines. Handwritten letters have to be read out to me. Anyway, you can cope with basic things.

RAFILUCCIO   I suppose so.

ANTONIO   And so can I. Look, I'm not going to ask what started this quarrel between you and your father. However, even the poorest church has two bells, and I'm used to listening to both. One bell's no good on its own: it tolls for the dead.

RAFILUCCIO   (*raising his right forefinger*) May I say something, Don Antonio?

ANTONIO   Go on.

RAFILUCCIO   Your advice carries weight, and I should be grateful if you would inform my father of my intentions. And unless he gives me what is rightfully mine as his son ...

ANTONIO   I've told you one bell is no good. I've got to hear the other one as well. (*Pause*) Are you armed?

RAFILUCCIO   (*pause*) Yes sir.

ANTONIO   Pistol?

RAFILUCCIO   Yes.

ANTONIO   Put it on the table.

RAFILUCCIO   (*takes a pistol out of his pocket and puts it on the table*) Here you are.

ANTONIO   Is that all?

RAFILUCCIO   That's all.

AMEDEO   (*enters*) Here I am, dad. I've taken care of everything. (*Notices* RAFILUCCIO) Good morning.

RAFILUCCIO   Good morning.

ANTONIO   Have you brought him?

AMEDEO   He's right outside. Shall I show him in?

ANTONIO   Wait. (*Turns to* IMMACOLATA, *who has just come in*) There's a gentleman outside. (*Points to the veranda*) Show him in.

IMMACOLATA   Yes, sir. (*Goes out*)

ANTONIO   Rafiluccio, I've got some urgent business to attend to. Amedeo will look after you.

AMEDEO   (*to* RAFILUCCIO) Come with me.

RAFILUCCIO   (*crossly*) Will you see me later ...?

ANTONIO   Yes, yes. I'll see you as soon as I'm through.

(AMEDEO *and* RAFILUCCIO *go out*)

IMMACOLATA   (*returns with* ARTURO SANTANI-ELLO) Step this way. Don Antonio is in here.

ARTURO   (*enters*) Thank you. (*He is a coarsely handsome man of about sixty, healthy and vigorous. He has the fixed stare peculiar to obtuse people. He is well and soberly dressed*)

ANTONIO   You are Don Arturo Santaniello?

ARTURO   The same. Your servant, Don Antonio.

ANTONIO   Pleased to meet you.

ARTURO   (*glancing beyond the veranda*) All your own property out there?

ANTONIO   You can't quite see it all from here. It's mine up to the olive grove three miles up the road, the same to the left, and right up to the sea-front on the other side. Yes, it's all mine.

ARTURO   Congratulations.

ANTONIO   I bought it when I came back from America forty years ago. It was a bargain.

ARTURO   Land was cheap in those days. It can't have cost much ...

ANTONIO   A pittance. And then, little by little, I developed it. I built a few houses, the odd villa ...

ARTURO   It's such a beautiful part of the world. I suppose you engage architects and builders yourself ...

ANTONIO   God forbid! Architects? Builders? They'd ruin me, man. No, no. I do everything myself. I've got an old jobbing foreman, a man of the old guard. There's no shortage of labour round here ... In other words, I build cheaply. My daughter does all the accountancy and purchasing: cement, stone, bricks, girders, plaster ...

ARTURO   But surely you've got to get plans approved.

ANTONIO   Well, this part of the world, as you call it, is quite isolated and nobody bothers much ... Besides, what are plans? Just bits of paper ...

ARTURO   Well ...

ANTONIO   You know, man's greatest discovery wasn't radio, or television, or the atom bomb, the sputnik ... no. Man's greatest discovery was paper.

ARTURO   (amused) You don't say.

ANTONIO   Think of the things you can make and do with paper.

ARTURO   Lots of things ...

ANTONIO   Drafts, contracts, stamps, books, newspapers ...

ARTURO   Passports, licenses, posters ...

ANTONIO   ... and banknotes.

ARTURO   Oh yes ... banknotes.

ANTONIO   And there's something else you can make with paper.

ARTURO   What's that?

ANTONIO   There was an inventor, obviously a man of remarkable genius, though I don't know who he was, who cut out a piece of square paper, folded four sides, stuck down three of them and left one open. On this last side he brushed a little gum and let it dry. It only gets sticky again if you lick it.

ARTURO   The envelope!

ANTONIO   It only becomes an envelope proper if, before you seal it, you put banknotes into it ... yet another paper product. There you have the greatest lubricant in the world. Don Arturo, without that sort of envelope nothing works. The atom bomb would refuse to go off without it. No need for architects or building contractors. Just a number of well-filled envelopes, which beget all the building permits one could possibly need.

ARTURO Yes. Very interesting. As I was saying, Don Antonio, it's a great pleasure to meet you.

ANTONIO My pleasure.

ARTURO I often see you in Via Giacinto Albino. They tell me you live in the district.

ANTONIO I do.

ARTURO And of course I remember seeing you as a young man, many years ago ...

ANTONIO You knew me in the States?

ARTURO No ... in Naples. About forty years ago. At your trial.

ANTONIO Ah, you were in court?

ARTURO Yes. Yours was such a fascinating case. People talked of nothing else. I was very keen on murder stories in those days.

ANTONIO Would it surprise you if I told you that it was I who asked for a re-trial? After the incident—I was only eighteen at the time—an acquaintance of mine in the States helped me get out of Italy. He's still alive, you know. He's eighty-three and we often write to each other, we keep in touch ...

ARTURO What's his name?

ANTONIO You want to know too much ...

ARTURO I'm sorry.

ANTONIO Anyway, I stowed away to the States, and over here I was sentenced in my absence. I was in America seventeen years. This acquaintance of mine took a fancy to me and with his help I did quite well for myself. What did I do? I worked for him. (*In answer to an ambiguous grimace on* ARTURO's *part*) No, nothing dishonest. Blood was spilt, yes, but in the pursuit of justice. I worked at the docks, as a shoeshine, in a pizza-parlour, as a fish-frier, house painter ... anything that was going.

Of course the few dollars I saved up wouldn't have gone far in America, but in Italy, with the rate of exchange applicable at the time, it was a fortune. So I came back and bought this estate and asked for a new trial. The famous De Fonzeca defended me. New evidence for and against, witnesses ... yes, I had eight witnesses for the defence. Result: acquittal. I had killed in self-defence.

ARTURO Were the witnesses genuine?

ANTONIO No. They were hired.

ARTURO What did De Fonzeca say?

ANTONIO He didn't know a thing. If ever you want to win a case, your lawyer is the last man you should confide in. A lawyer is like a father confessor, and I don't hold with confession. But although the witnesses were hired, right was on my side. Yes, I was in the right. I've two broken ribs, you know, and half my lower jaw is a metal plate, as a souvenir of that caper. Giacchino was responsible, the caretaker of the Marvizza estate. Oh yes, I killed him. May he rot in hell. Eighteen, that's all I was at the time, and a goat-herd. Yes, I come of humble stock. I used to look after goats. Giacchino always allowed other people's herds to graze round the Marvizza estate, but he wouldn't have me. Didn't like the look of me, or something. I used to say to him: But why just me and my goats? And he used to answer, his shotgun at the ready: Because I say so. I'm in charge here. Piss off, or I'll blow your brains out. One morning I'd had some bread and cheese and I fell asleep while the goats were grazing. I suppose that out of habit some of the goats trespassed into the Marvizza estate. I woke up to a shower of blows, slaps and kicks all over my body. I didn't know whether I was awake or dreaming it all. But I could hear the bastard's voice: This'll teach you to do as you're told! You know, Don Arturo, when he'd finished with me, my face was a mask of caked blood and dust. I said little at the hospital; just that I had fallen into a ravine. Days went by. I couldn't sleep, I couldn't eat. My poor sainted mother used to ask: What's the matter, son? And my father: Don't you feel well? I was really ill. I just wasted away. They called in doctors, but they couldn't decide what was wrong with me. If I was walking along the street, I could only see Giacchino in front of me. If a friend said hello to me, I looked up and there was Giacchino. At night, in bed, in the dark, all I could see was Giacchino. All I could think was that unless Giacchino died, I'd die myself. And I didn't want to die. (*Repeating the frenzied words he had said at the time*) It's him or me ... Him or me ... Him or me. I bought myself a flick knife and went to the Marvizza estate. Giacchino didn't even have time to aim his shotgun. You beat me up, I said.—It wasn't me, don't kill me!—It wasn't you?—No!—Swear it.—I swear it.—You swear it before God?—Yes, I do!—If he'd said to me: Yes, I did it ... I might have forgiven him. Fifty-seven years have passed since that day, Don Arturo, but still I haven't plunged my knife into Giacchino for the last time.

ARTURO   But surely, Don Antonio ... Two broken ribs, a smashed jaw ... couldn't you have had him arrested?

ANTONIO   He'd have denied it. When it happened, the only ones present were he and I and the goats ... and goats cannot testify. So. What would have been the good of that? They'd swear him in, and he'd swear before God he hadn't beaten me up. You see, humanity is divided into two categories: decent people and bastards like Giacchino. The law isn't elastic. The penal code consists of 266 pages and 734 articles. And do you know what people like Giacchino say to that? 'Tell me the law they're going to apply and I'll find a loophole.' What is the judge to do? He's got to go by the evidence, by the witnesses' testimony. Even if the judge, as a man, is convinced of the innocence of the accused, he's got to go by the book, and his sentence must comply with the rules ... like the result of a mathematical operation. It isn't the law that's at fault. It's people who gobble one another up, how shall I put it ... the clever ones gobble up the underdogs. I've taken up their case. I defend the underdog.

ARTURO (*unconvinced, smiles ingratiatingly*) Quite.

ANTONIO I'm sorry. I've gone off the point and I'm wasting your time.

ARTURO Don't mention it. It's an honour that you should speak so freely in front of me.

ANTONIO If I have spoken freely it's only because there's just the two of us here. If there had been a third person I wouldn't have done so.

ARTURO I get you.

ANTONIO Don Arturo, I have asked you to come to see me today as I'd like to ask you a personal favour, and if possible to contribute, with my help, to the solution of an unpleasant problem.

ARTURO Only too glad to oblige, Don Antonio. I'm at your service.

ANTONIO You are too kind. Well, now, I hear there's been bad blood between you and your son.

ARTURO (*hypocritically*) Have I a son?

ANTONIO Play-acting doesn't work with me, Don Arturo. Answer me man to man. You have a son called Rafiluccio, haven't you?

ARTURO Had. I had a son called Rafiluccio. If you hadn't mentioned his name I wouldn't have remembered.

ANTONIO Is the quarrel that bad?

ARTURO Let me put my cards on the table, Don Antonio. I started work as a baker when I was twelve years old.

Through sheer hard work and personal sacrifice and also, I suppose, because I'm good at my job, I now have two prosperous shops. I'm still working just as hard at my age. I get up at five every morning. But not him. No fear. He's bone lazy and doesn't give a damn for his father. I used to say to him, at first that is, because as time went by it was no use, I used to say: Stay in tonight, keep me company. We'll watch television, perhaps have a game of cards. No, sir! One excuse after another: I've got a date ... If only you'd told me this morning ... In other words, he cared more for his friends than for his father.

ANTONIO He's young. It's only natural he should want to go out with people of his own age.

ARTURO If there was an application to be lodged with the Town Hall I'd say: Don't forget, son, tomorrow's the last day. Don't worry, I'll see to it ... And the application was still in his pocket a week later. I'll give you another example. As a rule I eat steamed cod on a Friday. Tell me, Rafiluccio, I'd ask of a Friday morning, have you soaked the cod in water? Of course I have, he'd assure me. I'd get home the same night: no Rafiluccio, no cod. That's the consideration he had for his father. There's a photograph of my late wife which I've had enlarged and framed; as a matter of fact it's just like the one of myself over the counter at the shop ... Well, on the first Friday of every month I put some flowers by her portrait, and candles ... it's my way of showing respect. Don't forget Rafiluccio, I'd say, we'll need some candles tomorrow. Might as well have been talking to a brick wall. You know what this means, Don Antonio, don't you: that when I'm gone neither her portrait nor mine will get any candles. Besides, he's lazy ... I'm a worker and he's a parasite: that's why we don't get on. And he has no respect for his father.

ANTONIO But if you were to help him ...

ARTURO You mean if I cough up money ...

ANTONIO He's not exactly a stranger. He's your son.
However, I think I understand you. You think he would
only show respect if you handed out money.

ARTURO Right.

ANTONIO But didn't you know that this is often the
case? My dear Don Arturo, first we bring our children
into the world, then we have to start buying them.

ARTURO I'm not buying.

ANTONIO Haven't you got two businesses?

ARTURO If you're referring to the shop in Via Roma,
I'm afraid I couldn't possibly have him there. It's a
modern place, and it's exclusively staffed by girls, in
blue overalls and a matching ribbon in their hair ... It's
the smartest shop in Naples. There's a foreign woman,
a Swiss, who manages the place and is responsible to me.
I run the shop in Via Giacinto Albino, and he couldn't
possibly work there, with me on the premises. And
then ... with the greatest respect, Don Antonio, may I
say that these are private matters. I've no intention of
washing our dirty linen in public. This is a matter
between father and son. If my son has placed himself
under your protection, please bear in mind that he
is not seeking protection from a stranger, but his own
father. Setting himself against his own father. Do you
call that natural?

ANTONIO One moment. Your son didn't come to me
for protection. The reason he came here is a different
one, but I can't tell you what it is just yet.

ARTURO Very well, I believe you, but I beg you to keep
out of this matter. It's a purely private family affair. No
offence meant, Don Antonio. I hope you understand.

ANTONIO I do.

ARTURO You'll grant me that a man is master in his own house. (*Angrily*) And as for my money, Rafiluccio may as well forget it!

ANTONIO Yes, you're the master. (*Pauses, trying to think of another subject*) That's a fine gold chain you've got ...

ARTURO I bought it years ago at a public auction.

ANTONIO Did it come with the fob?

ARTURO It's a locket, actually. No. I bought it separately when my poor wife died ... it's got her photograph inside.

ANTONIO We're always buying. Buying ... Furniture, ornaments, clothes ...

ARTURO You're telling me. I've got a house full of stuff.

ANTONIO Me too. Acquisitions ... property ...

ARTURO But there comes a point when one stops. I haven't got the buying urge any more.

ANTONIO That's exactly what happened to me. After my second trial I got married. Then came the children ... and I went on buying. Armida, my wife, used to say: Antonio, stop it now, we've got everything we'll ever need. Too many possessions are a nuisance ... When he was about eight years old my boy Gennarino said to me: Daddy, is it true that when you die all this will be mine?

ARTURO He said that when he was eight?

ANTONIO Yes. I asked myself whether all that children were waiting for was their father's death. So I said to him: No, son, not when I die. It's yours now. I sent for my solicitor, divided the property in three equal parts and handed everything to my children in my lifetime. Now, when they say they are glad to see me and hope I'm well, I know they really mean it. (*Pause*) Would you excuse me for a moment?

ARTURO Of course.

(ANTONIO *leaves the room and comes back with* RAFILUCCIO, *who, unaware of his father's presence, is well into the room before he spots him. When he does he stops dead, as if petrified.* ARTURO *is just as shocked to see his son. Long pause*)

ARTURO (*grimly, to* RAFILUCCIO) So you've put yourself under his protection?

ANTONIO I've already told you that wasn't the reason he came to see me.

RAFILUCCIO (*hardly concealing the hatred he feels towards his father*) It was quite a different reason.

ARTURO What am I doing here then? Is it any of my business?

ANTONIO It's very much your business. Vitally so.

ARTURO I'm afraid I don't understand you, Don Antonio. This young lout shouldn't have put either you or me to all this trouble. We have nothing to say to each other. He's left my home, he's left my shop and he's over twenty-one. His life is no concern of mine. (*To* RAFILUCCIO) And don't forget, your little whore is never to set foot inside my house.

RAFILUCCIO (*with venom*) And who is going to instead?

ARTURO (*curtly*) Well, good day, Don Antonio. (*Is about to leave*)

RAFILUCCIO I suppose the only one to see the inside of your house is that filthy Swiss slag who's robbing you right left and centre. She gets in all right, the Swiss cow!

AMEDEO (*enters followed by* RITA) What's happening?

RAFILUCCIO I can't get a job because wherever I apply they ask me why my father sacked me, and slam the door in my face. And he keeps slandering me, telling all sorts of lies to justify treating me like dirt. But it's all right for you to spend money on your whore...

any amount of money on her ...

ARTURO I'll have who I like in my house. And the money's mine, understand? Mine! Don't let me ever see you again. As far as you are concerned, Via Giacinto Albino isn't on the map any more. I don't want ever to set eyes on you again.

RAFILUCCIO And I can't stand the sound of your voice! Christ ...! (*Seizes a chair and is about to hurl it at* ARTURO. AMEDEO *stops him*)

RITA (*rushes up to* RAFILUCCIO) Rafiluccio, please don't frighten me!

ARTURO (*ironically*) Here comes the fiancée with the bun in the oven ...

RAFILUCCIO (*held back by* AMEDEO) My God!

ARMIDA (*enters*) What's the matter, Antonio?

ANTONIO Nothing to worry about.

ARTURO You miserable creature! (*Turns to the others*) Look at him ... that's the way he treats his father. You see? (*To* RAFILUCCIO) You make me sick. (*To* ANTONIO) I'm going, Don Antonio. I'm sorry I haven't been able to be of more help. I am at your disposal for anything else that I can do for you. I want you to know that I look up to you and will always respect you. But where my family is concerned, I really must ask you to mind your own business.

ANTONIO I'm not very happy about a single word you've said, Don Arturo. Not just these last few words, but your whole conversation, ever since you came in.

ARTURO You've a right to your opinion.

ANTONIO Be quiet. When I am talking, mind you keep absolutely quiet. But I suppose I'd have been unhappy at anything you said, anything at all. The fact is, you are severely handicapped in any dealings you may have with me. You see, I can't stand the sight of you.

ARMIDA (*fearing the worst*) Oh, my God! (*Exchanges

glances and private signs with AMEDEO, *who leaves the room*)

ANTONIO   And another thing. No one's ever told me to mind my own business.

ARTURO   Perhaps this is the first time you've taken an interest in private family matters.

ANTONIO   I gave you an inch and you took an ell. I spoke to you with some familiarity, and for some reason you forgot who you were dealing with. I'll remind you: my name is Antonio Barracano.

ARTURO   (*irritated*) So what? I am a respectable man, an honest worker. I abide by the law and my name is Arturo Santaniello.

ANTONIO   (*grimly*) Are you armed? (*Produces a pistol and points it at* ARTURO)

ARTURO   I am not armed, Don Antonio.

GERALDINA   (*enters with* IMMACOLATA *and stops in her tracks*) Daddy ...

ARTURO   I am not armed. (AMEDEO *comes back with* FABIO *and both look on apprehensively*) I am sure Don Antonio Barracano knows how to act in front of an unarmed man.

ANTONIO   (*places the pistol on the table and goes up to* ARTURO, *looking at him steadily, with contempt in his eyes.* ARTURO *doesn't bat an eyelid and stands there as if paralysed*) You're a revolting man.

ARTURO   As it comes from you, I'm duty bound to accept your estimate of my character.

ANTONIO   You're a filthy swine.

ARTURO   I'll make a note of that.

ANTONIO   You're a louse ...

ARTURO   Then I'll ask you to forgive me for soiling your lily-white house with my presence. I'll go now, and thank you for your hospitality and all the useful knowledge you've passed on to me. Trials can be rigged ...

up to a point. Evidence may be fabricated ... but not always. Witnesses may be hired, though some will not be bribed. A little patience on my part and a little caution on yours. Good day, everybody. (*Goes out*)

ANTONIO   He's not a man. He's a worm.

RAFILUCCIO   So help me, I don't know how I could stop myself.

ANTONIO   He's your father. That's his advantage over you. He knows it all right, and you don't. You realise of course that your little project carries life imprisonment, don't you?

ARMIDA   (*alarmed*) What on earth ...

FABIO   Life imprisonment?

AMEDEO   Dad ...

RITA   Please, Rafiluccio. Let's think about ourselves for a change. Why destroy our lives?

RAFILUCCIO   Don Antonio, help me, do something ...

ANTONIO   He's your father.

RAFILUCCIO   I don't care.

ANTONIO   If you don't care, then you're a worm too. I don't think you've quite got the picture. Doctor, pay attention, and you too, Amedeo, and all of you. If I help you, Arturo Santaniello will be dead within the next twenty-four hours. I'll tell you how to do it. You walk past the shop in Via Giacinto Albino ... let's say the shop is over there ... (*Points to the upstage wall*) You go up to the shop and stop outside. As soon as you've spotted him and you're good and ready, you shoot five times. First you fire four shots on target and you're rid of him. Then you fire one shot to hit the shopwindow opposite ... Done. The gun? It was your father's. The minute he saw you he shot at you. You quickly disarmed him and the rest followed naturally. Wrongful dismissal, refusal to assist you financially, cohabitation with a known foreign prostitute ... self-defence will be duly proved and corroborated by reliable witnesses. I'll either get you off with a light sentence or get you acquitted altogether.

RAFILUCCIO But then ...

ANTONIO Christ! Do I have to spell it out for you? He's your father. You can't. You just can't. And I can't help you. (*The others exchange glances of approval*) And stop treating it as a question of principle. Are you afraid of what people will say if you change your mind?

FABIO You shouldn't care what people say.

IMMACOLATA You're young. You've got your whole life in front of you.

ARMIDA She's right. And you've got a kid on the way. Don't forget Our Lady never deserts us when children are involved.

RITA (*to the others*) He's such a good driver ... If only you could pass your driving test ... You could get a job ...

AMEDEO We can get you a job, man! We'll all give you a helping hand, me and Gennarino and dad here.

ANTONIO Think it over carefully, boy. And remember what I said half an hour ago. A man is only truly a man when he can back down gracefully, when he's not afraid of changing his mind.

RAFILUCCIO (*giving vent to his despair*) I can't back down. Don Antonio, it's not my fault ... believe me. When I think of that man ... I can't even bring myself to call him father! Look, look at my hands ... they're trembling. I can't think of anything else. I can't sleep at night. I can't eat or sleep ... I go on thinking the same thing. (*As if attempting to dismiss obsessive thoughts*) Go away! Go away! Understand? I don't want to think of this any more! But it's still there, Don Antonio, it won't go away. If a friend talks to me, it's my father's voice I hear. I close my eyes and I see his damned face. I open them and he's still there. I can't go on living like this. I'm losing weight. I don't want to die. I'm too young. It's either him or me, we can't both go on living! (*Deadly pale and shivering he collapses on a chair and covers his face with his hands, his elbows on his knees*)

ANTONIO (RAFILUCCIO's *words have reminded him of* GIACCHINO) Poor lad. You're right. You can't possibly go on living like this. It's as if you'd been bitten by a poisonous bug. It's just as if you were seriously ill. The germ of this disease is in the very dust of the earth we walk on. It clings to our shoes, penetrates through our feet into our bones and up to our brains. Once it's there it'll even suggest the most suitable place, the most propitious time, even the weapon you're to use. And by the time you feel better, you're in jail. No, there's nothing to be done, there's no other way: it's either him or you. You asked me to help you. All right. I will. But, you see, Giacchino was a stranger. Arturo Santaniello is your father. Therefore he must be told of your intentions, he must know why you came to see me, he must know why I'm taking a hand in this. Immacolata, my hat and stick.

IMMACOLATA Right away. (*Complies*)

ANTONIO When one wishes to acquire merchandise, it's usual to approach the owner and wait for his asking price. In this case the owner of the goods is Arturo Santaniello, and the offer you make him depends on his asking price. Then you'll be able to make up your mind ... and I'll make up mine. Doctor, will you drive me to town?

FABIO With pleasure.

(*They leave the room as*

THE CURTAIN FALLS

ACT THREE

(Later that evening. The Barracanos' town flat in the Sanità district. Large dining-room. As is her custom at the beginning of the summer, ARMIDA BARRACANO *has had all the furniture covered with dustsheets and the pictures taken down. The flat looks bare and apparently uninhabitable. The dining-table, however, is lavishly set for dinner and laid for eight. The chandelier is lit.* ANTONIO BARRACANO *is slumped in an armchair. He is very pale, and signs of physical pain are clearly visible on his face. Sitting beside him, in front of a typewriter placed on a chair, is* FABIO, *busy typing under dictation from* ANTONIO)*

FABIO *(has typed the last few words of a sentence)* Now all you've got to do is sign it.

ANTONIO Read it back to me first. Perhaps we've left something out.

FABIO I've written everything you dictated. We haven't got much time to waste. Still ... *(Takes the sheet out of the typewriter)* Listen and tell me if it's right. *(The doorbell rings)* That must be Luigi. *(Leaves the room and returns followed by* LUIGI *and* VICENZELLA)

LUIGI *(carrying a parcel containing eight roast chickens and a large boxed cake)* All you asked for. Eight birds, just as you said, salad, cheese and sweet: it's a special gateau.

FABIO Take it all into the kitchen. Put the birds in the big serving dishes.

VICENZELLA (carrying a basket full of vegetables, fruit and ice) I'll put the fruit on ice and get the salad ready. You can add oil and vinegar at the table.

FABIO Right. Be quick about it.

LUIGI You know, doctor, the man at the shop wouldn't believe the cake was for Don Antonio. He said Don Antonio was bound to be still at Terzigno with his family. It took me quite a time to convince him Don Antonio was back in town.

FABIO Really?

LUIGI Yes. He kept saying it was the beginning of September, and that Don Antonio as a rule never comes back before the middle of October.

FABIO We're only in Naples for the night. Tomorrow we're going back to Terzigno.

LUIGI Well, please come back soon, Don Antonio. We only ever see a bit of money when you are around. (Goes out to the kitchen) Come along, Vicenzella.

VICENZELLA Coming! (Goes out)

FABIO How do you feel?

ANTONIO I can't feel a thing.

FABIO It isn't possible. I know you've got a strong physique, but you're made of flesh and blood like everybody else. Don Antonio, the blade penetrated at least four inches. I've no instruments here, no disinfectant or drugs ... what could I do? I've made the bandage as tight as I could, but that's all. What a man you are! When it happened, instead of telling me you weren't feeling too well, you should have told me the truth and I would have rushed you straight to hospital.

ANTONIO ... where I'd have had to name names and lodge complaints. What would have been the good of that? This time I'm the injured party. You of all people should know how many tricky problems I've solved in my time without resorting to the authorities ... Now that I'm involved personally, what would you have me do? Stand up and say: Teacher, he's hurt me! Punish him ...

FABIO You could have said you'd been attacked by persons unknown ... that you might recognise the attacker if you saw him but that you couldn't remember what he looked like.

ANTONIO That's all right as far as the law is concerned. But what about my family? My sons? My sons knew I'd gone to see Arturo Santaniello. They would have put two and two together soon enough. Then we'd have had Gennarino and Amedeo against Santaniello. More blood, more revenge ... Enough is enough, doctor! We've worked together for thirty-five years to cut down crime and killings, not add to them.

FABIO But didn't he even give you the chance to reason with him?

ANTONIO Perhaps when he saw me walk into the shop he thought my intentions weren't peaceable ... I just had time to say: Don Arturo, I wanted to ask you ... He replied: Come in. There was nobody else in the shop. We walked towards each other. I don't know how it happened. Either he was already holding the knife or he picked it up from the counter. I just don't know. All I can remember is that he plunged it in here. (*Points to the left side of his abdomen*) At that very moment a customer came into the shop. Do you know who that was? Vicienzo Cuozzo. The carpenter who came to see me this morning ...

FABIO Oh, yes, the one who kept shouting: Don Antonio is our father! We all love you, Don Antonio! I could even hear him in my room.

ANTONIO The same. Anyway, Santaniello went to the

back of the shop and Vicienzo Cuozzo ran away.

FABIO   Weren't you armed?

ANTONIO   I had my pistol, but I thought of my sons. If I shoot now, I thought, the chain of killings will stretch out to infinity ... I put a hand on the wound and slowly got back to you waiting in the car. But I'm worried about Vicienzo Cuozzo. If he talks my sons'll end up in jail.

FABIO   I've carried out your instructions. When I went out to invite our friends and make arrangements for Arturo Santaniello, I went right up to Vicienzo's workshop. He assured me he'd come.

ANTONIO   Good. (*Pause*) So you'll be off the day after tomorrow. (*At a gesture from* FABIO) It's all right. You may leave. This will be a farewell dinner for you, with all good wishes for your new life in America. (*Short pause*) I really don't feel a thing. (*Mops his brow with the back of his hand*) I'm sweating a little ... Well, let's get on. So many arrangements to be made ... Would you give me a glass of water?

FABIO   You see? You're beginning to get thirsty. (*Gives him some water*) You've got a ruptured peritoneum and a perforated spleen.

ANTONIO   Would you read me the letter?

FABIO   (*reads out the typed sheet*) Dear Bastiano, the bearer of this letter is Doctor Fabio Della Ragione, who has been close to me for many years, has looked after my health and has served our cause loyally and selflessly. He is going to join his brother in the States, as he is tired and getting on in years. All he wants now is a little peace and quiet. Introduce him to our friends, and make sure that he is treated with the respect they would extend to me. He will give you any news you might like to hear concerning my health. My heart is not what it used to be and I don't think I shall live much longer. But don't let it worry you. I am seventy-five years old and I've had a good life. If I had to live it all over again I would wish to live it in exactly the same way, and that includes Giacchino. This may well be the last time I write to you. I kiss your hand gratefully for all you've done for me over the years. Keep fit and greet all our friends, yours most affectionately ... Will that do?

ANTONIO Give me the pen. (FABIO *hands him a ballpoint*) Antonio Barracano. (*Slips a ring from his finger and gives it to* FABIO) This is for you.

FABIO (*in some confusion*) Don Antonio ...

ANTONIO See whether it fits ...

FABIO (*tries it on*) Yes, it does.

ANTONIO It was given to me by Bastiano when I came back to Italy. He said: This ring must be taken from your finger by a friend when you close your eyes for the last time. This friend should bring it to me if I'm still alive. If not, he can keep it. You see, doctor, this ring used to belong to his father, who was framed and tried and died in prison. It's a long story. Anyway, show him the ring and he'll take his hat off. If he doesn't happen to be wearing one at the time, he'll go and put one on, come back and raise his hat to the ring. Give me some water. (FABIO *gives him another glass of water*) This business of the perforated spleen makes you thirsty.

FABIO It always does.

ANTONIO It happened an hour ago ... Have I got another hour?

FABIO Yes ...

ANTONIO You'll have time to go to Terzigno tomorrow. I don't want the two dogs to suffer. Would you mind seeing to them yourself? My family aren't any too fond of them. My wife's bound to give them away. Humanity is divided into two categories, as it were; Antonio Barracano on one side and Arturo Santaniello on the other. You'll be able to do it quickly and efficiently, I'm sure ... a couple of injections ... I dread the thought of my dogs in the hands of someone like Santaniello.

FABIO   I'll take care of it.

ANTONIO   (pointing to his clothes) This suit ... and shirt ... I've got to change. I don't want people to see me in these clothes tomorrow morning. I've got some things here. I'll change. Dispose of these in a suitcase. What about the death certificate? Hadn't you better get it ready?

FABIO   There's no need just now.

ANTONIO   Why not?

FABIO   I'll do it when the time comes.

ANTONIO   What will you give as the cause?

FABIO   Anything you want me to say.

ANTONIO   Heart failure.

FABIO   Very good. (The doorbell rings. VICENZELLA comes in from the kitchen and crosses the room) There's someone at the door.

VICENZELLA   I'll answer it. (Leaves the room)

FABIO   It's probably Cuozzo.

ANTONIO   Let's hope so. (Takes a sip of water)

FABIO   He's sure to come.

VICENZELLA   (enters with RAFILUCCIO and RITA) Come in.

RAFILUCCIO   Good evening, Don Antonio.

RITA   Good evening.

ANTONIO   Well, what is it?

RAFILUCCIO   Don Antonio, I simply had to see you. I didn't know where to find you, but I bumped into Vicienzo Cuozzo, who told me you were at home, that you were spending the night in Naples and that you'd asked him to dinner.

ANTONIO   Well?

RAFILUCCIO   Your wife has been very good to us, Don Antonio.

RITA   She said she'd let us stay in a small two-roomed flat which happens to be empty just now ...

RAFILUCCIO   She's taken a fancy to Rita, and told her that we needn't pay any rent till I settle down and get a job.

RITA   And your son will give Rafiluccio a job in his shop.

RAFILUCCIO   Then I remembered your advice about a man only being truly a man if he can back down ... Well, I've come to tell you not to worry any more about my father. I ... I won't do it.

RITA   It's a miracle, I tell you!

ANTONIO   I'm pleased to hear that. What's more, I can tell you that my conversation with your father was very satisfactory.

RAFILUCCIO   Really?

RITA   What did he say?

ANTONIO   What could he say? He had to bend. He asked me how much money he should give you, and I mentioned the sum of two million lire. He was a bit difficult at first ... old habits die hard ... but he gave way in the end.

RAFILUCCIO   It can't be true ...

ANTONIO   He didn't have it on him, so I told him I'd advance it to you, and he could reimburse me at his leisure. We shook hands on it, which is all you need do between gentlemen. Doctor, hand me my wallet ... It's in my coat pocket. My arm is hurting. I can hardly move it.

FABIO   Let me. (*Takes the wallet from* ANTONIO's *coat pocket*)

ANTONIO   Open it. There's a cheque book inside.

FABIO   Here it is.

ANTONIO Make out the cheque and I'll sign it. Date it Naples, 10th September 1960. (FABIO *writes out the cheque*) Raffaele Santaniello. Two million lire.

FABIO Done.

ANTONIO Give it to me. (FABIO *gives him the cheque and he signs it*) Here you are, Rafiluccio.

RAFILUCCIO Don Antonio, I don't know how to thank you. (*To* RITA) Kiss Don Antonio's hand.

RITA I'll kiss both his hands ... (*Kisses* ANTONIO'S *hands*)

ANTONIO All right, that's enough. Please go now. I'm expecting people.

RAFILUCCIO Let's go, Rita. Don Antonio's busy. Good night, doctor.

FABIO Good night.

RAFILUCCIO And thank you again. (*Goes out with* RITA)

ANTONIO Where's the letter?

FABIO The one to Bastiano?

ANTONIO No, that's for you to take to the States. The first one you wrote.

FABIO Here it is. (*Shows it to him*)

ANTONIO Hang on to it for the moment. Give it to me when I ask for it.

VICENZELLA (*enters*) Everything is ready. Is it to be white or red wine?

FABIO As it's roast chicken ... red wine. (*The doorbell rings*) Open the door. (VICENZELLA *goes out*) How are you feeling?

ANTONIO Quite well ... I'm sweating a bit.

VICENZELLA (*comes in followed by* VICIENZO CUOZZO) This way. (CUOZZO *comes in silently, stops by the entrance and lowers his eyes*)

FABIO Don Antonio was afraid you weren't going to turn up, but I was sure you would.

VICIENZO How could I fail to come if Don Antonio asked me?

FABIO It's as well you came. This may be the last time you see Don Antonio Barracano.

VICIENZO Doctor ... what are you saying?

FABIO There's nothing more a doctor can do.

VICIENZO Oh my God!

FABIO We shall mourn a great friend. (*Businesslike*) Now, the whole thing is extremely delicate. As you know, it happened about an hour ago. You were the only witness at the shop. There was nobody else, is that right, Don Antonio?

ANTONIO He came in just at the right moment, if you could call it the right moment.

FABIO Don Antonio knows how devoted you are to him. That's what worries him.

VICIENZO What are you talking about?

FABIO Of the knifing that took place in Via Giacinto Albino.

VICIENZO What knifing?

ANTONIO Wait a moment, doctor. What do you mean: What knifing? Didn't you come into the baker's shop in Via Giacinto Albino about an hour ago, as Don Arturo and I were talking?

VICIENZO No. An hour ago I was sitting quietly at home. I'm afraid you made a mistake.

ANTONIO (*bitterly*) I see. It wasn't you. You know nothing and you saw nothing. As a matter of fact all this suits me perfectly. Doctor, we needn't worry. This snotty bastard won't talk. (*To* VICIENZO) When you came in you looked at me and realised I'd had it. The doctor told you how things stood ... and you feel safe enough. I suppose the baker threatened you ... yes, I suppose you're right in your own way.

FABIO   What did I tell you? What have we got to show for our pains?

ANTONIO   You were wrong. I was right. There's an Antonio Barracano today, there'll be another one tomorrow, and yet another the day after that. Maybe my children's children and this swine's ... (*Pointing at* VICIENZO) children through our efforts may one day find themselves in a world that will have lost some of its gloss, but will be that much fairer ... Don't you agree?

FABIO   No!

ANTONIO   You and I haven't agreed about things for a long time now. (*Pause*) I'd like a change of clothes. Will you give me a hand?

FABIO   Of course.

ANTONIO   We must hurry. Our friends will soon be here. (*To* VICIENZO) It's a party for the doctor, who's just about to leave for the States. This, at least, is the excuse, but we can tell you the truth ... we know you'll keep your mouth shut. All our friends here tonight will be able to testify that I felt unwell at dinner. And a little later ... How did it happen? That's what they will be asked. Well, he was getting on ... Over seventy ... Heart failure. Stay to dinner as well, you can bear witness too ... false witness. (*Goes out supported by* FABIO)

(*After a short pause the doorbell rings*)

VICENZELLA   (*enters and crosses the room on her way to the main door*) Oh dear, they've left you all alone ...

(CUOZZO *does not answer.* VICENZELLA *answers the door and comes back with more guests. She goes back to the kitchen.* ARTURO, *visibly scared, is led in by two mysterious characters,* PEPPE' *and* ZIBACCHIELLO. *The two are silent, an enigmatic grin on their lips*)

ARTURO (*plaintively*) Won't you tell me what this is all about? Where have you taken me? Who am I to see?

PEPPE' We're friends, don't worry.

ARTURO But where are we? Whose house is this?

ZIBACCHIELLO It's just a house, can't you see?

PEPPE' And the dinner table is laid, the food is ready. There'll be other guests. You don't have to worry about a thing.

ARTURO (*angrily*) But I'm a grown man! I'm not a baby you can just pick up and put down somewhere else. (*Utterly exasperated*) Is there any justice in this world? I am a law-abiding citizen, why should I put up with the excesses of outlaws ... gangsters ... that's what you are. I am a worker. An honest man! Please, let me go home. I'm ill, just feel here ... (*Puts out his arm*) I've got a temperature. I've always minded my own business, never interfered with anybody else's affairs. Come the first Friday of every month I visit my poor wife's grave ... She was a marvellous woman ... If she were still alive today things would be different. I live alone, like a dog, and that criminal of a son of mine has got me into all this. He's succeeded in ruining his father ... they'll sling me into jail ... (*To* PEPPE' *and* ZIBACCHIELLO) I'm sure you are men of the world ... please help me. (*Kneels down at their feet*) Please, please let me go. I've got my ticket ready ... I'm off to Switzerland ... I'll give you anything you ask for. (*Takes a cheque book out of his pocket*) You name the sum. How much would you like? (PEPPE' *and* ZIBACCHIELLO *remain silent*) How much? Answer me ... say something!

FABIO (*enters*) What's the matter? Oh ... you must be Arturo Santaniello. You're a pretty sight!

ARTURO I'm an honest man ... I was minding my own business ...

FABIO   That's just the trouble. You shut your eyes, plug your ears and live as though you were the only man in the world. Then you're surprised when life winkles you out, takes you by the scruff of the neck and forces you to face reality. Whenever there's any trouble, all one hears from the likes of you is: I was minding my own business. But you're here now because it is your business to be here. The matter concerns you. It's something that you began with your eyes shut and you must now see through with your eyes wide open. (*The doorbell rings*) Vicenzella, the door!

VICENZELLA   (*enters*) Here I am.

FABIO   The door. (*Leaves the room*)

VICENZELLA   Very good. (*Goes and answers the door. She returns with* NAIT, PALUMMIELLO, PASQUALE NASONE *and his wife*) Come in, come in.

PASQUALE   Thanks. (*Notices* VICIENZO CUOZZO) You here, too? (VICIENZO *makes no answer*) Nice manners we've got ...

HIS WIFE   Don't talk to him you fool ...

PASQUALE   You're right. He's not worth it.

NAIT   It would have to be tonight! There's an English ship docking and I had a nice bit of business lined up ... Still, can't say no to Don Antonio.

PALUMMIELLO   One evening off won't hurt you.

FABIO   (*comes in*) Let's all sit down to dinner. (*Calls out*) Vicenzella, you may serve! (*They all sit round the table, except* ARTURO) Don Arturo, you sit here. (*Points to the place next to the one reserved for* ANTONIO) Next to me. (PEPPE' *and* ZIBACCHIELLO *lead* ARTURO *to the seat indicated by* FABIO *and sit him down*)

LUIGI   (*enters carrying food*) Here's the roast chicken.

VICENZELLA   And here's the salad.

FABIO You join us too. I've had instructions to ask you to have dinner with us. (VICENZELLA *and* LUIGI *sit down with the others*)

LUIGI Well, good health everybody.

FABIO If you'll excuse me just one moment. (*Goes out and comes back shortly after, arm in arm with* ANTONIO)

(ANTONIO's *appearance causes immediate silence and concern. His eyes are no longer bright or challenging. His step is unsteady and his pallor cadaverous.* FABIO *manages to take him up to the table and gets him to sit down. A half-hearted round of applause greets* ANTONIO *as he sits down.* ARTURO *and* VICIENZO *look down at their plates*)

ANTONIO You must forgive me, but I'm not feeling too well. That's the way of nature. The enemy is always lying in wait; you're standing there thinking all is well and he sticks a knife into you. Still, I expect it's nothing. Well, we're gathered here tonight to pay our respects to the doctor, who is leaving us for a new life in America. He has been our friend for many years and has helped us all, in one way or another, sometimes in extremely difficult circumstances. We are grateful to him and thank him from the bottom of our hearts. (*Round of applause*) He wanted to stay on with us and continue his good work, but I told him it was time to call it a day. I myself am getting on. I'm tired, as you can see my health isn't as good as it was and I want to retire. From tonight onwards I shall no longer manage the affairs of this district.

PEPPE' Don Antonio, you can't leave us just like that, from one moment to the next ...

ANTONIO I can't go on for ever. There's so much to be done. So much to be done. So many poor people to be helped, who need to be put on the right road, looked after ... who need protection. How can a man do all that on his own? There's a limit to human endurance. I'm not saying I've not achieved something in the course of all these years. On the contrary, I flatter myself I've done a lot to limit and contain crime. Let's hope that in times to come there'll be no need for people like Antonio Barracano.

NAIT You're really going to leave us?

ANTONIO Everything comes to an end, and how much better when it ends with a pleasant dinner and in good company. We are honoured tonight to have as one of our guests Don Arturo Santaniello. (*Round of applause*) I'm glad to see him and I am delighted to learn that the little difference with his son has now been ... composed. Don Arturo was very worried. Fortunately everything is now settled. Incidentally, Don Arturo, I've done as you asked me and advanced your son the two million lire you wanted me to make over to him. I also want to thank you for the letter you wrote me. I think the others should hear it. (*To* FABIO) Doctor, the letter ...

FABIO (*Takes a letter out of his pocket and hands it to* ANTONIO) Here it is.

ANTONIO You'd better read it, doctor. I can't see all that well and I'm a little tired.

FABIO (*reads*) Dear Don Antonio, I acknowledge receipt of two million lire and I note that you have advanced this sum to my son Rafiluccio. It was kind of you, as at the time I had no money or cheques on me. Needless to say I shall return this sum on demand. Thank you again, yours truly ...

ANTONIO (*to* ARTURO) You forgot to sign it ... would you mind?

ARTURO (*barely audible*) Not at all.

(FABIO *hands* ARTURO *a ballpoint, and he signs the letter*)

ANTONIO Have you got your cheque book?

ARTURO Yes.

ANTONIO Make the cheque out to Signora Armida Barracano. (ARTURO *writes out the cheque, tears it off and gives it to* ANTONIO) Doctor, would you kindly give this cheque to my wife?

FABIO Very well. (*Pockets the cheque*)

ANTONIO Go on, eat and enjoy yourselves. (*Slowly bends down and, pressing his right arm on his abdomen, collapses on to the table*)

EVERYBODY Don Antonio!

FABIO It's nothing serious. (*Helps* ANTONIO *to his feet*) Let's go into your bedroom, Don Antonio ... you'd better lie down a little and I'll examine you ... (*Without waiting for an answer he slowly leads* ANTONIO *out of the room*) He'll be all right presently. You carry on.

VICIENZO (*rises with tears in his eyes and goes up to* FABIO *and* ANTONIO) Don Antonio ... Don Antonio ...

ANTONIO (*thickly*) What do you want?

VICIENZO I was threatened ...

ANTONIO (*on his way again*) I know.

VICIENZO Don Antonio, don't leave me just like this ...

FABIO What do you want?

VICIENZO Don Antonio, say goodbye to me.

ANTONIO (*looking at him with glazed eyes*) Goodbye.

VICIENZO Give me your hand ...

ANTONIO (*after a short pause, smiles ironically and finds the strength to say*) No. I won't give you my hand. (*Leaves the room with* FABIO)

PASQUALE I don't like the look of Don Antonio.

HIS WIFE The man isn't at all well.

NAIT He isn't all that young, either.

LUIGI Don Antonio is as strong as an ox.

PALUMMIELLO (*to* NAIT) Pass me that bottle.

NAIT (*passing the bottle*) The chicken is smashing.

PASQUALE I can eat a whole chicken just like that.

VICENZELLA (*to* LUIGI) Dad, pass me the salad.

(*They settle down to eat and chat*)

FABIO (*comes back, his head bent. He goes up to the chair* ANTONIO *had been sitting in and looks with contempt at the assembled company, considering them one by one as if he were seeing them for the first time. After a long pause, during which the diners gradually fall silent, he announces flatly*) Don Antonio is dead. (*The diners exchange looks of consternation*)

PASQUALE Poor Don Antonio!

HIS WIFE Was it his heart?

FABIO Yes. He had an enormous heart, with a door to it that never failed to open when somebody knocked.

NAIT They don't make men like Antonio Barracano any more.

FABIO I was close to him for thirty-five years. I loved him. I respected him. Only I know what I am feeling just now. As for you, it's your turn to talk. (ARTURO *is silent*) Don Arturo, you must talk! (*Turns to* VICIENZO CUOZZO) You talk then. (VICIENZO *remains silent, his head lowered*) Wasn't it you who shouted: Don Antonio is our father! We all love you!..? (*Goes up to* VICIENZO *and grabs him by the scruff of the neck*) Have you nothing to say now?

VICIENZO What do you want me to say? I know nothing.

FABIO You know nothing. I suppose you know nothing either, Don Arturo. It seems we've all got into the habit of sending our conscience to the laundry, gentlemen. Not just us here, but everybody, from the most exalted in the land to the humblest peasant. Why should I follow Don Antonio's last wishes? Why? To protect scum like you? To save two swine who are afraid to tell the truth ... whose stock in trade is made up of lies, hypocrisy, threats, blackmail ...? It would suit you all, wouldn't it, if Antonio Barracano had really died of heart failure, after spending his whole life trying to limit and contain your criminality. He should have done the opposite and expanded it all. Yes. Because that's exactly what I am going to do. I'm not going to America. I'll stay put. (*Goes to the telephone and dials*) Hullo ... I'd like to call the Terzigno exchange ... get me the Barracano estate, will you? This is 314021. Thank you. (*Replaces the receiver, takes out of his pocket the cheque for two million lire and hands it to* ARTURO) You can give this to the widow yourself, if you feel like doing the decent thing. (*To* VICIENZO) And you can spill the beans if you feel you want to. (*To the others*) And you can tell what you've seen and heard tonight, that is ... if you feel like it. As for me, I am going to prepare the death certificate as my conscience dictates. Then Don Antonio's sons, and Don Arturo's relations will come out in strength, and their friends, their acquaintances, their hired help: there'll be a blood bath, it'll be total war till everybody's been wiped out. Better this way. Perhaps destruction on this scale will pave the way to a different world, the sort of world Don Antonio used to dream about, a world that will have lost some of its gloss but will be that much fairer ... Yes, I'll start the ball rolling by putting my full name to a genuine death certificate for a change: Fabio Della Ragione, MD. Butcher me, skin me alive, but I'll have the satisfaction of signing off with the words: THIS IS

A TRUE STATEMENT. *(Sits at the typewriter and begins to type as*

THE CURTAIN FALLS

Grand Magic

(*La Grande Magia*)

translated by Carlo Ardito

CHARACTERS

Mrs Locascio
Mrs Marino
Mrs Zampa
Miss Zampa *her daughter*
Marta Di Spelta
Calogero Di Spelta *her husband*
Mariano D'Albino *her lover*
A Waiter
Gervasio D'Aloisi *Otto's associate*
Arturo Taddei *Otto's associate*
Amelia *Arturo's daughter*
'Professor' Otto Marvuglia *Master of Occult
    Sciences and Celebrated Illusionist. Hypnosis
    and Telepathy a Speciality*
Zaira *his wife*
A Police Inspector
Roberto Magliano
Gennarino Fucecchio *Calogero's manservant*

Calogero's relations:
Gregorio *his brother*
Matilde *his mother*
Oreste Intrugli *his brother-in-law*
Rosa Intrugli *his sister, married to Oreste*
Hotel servants and patrons

*The action of the play takes place at
a seaside resort somewhere in Italy*

Grand Magic was first performed in this version on the Lyttelton stage of the Royal National Theatre, London, on 13 July 1995, with the following cast:

Mrs Locascio	*Gillian Raine*
Mrs Marino	*Marianne Morley*
Mrs Zampa	*Deirdra Morris*
Miss Zampa	*Jaq O'Hanlon*
Marta di Spelta	*Fiona Gillies*
Calogero di Spelta	*Alan Howard*
Mariano d'Albino	*Adam Henderson*
Waiter	*Mark Payton*
Gervasio d'Aloisi	*Christopher Ryan*
Arturo Taddei	*George Raistrick*
Amelia	*Anne-Marie Duff*
Professor Otto Marvuglia	*Bernard Cribbins*
Zaira	*Alison Fiske*
Police Inspector	*David Ross*
Roberto Magliano	*Michael Bott*
Gennarino Fucecchio	*William Osborne*
Gregorio	*Colin Haigh*
Matilde	*Gillian Raine*
Oreste Intrugli	*Edmund Kente*
Rosa Intrugli	*Naomi Capron*
First Policeman	*Edmund Kente*
Second Policeman	*Martin Chamberlain*

Directed by *Sir Richard Eyre*
Designed by *Anthony Ward*
Lighting by *Mark Henderson*
Musical Director *Dominic Muldowney*

ACT ONE

*(As the curtain rises the velvet draping or apron which
normally masks the orchestra pit also rises, revealing
a large garden with flower-beds and ancient palm trees
which partly conceal the sumptuous seaward elevation
of the Grand Hotel Metropole. This façade, which is
to be sited as far upstage as possible, shows some of the
windows and balconies on the upper stories, as well as
the vast lounge of the hotel, visible through large french
windows. As the orchestra pit draping is removed we
see in its place a rocky shore against which the gentle
waves of an imaginary sea softly break. The sea is to
be suggested by light effects and extends from the rocks
to halfway up the auditorium. Four sturdy cement
pillars support the edge of the garden. Painted silhouettes
will suggest brightly coloured boats moored by the rocks.
A small motor-boat sways gently between the two central
pillars. At the same time blue tubular railings will
emerge along the whole length of the footlights, denoting
the outermost edge of the garden. The railings trail off
on both sides to form banisters to the two small stairways
which lead down to the landing stage. Against the two
sides of the hotel façade upstage are three neatly arranged
rows of garden tables and chairs, surrounded by
thick, luxuriant myrtle bushes which are so shaped
as to leave a free central aisle. A number of deck chairs*

are to be seen on both sides of the garden. Well into sunset.

Downstage left, seated, are four women of the type one so often meets at grand hotels in the summer: MRS LOCASCIO, MRS MARINO, MRS *and* MISS ZAMPA. *They are playing cards.*

On the opposite side, downstage right, GERVASIO PENNA *has just had a cup of coffee and is now contentedly puffing away at his small briar pipe.*
ARTURO TADDEI *is seated at a downstage table closer to the hotel lounge, and is idly chatting with his daughter* AMELIA. *She is thin and large-eyed; her gestures and conversation are childish; she can as easily be moved to laughter as to tears)*

MRS LOCASCIO *(selects a winning card and blandly announces)* My hand I think ... and rubber!

(The others begin to add up points to settle up with the winner)

MRS ZAMPA   You've won yet again ... Lucky you! Well, that's my lot for today.

MRS LOCASCIO   Come, come, you haven't lost a fortune. A matter of a few hundred lire.

MRS ZAMPA   I'm joking, darling. In fact I don't know what we'd do with ourselves if we hadn't got our little game. It's so relaxing.

MRS MARINO   Where else would one find such peace and quiet? I've been here nearly a month and I haven't been to the cinema or the theatre even once.

MRS ZAMPA   No need to at all, my dear. Just sit out here any afternoon or evening and you'll get all the entertainment you'll ever want.

MISS ZAMPA   It's perfectly true. Every summer there's

always a couple who turn out to be the star attraction.

MRS LOCASCIO   How right you are! This year it's the Di Speltas. You should have been on the beach yesterday morning: it was like a Victorian melodrama. The husband, Calogero ... how can anyone go through life with a name like Calogero, I ask you! ... got there just as his wife was having her photograph taken: D'Albino was just pressing the release button. Calogero hadn't been expecting this. He was carrying half a water melon, of the really bright red variety. When he saw what was happening his face flushed a deeper red than the water melon in his hand and he put his lit cigarette back into his mouth the wrong way round. D'Albino for his part— you know the cheek of the man—just vanished. Only husband and wife were left on the scene. They were speechless and couldn't look one another in the eye.

MRS ZAMPA   She's a good-looking woman. I can't blame her husband if he's jealous.

MRS LOCASCIO   Why doesn't he show it then? No, he bottles it all up. I think he's wrong. Unless one lets off steam in these cases one just gets more and more bitter. Haven't you noticed how ill-mannered he is to every-body? I put it all down to the fact he doesn't want his jealousy to show through.

MRS MARINO   But then how do you account for the fact that she's never allowed out for a walk on her own, that he locks her in her room when he goes out?

MRS LOCASCIO   Because a lot of men get a feeling of inferiority if they suspect others know how passionately attached they are to their wives. They put up a barrier of contemptuous, detached silence and that makes them feel better and rather superior. Frankly I find it quite gratifying when these types end up in homes for nervous diseases.

MISS ZAMPA   How is Mr D'Albino taking it?

MRS LOCASCIO He's going out of his mind with
   frustration. Despite all his clever tricks and stratagems
   he never seems to be able to have five minutes alone
   with her. Apparently that's why he took her photograph.
   He said to me last night: Now I've taken her picture
   she won't slip through my fingers. Let's see if her
   husband manages to stop me now. I wonder what he
   meant?

MRS ZAMPA (looking to her left notices the approach
   of MARTA and CALOGERO) Here they come. She looks
   as if she'd been sentenced to death, and he's the very
   picture of gloom.

MRS LOCASCIO What I don't understand is why they
   don't part, having reached this sorry stage.

MRS ZAMPA You never know. It may well happen.

(From the left MARTA enters followed by CALOGERO.
He is a man in his middle years, slightly dreamy, with a
very black moustache and a highly coloured complexion.
He dresses rather showily: a jacket with large checks,
double vent and button-up pockets, drainpipe trousers
and a brash straw hat on his head; in short, a garish
tailor's dummy. MARTA is a beautiful young woman.
She affects an air of indifference but is slightly on edge.
They are both tormented by a private inner argument
which has sunk them in deep dejection. He hides this
mood by a somewhat grotesque manner and at the same
time attempts to appear cool and nonchalant. The ladies
look at the couple out of the corner of their eyes while
pretending to be deep in conversation. CALOGERO
walks a step or two behind MARTA as they take a turn
in the garden)

MRS ZAMPA Do join us, please.
MARTA Thank you. I think I will. (Sits down)
MRS LOCASCIO (to CALOGERO) Won't you join us

as well? I have the impression you're always avoiding us.

CALOGERO You're wrong. I never avoid anyone. Especially people whose company I detest.

MRS ZAMPA You see? You've hardly sat down and you've already come out with your first uncivil remark.

CALOGERO Not at all. I've told you my first home truth.

MRS LOCASCIO Then I'll tell you another home truth: we forgive you because you're not quite yourself.

CALOGERO What makes you think I'm not? I hate these hasty opinions. They're like sentences against which there's no appeal. I'll have you know I'm extremely happy and even-tempered at the moment. If only you knew how much importance I give to facts and facts alone! I want you to bear this in mind: I am a happy man because I am a realist. I call a spade a spade in and out of season.

MRS LOCASCIO What's that supposed to mean?

CALOGERO I mean that I'm ready for anything. I don't expect any surprises from life because I don't trust anyone, not even myself, an inch.

MRS ZAMPA You don't even trust women?

CALOGERO Especially women. No offence meant.

MARTA Can't you see you're making yourself ridiculous? (To the others) Don't mind him. He's pulling your leg.

CALOGERO You're quite right! And you may be sure of something else, too: I would never allow myself the liberty of taking any one of you seriously.

MRS MARINO Never mind. We won't take you seriously. I suppose you yourself know the things you take seriously.

MRS LOCASCIO Oh ... Mariano D'Albino.

CALOGERO You must be mad. As far as I am concerned he doesn't even exist. My wife will vouch for this. I've never been jealous of anybody, let alone this fellow ...

MRS LOCASCIO Please, don't take on so! I said Mariano D'Albino because I've just noticed he's coming this way. (*Points to the left*)

CALOGERO (*apologetically*) I'm so sorry. I misunderstood.

MARIANO (*approaching from the left*) Here I am Mrs Di Spelta. I hope you'll appreciate my promptitude. I rushed to the chemist's and they had the photographs developed in a trice. They're beauties. (*To* MRS ZAMPA) You're in them, too.

MRS ZAMPA The ones you took of us as a group?

MRS LOCASCIO The ones with the dog?

MARIANO That's it. (*Opens an envelope and shows the snapshots round*)

CALOGERO You don't let the grass grow under your feet ...

MARIANO Ah well, the ladies expect me to keep my promises, you know ... (*The others look at the snapshots appreciatively*) By the way, Mrs Di Spelta, yours came out so well that I had six prints made.

MARTA Thank you. It's awfully kind of you.

MARIANO (*handing a snapshot to* CALOGERO) You're in this one as well ... I see you're carrying a water melon. (*To the others*) I pressed the button and he didn't even notice. Looks as if you were peddling the things ...

CALOGERO May I have the six copies of my wife's photograph?

MARIANO (*hands them over*) Here they are.

CALOGERO (*counts them*) There's only five here.

MARIANO I suppose they only printed five and I didn't notice.

CALOGERO Have you got the negative? (*Takes a cigarette from a packet and puts it between his lips*)

MARIANO Of course. (*Finds it among the other negatives and hands it over*) Here it is.

CALOGERO (*takes the negative and holds it up to the light*) It's very good. (*Pretends to light his cigarette and*

as if by accident the lit cigarette sets fire to the negative)
Oh, dear! I've burnt it. (*The others exchange meaning-
ful glances*) There goes the negative ... I'll keep the five
prints. (*Pockets the snapshots*)

MARIANO   Well, I'm glad I've been of some use. (*Goes
out right*)

MRS ZAMPA   (*changing the subject*) We're going to have
a performance in this garden tonight.

CALOGERO   No one asked you to stay here. If we're
troubling you, you can get up and leave.

MRS ZAMPA   Why on earth should I?

CALOGERO   You've just said we're making a spectacle
of ourselves.

MRS ZAMPA   My dear Mr Di Spelta, you seem to imagine
that the world revolves round you and your affairs. I
said there was going to be a performance in this garden
tonight, as a famous conjurer is coming to entertain
us all.

CALOGERO   Forgive me. I didn't understand.

MARTA   Oh, I do like conjurers!

CALOGERO   They're a bit old hat these days.

MARTA   I didn't for a moment think you'd share my
preferences.

CALOGERO   Look, people are much too sophisticated
these days. At one time conjurers and illusionists used
to be extremely popular, but we've moved on. People
are no longer impressed.

GERVASIO   (*who has overheard, butts in*) And yet I
think you're in for a surprise. You'll have to reconsider
what you've just said when you've seen the show. (*Gets
up, walks over to their table and introduces himself*)
How do you do? My name is Gervasio D'Aloisi.

CALOGERO   What makes you think I'll have to reconsider what I said?

GERVASIO   Because I know this conjurer. He rarely

appears at all. He gives a few performances in large hotels now and again, but that's about all.

MARTA   Is he any good?

GERVASIO   Good is hardly the word I would use to describe him: more like a wizard. The things he can do are beyond human comprehension.

ARTURO   I know him too. I saw his act in Paris. (*He and* AMELIA *move closer to the others*)

AMELIA   Only last year: what an unforgettable evening! I really got scared! (*Laughs without conviction, a short, rhythmic, infantile laugh*) Ha ha ha!

MRS LOCASCIO   Well, don't let's get carried away. A conjurer after all can only be a charlatan, a trickster and nothing more.

ARTURO   That's what I thought at first! (*Introduces himself*) Arturo Taddei. How do you do? ... (*Points to* AMELIA) My daughter. I thought he was just a mountebank to begin with, but I soon knew better, to my cost.

GERVASIO   As for me, he put me through the most frightening ordeal.

ARTURO   My daughter fainted ...

AMELIA   I fainted, that's right ... (*Laughs, as above*) Ha ha ha!

MARTA   But what does he do?

ARTURO   We were watching the show, my late wife, my daughter and I, when ...

GERVASIO   Forgive the interruption, but I must really insist that no one can possibly have been through a more harrowing experience than mine at the hands of Professor Marvuglia. He started off with a few of the usual tricks, you know, rabbits out of top hats, vanishing tricks, just what one would expect. Then he went on to experiments in telepathy and hypnosis. This is when it all started. He asked members of the audience to join him on the stage and I was stupid enough to volunteer. He looked

me straight in the eye and said: You are under sentence
of death. You are a persecuted man. Run away, flee, or
you're lost. There's a passport in your pocket. Get the
next train, and good luck to you. With that passport I
travelled the world over: France, England, Russia,
Japan ... for years and years, without ever stopping in
any one place too long for fear of being arrested. I went
by train and sea and air. I climbed mountains. I found
myself knee-deep in snow. And in icy wastes ... I crossed
desolate deserts and primeval forests ...

CALOGERO Using the same passport?

GERVASIO I had no passport, can't you see? Or rather,
I had it and yet I hadn't. I was under a spell. Anyway
at the end of the journey I found myself in the professor's
presence again, in front of an amused audience. Only
a few seconds had elapsed, don't you know, but I felt I'd
been on the move for countless years.

CALOGERO I'm not doubting what you're saying, Mr ...

GERVASIO D'Aloisi.

CALOGERO ... Mr D'Aloisi, but you will admit what
you've just told us stretches one's credulity a bit.

GERVASIO Wait till tonight. Then you'll see.

MRS ZAMPA (to AMELIA) And you say you ... fainted?

AMELIA Yes, I did ... when I saw daddy turn into a
stag ...

MRS ZAMPA A stag?

ARTURO That's right. A stag. The transformation took
place in a second, and there I was—a stag.

CALOGERO It isn't possible ...

ARTURO Why should I be having you on? Everybody
in the audience was under the impression I was a stag
and saw me amble and canter gracefully and with the
greatest agility. It was odd in the extreme, because
though the others saw me caper round as a stag, I was
just quietly sitting on a chair. And I heard people

shout: Look at his antlers! Aren't they magnificent? I passed a hand over my forehead and could feel no antlers at all.

CALOGERO   It was just a case of mass hypnosis.

GERVASIO   Call it what you will. But you should have been there. You'd have changed your tune ...

MRS LOCASCIO   What sort of man is he?

GERVASIO   He isn't young. In his sixties I should say. He's got a deeply lined, ravaged face ... He talks slowly; he seems to articulate words more with his hands than with his lips and mouth. But his eyes are his most extraordinary feature: you feel they're always on you. Strangely enough, from the way he dresses and his general appearance you could quite easily take him for a tramp. But if he claps his eyes on you, you can't stare him out.

MRS ZAMPA   I'm not sure I'm going to come to the show. It sounds too creepy.

MISS ZAMPA   Come on, mummy, don't let's exaggerate ...

THE WAITER   (*approaches from upstage right followed by two porters carrying a large wicker basket*) Put it here, right here. (*Points to the appropriate spot. The porters put down the basket*) Bring over the rest of the equipment as directed by the Professor. Be quick about it as it's getting late. The Professor's here already. (*The porters leave upstage right*)

CALOGERO   Is it the conjurer you're talking about?

THE WAITER   Yes. This is his gear. There's more to come. He's got another cartload on the way!

(*The porters return carrying two chromium-plated round tables, two chairs in the same style and a larger rectangular table, also in metal, as well as an Egyptian sarcophagus large enough to accommodate an adult*)

CALOGERO (*sceptically*) Tricks. Just tricks. That's all they are.

GERVASIO Please yourself. But watch out.

MARTA (*to* THE WAITER, *referring to the conjurer*) Is he here yet?

THE WAITER He got here a few minutes ago. I believe he's having a word with the manager. (*Glancing at the central entrance to the lounge*) Oh, there he is. That's him.

OTTO (*comes in through the lounge entrance. Physically he answers* GERVASIO'*s description to the letter. He walks slowly, and seems lost in thought. He is wearing an old-fashioned suit, possibly altered to fit him. He wears a bow-tie over a wing collar. On his head sits a Panama hat, yellow with age. An altogether tired and resigned presence, though not devoid of a hint of grotesque dignity, especially when he indulges in the histrionics peculiar to his calling. He is a thoroughly professional charlatan. As he enters he looks around carefully and scrutinises every individual present. Long pause, during which the others look at him, and study his every gesture with great interest. At length he turns to* THE WAITER) Here?

THE WAITER Here, Professor. As you see there's plenty of room.

OTTO (*looking at the landscape*) A truly charming view.

THE WAITER It's an enchanting place. Look at the colour and the sheer size of the sea. (*Points at the auditorium with a sweeping gesture*)

OTTO (*looks at* THE WAITER *with infinite pity*) So you think the sea is vast. You poor, ignorant man. There was a time when I, too, thought exactly the same thing and I took a dive into the sea. The moment I was in the water I failed to find enough room to move about freely. The whole of humanity had jumped in before me. One thousand pairs of hands pushed me back roughly and I was, as it were, squirted back to the shore. (*Pointing at the auditorium*) It's no more than a drop of water, my dear friend. Its only prodigious characteristic is that it never dries up, or at least if it does the process must be too slow for the human eye to perceive it. A mere drop of water in the centre of darkness, darkness without end, darkness which persists even during those hours when we imagine the sun has done away with it ... (*Now turns to everyone generally and goes on with typical conjurer's patter*) Yes, ladies and gentlemen, the sun may be beating down, but through it I perceive darkness. The sun runs its course, it cannot help it, just as a sentenced man cannot help going to prison. The sun cannot destroy its circumambient darkness. But we could, oh yes: we could destroy darkness with what I call our third eye, if only it were granted to each and everyone of us to possess it. Yes, the third eye; the eye without window, the eye of thought, the only eye I am now left with. The other two, alas, the ones that are visible and which in my youth saw everything as larger than life ... enormous and full of wonder, the other two, I was saying, I have lost irretrievably. They were extinguished shortly after my fiftieth birthday ...

MRS ZAMPA   (*in an undertone*) My God, is he blind then?

OTTO   No, madam. I am not blind. But you are, madam, blind in the extreme, since you form part of that large band of blind people who may be well into their fifties yet will never acquire the third eye. Of course that's just as well and could be a blessing in disguise. Heaven help us if it were given to everybody to acquire it. Very few ever do, anyway, and its potency varies greatly. My third eye is not particularly important. I only use it for my modest performances. My tricks are simple and innocent in nature. But there are those who, having acquired the third eye, are driven to become illusionists of an altogether different and more sinister calibre. When their third eye is at work, illusions and deceptions multiply to infinity, all sorts of forces are brought to bear, to the detriment of all concerned. Surely you, Mr D'Aloisi, can vouch for the innocence of my tricks! True, I made you travel, but not for long, you'll admit. And what about you, Mr Taddei, would you object if I made you jump around once again as a stag in its wild habitat?

ARTURO   Please, Professor, don't even say it in jest.

OTTO   I wonder what Mr Di Spelta would say if during my performance I were to turn him into a garrulous parrot?

CALOGERO   (surprised) You know me?

OTTO   I know you all. Mrs Locascio, Mrs Zampa and Miss Zampa her daughter. I know you all because of my third, all-seeing eye. I promise you we'll have fun later on. The performance will be most interesting. I trust you will honour me with your presence.

EVERYBODY   Yes, of course ...

MRS ZAMPA   (rises to leave) Will you excuse me?

OTTO   Certainly.

MARTA   Till later then, and all the best of luck with the show.

(They all go out except OTTO, GERVASIO, ARTURO, AMELIA and the porters. THE WAITER makes way for them and follows them out)

OTTO   (to the porters) I'd like you to wait for my wife at the main entrance. (The porters leave)

GERVASIO   (confidentially, to OTTO) Didn't Zaira come with you?

OTTO   No.

GERVASIO   Another row?

OTTO (*dropping his 'professional' educated accent, lapses
     into something more common, say a tinge of Cockney
     or North-Country. This will recur throughout the play
     whenever he is talking with his intimates*) She's an
     impossible woman. Do you know, I sometimes wake up
     in the morning and the moment I'm aware of being
     awake I keep my eyes shut tight. I just say to myself:
     The moment I open my eyes she'll catch on I'm awake
     and start a row.

ARTURO (*in a conciliatory tone*) Why don't you both
     try to make a go of things? Life's difficult enough as it is.

OTTO Is everything ready here?

GERVASIO Absolutely.

ARTURO (*hands a sheet of paper to* OTTO) Here is the
     list of all the guests in the hotel. Not a single name
     missing.

GERVASIO (*hands* OTTO *a photograph*) And this is
     what Mrs Di Spelta looks like.

OTTO (*looks at it admiringly*) The female who was here
     just now with her husband? It's a very good likeness.

GERVASIO Yes. Have no fear. You can't go wrong.

OTTO Has Mariano D'Albino turned up?

GERVASIO I saw him about an hour ago. But his motor-
     boat is down there. (*Leans over the railings and looks
     down*) There it is.

OTTO (*leans out over the railings*) Hm ... Well, that's
     his business.

GERVASIO We've done some quite good work. The
     atmosphere is favourable. You'll see.

OTTO Let's hope so. (*Goes up to the wicker basket, opens
     it, takes out various items and begins to arrange them in
     the centre of the garden, in preparation for the evening
     performance*)

ARTURO (*solicitously, to* AMELIA) How do you feel?

AMELIA I'm all right, daddy.

ARTURO *(carefully takes a small parcel out of his coat pocket, unwraps it and produces an egg, which he hands to* AMELIA*)* It's a really fresh one. Go on, eat it ...

AMELIA *(exasperated)* I don't want it!

ARTURO But look, I got it out in the country ... I saw the farmer get it from under the hen with my own eyes ... It cost fifty lire.

AMELIA I won't eat it. I wouldn't eat it if you'd paid a million for it. Just the sight of it makes me feel sick. No. I won't eat it.

ARTURO But why?

AMELIA Because it wouldn't do any good ...

ARTURO You'll drive me mad, you will ... I'm desperately short of money as it is ... and yet I try to get you all the food the doctor recommends ...

AMELIA Pay no attention to the doctor. I'm feeling quite well; besides, if what he said is true ... when your time is up, it's goodbye ... and that'll be that.

ARTURO Goodbye ... and that'll be that! Is that supposed to cheer me up? Listen to me, child: provided you keep to a wholesome, nourishing diet ...

AMELIA You are pigheaded! It's got nothing to do with diets ... Diets never cured heart trouble.

ARTURO Come on ... just to please me: eat your egg.

AMELIA All right ... I will. But later.

GERVASIO Listen, Arturo, let's go for another little tour in the hotel and spread a few enticing rumours. Better not to be seen together, though. *(To* OTTO*)* See you later. Don't work too hard. *(He and* ARTURO *go out upstage followed by* AMELIA*)*

MARIANO *(enters after a short pause)* Professor ...

OTTO Good evening to you.

MARIANO Everything going according to plan?

OTTO Naturally.

MARIANO Did your friend give you the photo?

OTTO   Yes. He did.

MARIANO   (*writes out a cheque*) And here's the fifty thousand lire. (*Having signed the cheque hands it to* OTTO) Here you are. All I need is fifteen minutes with her.

OTTO   Well, I'm not so sure ...

MARIANO   Now, look here, I've been to no end of trouble to fix things. I've had to persuade the management to engage you ... Is fifteen minutes too much to ask for in return?

OTTO   I can but try.

MARIANO   It's your business to succeed.

OTTO   I'll see what I can do.

MARIANO   I'll be waiting in the boat.

OTTO   Very well.

MARIANO   Now Professor: I've done my bit. Mind you do yours or there'll be trouble. Goodbye. (*Goes out through the garden*)

(*After a pause,* ZAIRA, *in a towering rage, enters and bears down on* OTTO *like a fury. She is in her midforties, exuberant, vulgar and irritating. She dresses with the affected smartness of an elderly music-hall soubrette. The two porters follow close behind carrying large bundles*)

ZAIRA   Now just you listen to me, Mr High-and-Mighty: don't you ever again walk out on me in the middle of an argument and leave me behind with half your gear or I'll slap your face so hard you won't know what's hit you. (OTTO *does not react. With studied calm he takes the bundles from the porters and dismisses them with a nod. The porters leave as* OTTO *quietly disposes his props in the centre of the garden: the two round tables on each side of the set, the larger rectangular table in the centre. He places the sarcophagus to the right of the*

auditorium, as far downstage as possible. Helped by
ZAIRA *he takes the oddest objects out of the wicker
basket: swords, pistols, top hats, two enormous dice,
Japanese fans, an Italian flag, scarlet velvet material
with a gold fringe, a rectangular Japanese box bearing
intricate designs and inlaid with small mirrors of all
shapes and sizes, as well as various other items)* Will you
kindly tell me whether we'll ever stop living like tramps,
working in hotels, hospitals, barracks and fairgrounds?
Can't you get yourself a good safe contract in some
theatre?

OTTO How many times must I tell you that conjurers
are out of fashion in the theatre? I might land the odd
engagement here and there if I had a sexy young partner.
But as you insist on fulfilling that role I'm afraid you'll
have to make do with hotels, barracks and hospitals.

ZAIRA That's what you like to think. For your information a great many people still find me young and attractive. When I'm made up and properly dressed I can
knock girls of eighteen into cocked hats, and that's a
fact!

OTTO You forget I can see you with my third eye ...

ZAIRA I'll blind the three of them if you're not careful!

OTTO You really are impossible! Don't you see we're
skint? That I've got to take any job that comes along?
That unless we pay all the back rent we owe, the landlord'll throw us out? (*Referring to some coins he needs
for his act*) Hand over the sovereigns.

ZAIRA (*gives him a purse*) Here you are.

OTTO By the way, they've cut off the electricity at home.

ZAIRA I'm delighted to hear it. How wonderful!

OTTO And I calculate that in three days' time they'll
cut off the water supply, too. (*Empties the purse into a
top hat*)

ZAIRA Better still.

OTTO   ... and as far as I know there's no food left in the house.

ZAIRA   Good! We'll all starve. It had to come to this. We'll all end up begging in the street. It's your fault, you're just a fool, with no initiative, no push in you. You couldn't care less. That's the story of our life together. And if I stick to you at all it's because I've got to keep tabs on you every minute of the day. Oh yes, do you think I've forgotten the days we were working the halls? Do you think I've forgotten the number of times I found you in a passionate clinch with chorus girls?

OTTO   Better leave that side of things alone, my love. You did exactly the same. What about the time I caught you with the acrobat?

ZAIRA   (*nostalgically recalling her past*) Sandro ... what a chest that man had ... Such gorgeous muscles ...

OTTO   And the time I walked in and caught you with the *Human Submarine*?

ZAIRA   (*dreamily*) Demetrio. What a sense of humour he had! A laugh a minute ... And so strong, such stamina ...

OTTO   Not to mention the occasion I caught you with *The Living Skeleton* ...

ZAIRA   (*voluptuously relishing the memory*) Hm ... Don't remind me of him ... He was so lovely, so dishy ... Thinner than Gandhi, but my word ...

OTTO   Allow me to remind you that when I say 'caught you' I am not referring to purely illusory, intuitive conjectures. I always 'caught you' in the crudest and most positive sense of the expression: in the act! There were only two solutions open to me: either a revolver shot or a shrug of the shoulders. It must be clear and evident to you that I chose the second.

ZAIRA   (*apparently offended but with a hint of inner*

pride) You were so jealous in those days ... and you still are, you know ...

OTTO (*condescendingly and with tired resignation*) Yes, my dear. I still am.

ZAIRA That's why you treat me so badly. I know. But please bear in mind that even my patience can wear thin, and if you carry on like this I'll up and run off with the first man I fancy.

OTTO (*coldly and with calculated menace in his voice*) You will never do that. Take care, Zaira. Where's my magic wand?

ZAIRA (*appeased and cloyingly loving*) You know I'd never leave you. That's why you take advantage of me.

OTTO (*stroking her hair with a gesture which is now habitual and monotonous to him*) Zaira, my darling ... I love you so much.

ZAIRA Give us a kiss then.

OTTO Of course. (*Kisses her*) There you are. (*With a yawn*) Let's go and get ready.

ZAIRA (*half yawning too*) Right.

(*They carry the empty wicker basket between them and walk away*)

OTTO Did you bring a bit of something to eat?

ZAIRA I've scraped a few sandwiches together and a thermos flask of coffee.

OTTO We'll send for a bottle of wine.

(*They go out right. Night has fallen. The garden is lit up by moonlight and by lamps placed in the most suitable spots. People begin to trickle in from upstage and occupy tables at random. They chat and laugh. We see* MRS MARINO *and* MRS LOCASCIO *at one table, at another* MRS ZAMPA *and her daughter. Somewhere else* CALOGERO DI SPELTA *and his wife* MARTA, *also* GERVASIO, ARTURO *and* AMELIA. *After this long pause, during which the public will settle down in their various places, including the arrival of one or two latecomers,* THE WAITER *appears from upstage and takes up his place in the centre, his back to the auditorium, to address the spectators)*

THE WAITER   The management have great pleasure in announcing that this evening's entertainment is about to begin. In a few moments Professor Otto Marvuglia, whose services we were lucky enough to secure, will step into our midst. We have all heard of his powers, which until today have all been hearsay as far as we were concerned. Now we're about to share in the privilege of witnessing the most remarkable experiments. Please be seated and enjoy yourselves. (*Walks upstage and will remain standing during* OTTO's *performance by the central door leading into the hotel lounge*)

(OTTO *enters from the right. He has replaced his jacket with a large black frock-coat, secured at the waist by a red silk sash with gold fringes, knotted on his left hip so as to produce a rich golden tassel. He walks in slowly and mysteriously. As he reaches the centre of the garden he greets the spectators with a slight nod. He is in turn greeted by scant applause. He is followed in by* ZAIRA. *She is wearing a grand evening dress, long black gloves. Her hairdo is elaborate. Briskly and merrily she curtsies several times. Again scant applause, this time mixed with barely suppressed laughter*)

OTTO   Ladies and gentlemen, I must warn you that my act is not always successful. Why, you may well ask. Because I need your help, trust and understanding if I am to succeed. I can take care of conjuring tricks without any help, but in order to demonstrate my supernatural powers as well as hypnotic suggestion and telepathy you must come to my aid. I cannot transmit my thoughts to you unless you are prepared to receive them. If you wish to help me then relax, yield to your instincts, and I shall demonstrate to you phenomena of the highest scientific interest. Let us take an example: I cannot add a large orchestra to my performance. It would cost too much. On the other hand an illusionist is always handicapped by the absence of music. What can I do? What can you do? Let us concentrate and think hard of the sort of music which is usually heard at entertainments such as mine ... (*A man hums a typical fairground air. The audience laugh*) No, please ... If I could have some silence I'll do my best to transmit the right sort of music. (*After a short pause, a faint melody which eventually grows in volume is recognisable as* The Skaters' Waltz) Here it is: can you hear it? (*The music increases in volume and gets much louder. At length some applause is wrenched from the public*) Right. I can work much better with music. But before going into my act proper, it is my custom to think of the charming ladies in my audience. Zaira! (ZAIRA *hands him a large sheet of white paper. He shows first one side, then the other, then rolls it into a cone from which he begins to extract flowers, which he throws at the tables occupied by ladies*) Here's one for you ... and for you ... flowers for the beautiful ladies. (*Another small round of applause*) As for the gentlemen, perhaps a cup of coffee wouldn't come amiss. (*Picks up a minute chromium-plated coffee percolator and shakes it to ascertain whether there's anything inside*) It's full— but will there be enough to go round? I hope so. Let's share it like good friends ... (*Approaches the tables and, holding his left arm high in the air moves his hand rapidly as though trying to catch something from the void. In fact, as if by magic, a china coffee cup appears in his hand.* OTTO *repeats the gesture with every single man present among general merriment. This trick is an extremely simple one: each spectator with some dexterity hands the cup meant for him to* OTTO *who then 'produces' it)* And now we'll go on to a more important experiment.

GERVASIO (*decisively*) I'm leaving. (*Gets up as if to leave*)

ARTURO So am I. (*Rises*)

OTTO (*stopping them*) But please ...

GERVASIO If you think you're going to get me to make a fool of myself again, you're wrong! Don't forget the trick you played on me at the Majestic in Brighton.

ARTURO Or what you did to me in France.

OTTO Please, please go back to your places, gentlemen. I never repeat my experiments with the same people. What have I asked for? Just a little cooperation from you all. Now if there is a lady in the audience prepared to help me, would she kindly step this way ... A lady with courage, I should hasten to add.

MARTA (*rising and with a smile of complicity at* OTTO *steps forward a few paces*) Will I do?

OTTO Will you do? Admirably, dear lady, admirably! (*Quickly glancing at the photograph* GERVASIO *had given him earlier*) I couldn't have picked a more suitable candidate if I tried. Please come forward.

MARTA (*confidently goes up to* OTTO *and stands beside him, pleased at the admiring glances and applause from the spectators*) Here I am.

(*The music stops*)

OTTO I congratulate you, madam, on your beauty and on your courage. Would you kindly step nearer this Egyptian sarcophagus? (MARTA, *preceded by* OTTO *and* ZAIRA, *complies*) Observe it closely: it's an authentic piece. (ZAIRA *opens the sarcophagus*) Would you step inside?

MARTA But of course. (*Makes as if to get into the sarcophagus*)

OTTO (*stops her*) One moment. A second after the lid of the sarcophagus is closed you will vanish. You will be drawn into a world of dreams, you will experience a beatific, euphoric feeling, your body will lose itself insubstantially after your soul has parted from it. But above all—and listen carefully now—when the experiment is over, when body and soul reintegrate, remember this, dear lady: let your soul ignore your body's sensations, let your body ignore your soul's adventures! You may enter now.

(MARTA *gets into the sarcophagus.* OTTO *closes it. The lights in the garden slowly dim until it is only light enough to distinguish the characters as shadows. The music starts again.* OTTO *moves about as though he were explaining some important aspect of the experiment to his audience. Just as the lights dim in the garden, the landing stage lights up.* MARIANO D'ALBINO, *in yachting attire, appears from the rocks and athletically leaps into the motor-boat. With an expert manoeuvre he gets the motor-boat closer to the left stairway. While this is taking place,* ZAIRA, *pirouetting, reaches the rear of the sarcophagus, the part visible to the 'real' public, opens a concealed flap and beckons to* MARTA. MARTA *gets out smartly, softly tiptoes to the stairway on the left and rapidly descends. At the landing stage, helped by* MARIANO, *she gets into the boat.* OTTO *opens the sarcophagus. It is empty. He shows it to the public. Round of applause.* OTTO *closes the sarcophagus. Very soft music*)

MARIANO (*a trifle irritably*) At last!

MARTA As if you didn't know what my husband
is like. The life I have to lead! All his relations spying
on me, especially that dreadful brother of his. Just
imagine if they knew about us: the gossip, the malicious
comments, there'd be hell to pay! They'd love to get rid
of me. They're after Calogero's money; they'd squeeze
the last penny out of him. And Calogero himself never
leaves me alone. His jealousy has reached such a stage
I can't stand it any more. Why, if he has to go to the
bathroom he locks me in the bedroom and takes the key
with him. (*Pause*) I can't stay more than a quarter of
an hour.

MARIANO We're leaving immediately.

MARTA What on earth do you mean?

MARIANO I said we're leaving. We'll be in Venice by
the morning.

MARTA Are you out of your mind?

MARIANO Just leave it to me.

MARTA (*rising*) Let me go. (*Makes as if to leave the
boat*)

MARIANO You're not getting off this boat. You're coming
with me.

MARTA Mariano ...

MARIANO You're coming with me.

(*Louder music. With a lightning gesture* MARIANO
*starts the engine. He steers expertly and once he has
gained the centre of the landing stage between the two
pillars he points the prow towards the central door at
the back of the stalls.* MARTA *protests, but* MARIANO
*pays no attention. Slowly, through the central aisle, the
boat crosses the whole of the auditorium. The lights
fade on the shore and go back to normal in the garden*)

OTTO (*on hearing the throb of the engine looks out to*

sea with a troubled look, endeavouring to spot the fast-disappearing boat, then turns back to his audience, his first remark a personal allusion) Yes, ladies and gentlemen: we always know how to begin an experiment, but we are never quite sure how it will end. Let us hope for the best. Zaira! (*Picks up a small cage containing a canary from the central table*) Please observe, ladies and gentlemen, my poor feathered prisoner. (*Goes up to the various tables showing the canary to the spectators*) He's happy and oh! so lively ... The poor little bird is unaware of his own unhappy situation. (*Now and then glances nervously over his shoulder in the hope of sighting* MARIANO's *boat*) But if he were to escape who would ever catch him again? (*Addressing the canary*) But you're not to go away for ever. I'll allow you a little freedom, say a quarter of an hour. At the end of that time you must come back. Agreed? (*Calls out*) Zaira! (ZAIRA *goes up to him, takes the cage from* OTTO *and places herself on the left, showing the cage to the public.* OTTO *covers the cage with a square of black material, picks up a pistol from the central table and after walking away a few steps points the pistol at the cage*) May I have your attention please, ladies and gentlemen ... One, two, three! (*Shoots.* ZAIRA *at the same time uncovers the cage, now empty. Another small round of applause*) Let us now move on to another experiment.

CALOGERO (*rises and courteously addresses* OTTO) Excuse me, would you be kind enough to conjure my wife back?

OTTO (*equally urbanely*) But ... forgive me: who are you?

CALOGERO Who am I? I'm her husband. That's why I'm asking you to make my wife reappear.

(The spectators are amused by this exchange)

OTTO   Yes ... Have a little patience, sir, please ... Zaira!
(ZAIRA *takes one of the outsize dice from the table and
hands it to* OTTO, *who holds it up to the audience*) Now
then, kindly verify that all the numbers are correct. I
feel sure you will judge quite dispassionately. This
deception will not fail to amaze you.

CALOGERO   Just a moment. Before you go on, would
you mind completing the deception you left hanging in
the air earlier on?

(The music stops)

OTTO   I'm afraid I don't understand.

CALOGERO   Come now, it's perfectly simple. Just make
my wife reappear.

OTTO   With respect, sir, who is in charge of the experiment? You or me?

CALOGERO   You, of course. I'm involved to the extent
that my wife has disappeared and I want her back.

OTTO   (*seemingly amused*) I like that! Most diverting.
You are firmly convinced, I take it, that your wife has
vanished.

CALOGERO   Yes I am. The sarcophagus is empty.

OTTO   I beg your pardon—what has the sarcophagus got
to do with it? What can a sarcophagus do? Are you so
naive as to think that a painted wooden cabinet has the
power to make people vanish—your wife in this case?
Haven't you given any thought to the possibility that
you yourself might be responsible for your wife's disappearance?

CALOGERO   Me?

OTTO   Unintentionally, of course: let's say you did it
in good faith. Let me ask you again, all the same: are
you firmly convinced that your wife vanished a moment
ago?

CALOGERO Yes I am. She was sitting next to me, over there.

OTTO Next to you? Never! What a thing to say ... Your wife was not sitting next to you. For all I know she never even came to this hotel with you. Heaven knows when your wife disappeared. You see, everything that is happening before you is sheer illusion. You are here alone. We've never seen your wife. (*Turns to the spectators*) Have we, any of us, ever seen this gentleman's wife?

THE SPECTATORS (*joining in the game*) No ... No ...

CALOGERO But I swear to you I haven't done a thing to bring about my wife's disappearance ...

OTTO That is what you think. That is what you persist in thinking, because you do not possess what I call the third eye, the eye without window, the eye of thought ... Can't you see you're the architect of your own delusions? I'm afraid if your wife has vanished at all, you yourself made her vanish. It's now up to you to make her reappear. It's got nothing to do with me. At most I could try to help you ... In fact I'll do it with pleasure. Would you kindly step this way, right up here where I am standing?

CALOGERO (*impatiently*) Look, I'm not a charlatan and I won't have you make me look ridiculous.

THE SPECTATORS Go on, be a sport ... it's just a bit of fun!

CALOGERO Sorry, but no. There's a limit to impudence and bad manners. He must be made to realise he's dealing with a gentleman. I can't lend myself to this kind of buffoonery.

OTTO Do you want to lose your wife for good?

CALOGERO (*laughing at* OTTO'*s remark, turns to the spectators*) The cheek of the fellow ... He's a real card, he is ...

THE SPECTATORS Go on, don't be a spoilsport ...
We're having such fun!

CALOGERO (*giving in reluctantly*) All right. Let's see.
(*Approaches* OTTO)

OTTO Very well, then. (*The spectators fall silent and
pay attention*) Be good enough to answer a few questions.
Are you a very jealous husband?

CALOGERO I'm afraid you're being too personal. These
are matters which concern neither you nor anyone
else.

OTTO But answer me all the same. I'm trying to help
you. Are you a jealous husband?

CALOGERO Well ... yes, I am.

OTTO Did you get that, Zaira? The gentleman is jealous.

ZAIRA (*playfully reproachful, makes the sort of gesture
one associates with telling off a child*) Now ... now ...
now ...

OTTO Does your wife have to put up with jealous scenes?

CALOGERO (*offended*) Would you mind stopping all
this nonsense?

OTTO Please don't get upset. Answer me as calmly as
possible. Have you ever had reason to doubt her ...
fidelity?

CALOGERO (*readily and with some pride*) Never!

OTTO Good. Very good. Now pay attention. Your wife
has vanished. Have a good look inside the sarcophagus.
(CALOGERO *scrupulously inspects the interior of the
sarcophagus*) Are you satisfied she isn't there?

CALOGERO Yes.

OTTO Now come here. (CALOGERO *obeys*) Careful
now. (*Picks up from the central table a rectangular
Japanese box, seven inches high and sixteen inches
long*) Take it. (CALOGERO, *full of curiosity, takes the
box from* OTTO) Your wife is in that box. Open it.

CALOGERO Of all the silly ... (*Makes as if to open it*)

OTTO (*stops him opening it with a jerk of his hand*) One
     moment. Are you in good faith?

CALOGERO In what way?

OTTO Are you sure that your wife is in that box? Now
     look, unless you believe it, and very firmly at that,
     you will not see her. Do you understand? Unless you're
     certain she's there, please do not open it.

THE SPECTATORS (*egging* CALOGERO *on*) Go on,
     open it, don't hesitate ... what are you waiting for?
     Open it!

OTTO (*intervening*) Please, please, ladies and gentlemen.
     Don't influence him. He alone must decide. The
     responsibility is his. (*Turns to* CALOGERO) You said
     just a little while ago that you have never doubted your
     wife's fidelity. I wonder ... I have doubts as to your
     sincerity on this point. However, think it over carefully.
     If you open the box in good faith you'll see your wife
     again, if you open it in bad faith you will never set eyes
     on her again. Therefore if you're in good faith, go on,
     open it! (CALOGERO *seems perplexed. He is un-
     certain. He smiles stupidly,* OTTO *senses his advantage
     and exploits the situation*) Now look here: are you or
     are you not in good faith?

CALOGERO Of course I am.

OTTO Then what are you waiting for? Open it. (CALO-
     GERO *doesn't bat an eyelid. He stands silently, lost in
     a sea of doubt. He doesn't know what to do. By doubting*
     OTTO's *affirmation he implicitly admits his wife's in-
     fidelity. On the other hand there is no guarantee that
     his wife is inside the Japanese box. The spectators look
     on as if aware of* CALOGERO's *terrible dilemma.
     Finally, after a long pause, he makes up his mind. He
     slowly puts the box under his left arm and dejectedly,
     like a whipped dog, goes back to his table. The spectators
     have been following his movements without taking their*

eyes off him and now begin to exchange malicious comments. OTTO, *with calm deliberation and outwardly serene, as if nothing out of the ordinary had taken place, regains the centre of the stage and continues his act)* May I have your attention now, ladies and gentlemen, as I am about to embark on a truly remarkable experiment ... *(The music starts again)* Zaira!

THE CURTAIN FALLS

ACT TWO

(Four days later.

OTTO MARVUGLIA'*s pitiably shabby home. An atmosphere of seedy melancholy hangs over the room. Through a large window upstage left the rooftops and terraces of equally shabby dwellings are visible. The main entrance door is upstage right. Downstage left another door. The room is littered with every kind of junk: the familiar chromium-plated tables, top hats, boxes, flags, helmets, swords. Poor furniture, odd chairs. Hanging by the centre of the large window is a large birdcage full of canaries. On the window sill another cage containing four or five doves.*

Early morning)

AMELIA *(leaning out of the window, talking to someone in the house opposite)* No, I won't let you do that! You mustn't ... Look, I'll be quite frank with you: if you dare come and talk to daddy I'll never see you again! *(Listens to the answer, then carries on)* Why, you ask? Well ... let's say I don't want to get married at the moment. Do you feel any better now I've told you? *(Listens)* I won't give you a reason ... You'll know soon enough. Maybe I'll tell you tomorrow—and tomorrow's my birthday. I'll be eighteen. If you're patient enough to wait three or four years we'll get married. *(Listens)*

You are pigheaded! No, I'm not going to tell you. Let's talk of something else. You know, I'm not so sure you really love me, because you haven't yet asked me the question all lovers put to their sweethearts. (*Listens*) You haven't asked me which is my favourite flower. (*Listens*) But of course! That's the first thing one should ask. A girl I know told me ... and her boy friend is madly in love with her ... (*Listens*) Well, naturally, but only because I told you first. (*Listens*) It's carnations ... I love pale pink carnations ... the tiny ones ... fruit sellers use them to decorate their baskets ... I simply adore them. When I was small, I remember standing alone on our balcony—we used to live on the first floor— and I saw one of those pale pink carnations mixed up in some hay that a coachman was feeding his horse. Bit by bit the horse ate the hay, and his mouth got closer and closer to the carnation ... (*Listens*) Yes ... the horse ate the poor carnation in the end. (*She sobs*) I can't help it ... I can't help crying whenever I think of it ... Remember, won't you? Pale pink carnations, but the tiny dwarf variety ...

(OTTO *enters from the left, wearing trousers, a shirt unbuttoned at the neck and a pyjama jacket. As he comes in he is talking to* GERVASIO, *who follows him into the room*)

OTTO No, no, Gervasio. Give me the flex. It's better if I keep the switch in my pocket, as I've got to synchronise things.

GERVASIO (*hands over to* OTTO *a small plastic switch connected to an extremely fine piece of electric bell wire which trails into another room*) But wouldn't it be better if I operated the switch? If the audience sees you with it you're sunk.

OTTO They won't notice a thing. When the number's

over the audience will not be concentrating, they won't be expecting another trick. Let's rehearse. Go into the other room and plug in, but mind you don't damage the record ... (GERVASIO *goes out left*) Tell me when you're ready! (*Places himself in the centre of the stage and waits*)

GERVASIO   (*offstage*) Ready!

OTTO   (*begins to fiddle with the small switch with his right hand and holds it behind his back in an attempt at concealment. As though broadcast by an invisible loudspeaker, a short deafening crackle of static is heard*) My fault. Sorry. I haven't quite got the hang of it. Let's try it again. (*He has an idea*) Listen! (*Turns to the door on the left*) I say, come in here. Arturo as well. We'll have a proper dress rehearsal.

GERVASIO   (*comes in with* ARTURO) Here we are.

OTTO   You can be the audience. Over there. You too, Amelia. (*Places them downstage right, by the footlights*) Just imagine the number is over. I'll take my bow. (*Bows. The three begin to clap*) Good.

(*As before he begins to work the switch. This time the beginning of an enthusiastic applause mingled with cheering is heard. It gradually increases in volume and blends with* GERVASIO's *and* ARTURO's *clapping. It slowly turns into an overwhelming ovation, reminiscent of large political rallies, when just as one thinks the noise is dying down it gets going again, louder than before.* OTTO's *face lights up. The illusion is perfect. He is now famous. He is understood. With quiet dignity he bows repeatedly before the imaginary masses who are busy cheering him so frenetically*)

ZAIRA   (*enters upstage. She is wearing a cheap thread-bare dress, not devoid of a few touches of impudent*

*dignity which only add to the grotesqueness of her
appearance. She is carrying a shopping bag full of vegetables, also parcels of groceries under her arm. On seeing*
OTTO *she looks on intrigued and stops still by the
entrance door)* Are you all going mad? You're clean off
your heads! What on earth is all this noise?

OTTO   *(switching off the applause)* Our number was just
over and the public were showing their appreciation.

ZAIRA   What public?

OTTO   *(innocently)* Am I or am I not an illusionist? I have
just created a new deception and I have christened it
'the multiplication of applause'. We'll work it after each
turn in future and get the impression we're playing to
full houses every time. A friend of mine in broadcasting
gave me an old record they don't use any more; it produces the best round of applause I've ever heard. Just
listen ... the illusion is perfect. *(Stands in the centre)*
The number is over, right? *(Turns to* GERVASIO,
ARTURO *and* AMELIA*)* You start it off. *(The three
begin to clap.* OTTO *now more expertly works the switch
so as to bring about a slow progression of louder applause,
at the climax of which he reverses the process decreasing
the volume until he eventually switches off. Turns to*
ZAIRA, *evidently pleased with himself)* It's perfect, I
tell you! Who wouldn't be proud of this discovery?

ZAIRA   *(stares long and hard at* OTTO *with contempt.
Then turns to* GERVASIO *and* ARTURO*)* I take it you
realise we're dealing with an irresponsible fool. Worse
luck for me ... While he's busy multiplying applause
he's quite unaware of the constant subtraction from our
funds. I had to pawn my last earring to get these few
groceries this morning. *(Points to the shopping bag and
parcels)* The money we got the other day all went to
pay off debts.

OTTO   All of it? It was fifty thousand lire.

ZAIRA   That doesn't go very far these days. Back rent to
the landlord, ten thousand to get the electricity put back
on—incidentally, please don't mess around with electri-
cal experiments or they'll cut us off again at the end
of the month. Then the grocer, the butcher ... I could
tear my hair ...

AMELIA   (*hopefully*) Don't worry. You'll see, something
will turn up.

ARTURO   Now that I think of it, something has turned
up ... I'm afraid. Guess who I bumped into yesterday?
Roberto Magliano.

OTTO   (*on hearing the name starts violently*) Magliano?

ARTURO   I hardly recognised him at first. He's in tatters,
in a terrible state. It was he who recognised me. He
wanted your address.

OTTO   Did you give it to him?

ARTURO   I'm not that stupid! I said I hadn't seen you
for ages and didn't know where you lived. He wants his
money back. The hundred thousand he lent you. He said
he won't leave a stone unturned to find you. Be careful,
he's on his uppers and is quite capable of taking a pot
shot at you. You know his record.

OTTO   (*philosophically*) Shoot me, eh? Right. Have you
ever played roulette? The wheel is made up of thirty-
six numbers. A city like ours might run to two hundred
thousand houses. How is he going to find me? He'll be
lucky!

ARTURO   Listen to me, Professor: I've played roulette
umpteen times. And I tell you there's a devil inside that
ball. It goes round and round and round and all of a
sudden ... you'll find yourself face to face with Roberto
Magliano in this very room.

OTTO   Let's hope not.

AMELIA   (*to* ZAIRA, *pointing to the shopping bag*) What
did you buy?

ZAIRA Just a few things ... what little we could afford ...
(*Takes a small bunch of pale pink carnations out of the
bag and gives it to* AMELIA) Here ... I got these
for you.

AMELIA (*ecstatically happy*) Oh they're lovely! Thank
you! I do love you!

ZAIRA And I love you, child.

AMELIA Such a heavenly scent! They remind me of
the one ... (*Bursts into tears*)

ZAIRA Come on now ... don't ...

ARTURO (*goes up to them, worried*) What's the matter?

(*The doorbell rings.* GERVASIO *goes and answers it*)

ZAIRA Nothing. She saw the flowers and started crying.
(*To* AMELIA) If you go on crying I won't buy you flowers
any more. (AMELIA *arranges the carnations in a vase
upstage*)

GERVASIO (*comes back followed by* THE WAITER)
It's the waiter from the Metropole. He'd like a word
with you.

THE WAITER Good morning, Professor.

OTTO Good morning. What's up?

THE WAITER (*gives* OTTO *a letter*) This arrived for
you yesterday. Perhaps they didn't have your private
address. As it's my day off and I live round the corner I
thought I'd bring it myself.

OTTO Thank you. You're very kind. (*Opens the envelope, unfolds the letter and reads it*)

THE WAITER Anything important?

OTTO Yes it is. And thank you again. Won't you sit
down for a moment?

THE WAITER No, thank you. I must be off.

OTTO What about a cup of coffee?

THE WAITER No, thank you.

OTTO You know, it's child's play in a conjurer's home.

I can produce cups of coffee out of the blue. Doesn't cost a penny.

ZAIRA (*ironically*) Of course he can! Here everything appears as if by magic. (*Points to the groceries and now addresses the room at large*) You see all this stuff? He conjured it up with his magic wand. Come the end of the month, this is what he'll do—(*Lifts up her right arm and opens and shuts her right hand as though to catch something*) ... and pay the rent. When his shoes need mending, he hypnotises the cobbler, who repairs them free of charge. Then of course I'm very good at vanishing myself. One of these days I'll just say: One, two, three! And I'll vanish in a puff of smoke and that'll be that! (*To* THE WAITER) Come with me, I'll give you a cup of coffee.

THE WAITER There's no need to, madam, really.

ZAIRA Never mind that, you've been very kind.

AMELIA Besides, we're going to have some ourselves. Come along.

THE WAITER Thank you. (*Goes out left with* ZAIRA *and* AMELIA)

ARTURO I'll go and have a shave. (*To* GERVASIO) Can I borrow your razor?

GERVASIO I'll get it for you.

(ARTURO *and* GERVASIO *go out left.* OTTO, *now alone, rolls up the bell wire and switch and places them on a table, left. The doorbell rings.* OTTO *goes out through the door upstage to answer it. Comes back shortly after, preceding a police inspector and* CALOGERO DI SPELTA, *who is clutching the Japanese box under his left arm*)

OTTO Please come in, Mr Di Spelta. This is an unexpected pleasure.

CALOGERO (*darkly*) We'll see about that. What I had to

say I've passed on to the Inspector. He'll talk to you.

OTTO I see. Well, Inspector, what can I do for you?

THE INSPECTOR (*ironically*) Come now, sir. You know what I'm here for, surely. Four days ago, in the garden of the Metropole Hotel, you indulged in conduct which led to the disappearance of this gentleman's wife, namely a Mrs Marta Di Spelta.

OTTO (*tentatively*) But ...

THE INSPECTOR (*firmly*) Let me go on, sir. Now his good lady wife happened to be wearing valuable jewellery, such as diamonds ...

CALOGERO Don't forget the ten-carat emerald!

THE INSPECTOR Do let me proceed, please! Such as diamonds and emeralds. Now, I put it to you that you murdered the good lady in order to gain possession of her jewellery. All we've got to establish is the whereabouts of the body. Sir: I must warn you that anything you say ...

OTTO Please, please, Inspector. Don't be absurd. I have already and quite patiently explained to Mr Di Spelta that the whole matter was just a simple conjuring trick. And what is more it was he who started it off, heaven knows how long ago. But I refuse to be held responsible for the lady's disappearance. All I did was to summon up and materialise for him for a few seconds the archetypal images of his racial memory.

THE INSPECTOR (*puzzled but determined*) But the lady vanished. Yes or no?

OTTO No doubt about it. The lady vanished. (*Points to* CALOGERO) And her reappearance depends exclusively on him, on him alone. Show us, Mr Di Spelta! Be of stout heart, don't waste the valuable time of hardworking members of our civic arm: make your wife reappear!

CALOGERO (*has understood* OTTO's *allusion*) I'm not

going to open the box. I'm not going to be such a fool
as to lend myself to an imposture.

THE INSPECTOR (*even more puzzled than before*)
Box? What box?

CALOGERO (*shows it to him*) This one.

THE INSPECTOR What's the box got to do with it?

CALOGERO He insists my wife is inside.

OTTO (*insinuatingly*) So, Mr Di Spelta ... we haven't
taken a little peep yet, I see ...

CALOGERO (*determined*) I'm not going to open it.

OTTO Why on earth won't you?

THE INSPECTOR (*suspiciously*) Excuse me, gentlemen,
but what leads you to believe we'd find Mrs Di Spelta in
that box, unless ...

OTTO Not only Mrs Di Spelta, my dear Inspector. A box
like that, even a smaller one, may well contain a
hundred ... a thousand wives!

THE INSPECTOR (*has been looking at* OTTO *but averts
his eyes as if he found the experience uncomfortable*)
Enough of this tomfoolery. You're pulling my leg. The
lady's vanished. You'll find it'll go better for you if you
come clean and confess. Why did you kill her? How did
you kill her? Where is the body?

(CALOGERO *nods with satisfaction as the* INSPECTOR
makes his accusation)

OTTO (*after a pause, makes up his mind*) I see. I had
better come clean, I suppose.

THE INSPECTOR That's more like it. Fire away.

OTTO I'd prefer to tell you in private. Would you ask
Mr Di Spelta to leave us alone?

THE INSPECTOR (*to* CALOGERO) Step over there,
will you? (*Indicates a place upstage right.* CALOGERO
complies)

OTTO (*taking the* INSPECTOR *aside*) Please sit down,

Inspector. (*They sit*) Mrs Di Spelta, the wife of that man over there who lodged this complaint against me, is in Venice.

THE INSPECTOR   Is she dead?

OTTO   She's never been more alive than she is now. On the evening of my performance in the garden of the Metropole, she picked the most propitious moment to run off with her lover, Mariano D'Albino ...

THE INSPECTOR   (*slowly turns his head towards* CALO-GERO *and looks at him from head to foot*) So the lady had a lover?

OTTO   Correct. And it was for the sake of protecting the poor devil from stark reality that I attributed the whole incident to a skilful deception. I mean the business of the box.

THE INSPECTOR   (*worried*) What if he opens the box?

OTTO   He'll think he's opened it in bad faith.

THE INSPECTOR   And if he doesn't open it?

OTTO   He'll blissfully go on believing in his wife's fidelity.

THE INSPECTOR   I'm not with you.

OTTO   It doesn't matter.

THE INSPECTOR   Hm ... (*Amused at first, his mood changes into one of suspicion*) Can you prove you're telling me the truth?

OTTO   I have the proof right here. (*Produces from his pocket the letter which* THE WAITER *delivered and shows it to* THE INSPECTOR) This letter is from Mrs Di Spelta. She sent it from Venice. (*Reads out*) Dear Professor Marvuglia, I am sorry if I've caused you any embarrassment through my disappearance, especially vis-a-vis my husband. But believe me, it wasn't my fault. It was Mariano D'Albino who dragged me to Venice. I am with him now, and it's sheer paradise! I am truly concerned about poor Calogero. Do have a word with him and tell him not to look for me. He is not the man for me. Forgive me and believe me, yours sincerely, Marta di Spelta.

THE INSPECTOR I see. Let me have the envelope. (OTTO *gives it to him.* THE INSPECTOR *goes up to* CALOGERO *and holds the envelope up to him*) Do you recognise this handwriting, sir?

CALOGERO It's my wife's.

THE INSPECTOR Right. (*Goes back to* OTTO) It's clear now from the evidence that we haven't got a murder on our hands, not even a case of kidnapping. What am I going to do with him, Professor?

OTTO (*quietly*) I'd arrest him if I were you. It'd be a good thing if he were kept out of the way for a little while.

THE INSPECTOR Arrest him? On what charge?

OTTO Lodging a false complaint. What about that?

THE INSPECTOR (*perplexed*) I don't think that's an offence.

OTTO What about defamation of character—my character?

THE INSPECTOR Can't run him in for that. Look here, why don't you tell him what's happened straight out? Make him face up to the truth. Say to him: Your wife has run away with another man.

OTTO Why don't you tell him yourself?

THE INSPECTOR It's none of my business.

OTTO Come to that it's none of my business either.

THE INSPECTOR I've got to say something to him ...

OTTO (*enticingly*) Inspector, why don't you join in, become part of our experiment as it were? You'll not only solve your present problem, but you'll enable that poor fellow to go on living with his illusion. (*Pause*)

CALOGERO (*who has been waiting impatiently for the end of the* INSPECTOR's *and* OTTO's *conversation*)

Would you mind telling me what's happening?

(OTTO *and* THE INSPECTOR *look at one another in silence*)

THE INSPECTOR   (*reacts almost truculently to* CALO-
GERO'*s question*) You'd be well advised, my dear sir,
to keep quiet. And thank your lucky stars that so far
I have taken a lenient view of this whole situation.
(CALOGERO *seems astounded*) The Professor here could
quite rightly bring an action against you for defamation
of character, and I could easily lock you up for a couple
of days for daring to waste the time of a police officer.
CALOGERO   (*astonished*) What? Me?
THE INSPECTOR   (*sternly*) You, you, you! Yes, my dear
sir. You should have thought of the likely consequences
of your actions, especially where the administration of
justice is concerned. You wish to report an offence?
Theft, robbery, murder ...? What are the facts? Facts,
facts: you need facts to set the wheels of justice in
motion. Facts, documents, evidence ... irrefutable proof!
If you come to me and say: My wife has been murdered
... I shall expect you to produce the body, however badly
dismembered. If, on the other hand, you were to tell
me that your wife has been enticed or better still kid-
napped by another man, let me know where they are
and I'll arrest him. Can you give me any such information, duly corroborated by sound evidence? In writing,
signed by you and witnessed?
CALOGERO   No.
THE INSPECTOR   So what am I supposed to do? It
looks as if all this has been some kind of conjuring trick,
an illusion. And that you are the one who can put an end
to the deception. You and you alone are responsible.
You know the saying, that dirty linen should not be

washed in public, if you know what I mean ... you get the point? (*Turns to* OTTO *and takes his leave with a wink*) Good day, Professor, and congratulations. (*As he leaves the room he turns again to* CALOGERO, *slowing down as he passes him*) Faced with such grand magic, sir, what can a poor policeman do but reverently raise his hat? (*Goes out*)

CALOGERO   (*after a long pause during which, as in a film dissolve, his face registers all the expressions of his inner confusion, he slowly sits down*) I understand! (*Breaks into tears like a child.* OTTO, *from where he is standing, regards him with compassion.* CALOGERO, *still sobbing, repeats*) I understand!

OTTO   (*goes up to him*) No, no, Mr Di Spelta. This won't do. What is it you think you understand? I am really deeply sorry. I had no idea you had got so thoroughly involved in the game.

CALOGERO   (*dejected*) What game?

OTTO   The experiment I am carrying out in front of the public, here, in the garden. You see, I am in the middle of my performance. Thanks to my third eye I have been able to project into your brain, for a split second, a number of archetypal images. I have injected into your thoughts racial memories which you accept as reality, while they may simply be defined as phenomena from our atavistic heritage—in a word: time!

CALOGERO   (*suspiciously*) What?

OTTO   How shall I put it ... Your present condition could bring about a breakdown. It might prove fatal. That's why I am going to betray my professional secret and give you a share in my third eye. But you'll have to go on with the experiment right to the end, because unfortunately once you've started on one you cannot bring about its completion unless you, as the subject, can quite dispassionately talk about it with others, even have a good laugh over it. Now listen. Do you think that time ... passes? It isn't true, you know. Time is a convention. If men were not socially organised in this world, how could you possibly keep an appointment? If each and everyone of us were able to live without commitments or business or cares, I mean a truly natural, primitive life, why, you would endure. You would endure and not even be aware of it. Therefore you are time.

CALOGERO   Me?

OTTO   Take a man, for example, a man who's just been sentenced to thirty years' imprisonment. How long will he have to wait before he regains his freedom?

CALOGERO   Why ... thirty years.

OTTO   Very good. And if, let us assume, the sentenced man were to drop dead a minute after sentence was passed, according to you the thirty years would pass all the same?

CALOGERO   But of course.

OTTO   Who for?

CALOGERO   For those who survive.

OTTO   But why should the survivors be aware of the thirty years which the sentenced man failed to serve? The thirty years existed only in the consciousness of the prisoner and of those who sentenced him. Believe me, we're just piling convention upon convention. By the way, at what time do you usually lunch?

CALOGERO   About one-thirty or thereabouts.

OTTO   Very good. Consequently come one o'clock, one-fifteen, you begin to feel peckish, I take it.

CALOGERO   True enough. I start getting hungry as early as half past twelve at times.

OTTO   Try to follow my argument. Do you get hungry because it's half past one, or is it half past one because you get hungry?

CALOGERO   Isn't it the same thing?

OTTO It is most certainly not the same thing. It is half past one because you get hungry. The clock is built into your organism, and from what you tell me it seems to function. Therefore you are time.

CALOGERO (*appears convinced*) True ... When I'm not feeling well, in fact, I'm not hungry ...

OTTO When did your wife disappear?

CALOGERO Four days ago.

OTTO I expected that reply. And you believe it?

CALOGERO I can't help believing it.

OTTO Why can't you help believing it? When you say you believe four days have elapsed, this sounds to me more the result of personal experience than demonstrable fact. I say this because I can, now, having betrayed my professional secret. A fine sort of experiment I'm conducting! (*Points upstage*) Look ... over there are the patrons of the hotel sitting watching my show. You are convinced you're in my home, but we are in fact in the garden at the Metropole. All the sensations you are experiencing, all the images your eyes perceive are transmitted by me. I am exploiting your racial memory. You, for one thing, firmly believe that you have looked everywhere for your wife ...

CALOGERO I came here with a police inspector ...

OTTO Wrong again. It isn't true. You think you did. You even imagine you're at my place, but that isn't true either. Anyway you're playing your part in this deception like anybody else. In other words, you're impelled by racial memories. You are undergoing all the sensations caused by this particular deception, but in reality you're not its protagonist.

THE WAITER (*enters from the left and offers* OTTO *a cup of coffee on a small tray*) Here you are, Professor, a fresh cup of coffee.

(CALOGERO recognises THE WAITER and registers surprise)

OTTO *(taking advantage of THE WAITER's arrival to reinforce his argument)* Thank you, my dear fellow, but I'm not alone. I have a guest. Give it to the gentleman and bring me another cup.

THE WAITER Right away, sir. *(Gives the coffee to CALOGERO and on recognising him bows respectfully)* Always a pleasure to serve you, Mr Di Spelta. *(CALOGERO, stunned, takes the cup from THE WAITER and sips the coffee)* Mr Di Spelta is one of our oldest clients.

CALOGERO So I am.

THE WAITER If you'll excuse me. *(Goes out left)*

CALOGERO *(still sipping the coffee, looks around carefully to establish the authenticity of the objects round him. Whenever his eyes catch OTTO's he smiles, with a mixture of incredulity and shrewdness)* In fact each year I come ... go ... yes, I come to this hotel. I'm sorry I've deprived you of your coffee.

OTTO Don't give it a thought. They'll bring me another cup directly.

CALOGERO The service at this hotel has always been absolutely first class.

OTTO And what about the cooking? What a restaurant!

CALOGERO The cuisine is excellent. After a spell in the hotel I even complain about home-cooking.

THE WAITER *(enters left, with another cup of coffee)* Here you are, Professor. Your coffee. Forgive me, but I have things to attend to. If you should need me ...

OTTO I'll call you, have no fear.

THE WAITER Mr Di Spelta, always at your service.

CALOGERO You're still ... at the hotel.

THE WAITER Yes.

CALOGERO Even now?

THE WAITER Yes. Even now. Goodbye sir. (*Bows and goes out*)

CALOGERO (*after long deliberation*) Excuse me, Professor, but I recognised the chap who has just left. He's a waiter at the hotel. Now isn't there something wrong here? If you are transmitting ... images to me in order to bring about the end of the experiment, surely you shouldn't have produced the waiter. He's part of reality, not one of your illusions.

OTTO Good man. I like you because you go into these things thoroughly. I was really moved when you broke down just now, so much so that I let you into my professional secret.

CALOGERO Ah, yes. The business of the third eye.

OTTO Precisely. (*Begins to hum* The Skaters' Waltz. CALOGERO *joins in*)

ROBERTO (*enters upstage right. He is fortyish, pale and in a dangerous mood. The suit he is wearing is worn and threadbare but in good taste. As he enters he immediately spots* OTTO, *and his expression shows he is prepared to take the most drastic steps*) Good morning. (*Sits down wearily on the first chair by the door*)

OTTO (*momentarily at a loss, quickly regains control of himself*) My dear Roberto, how are you?

ROBERTO You didn't expect to see me, did you? Hm ... You're really quite shaken. I warn you that excuses and pretexts won't wash. You shouldn't have acted as you did. You even vanished from circulation so as to give me the slip, but when you needed my help you always knew where to find me. You've no idea how bad my present circumstances are. I wrote to you. I asked people to give you messages. No response. Useless.

OTTO Look here, Roberto, I'm in just as bad a fix financially as you are.

ROBERTO Your situation doesn't concern me in the least. It's mine I'm worried about. I have three kids to feed and my wife's just about to go into hospital. (*Rises and walks up to* OTTO) Have you forgotten that when you came to me for help I forked out without a murmur? I gave you one hundred thousand lire. One hundred thousand lire which today could save me from disaster ...

OTTO Have you no friends who could ...

ROBERTO Why should I? Why should I go round begging, or see my kids starve just to do you a favour? Now look: I'm in a desperate state and unless you come across you'll be in trouble, friend. Big trouble. In fact I'll kill you. Make up your mind. (*He calmly takes a pistol out of his pocket and points it at* OTTO)

OTTO (*equally calmly, to* ROBERTO) One moment. (*Turns to* CALOGERO *and, aside, talks to him*) You see, this gentleman is part of another experiment, which God knows who started, or when.

CALOGERO Another game?

OTTO Part of one. Quite unconsciously he plays a part in it, but he's not aware of it—just like you. What is going to happen now? I'll tell you. The experiment is at a crossroads. If I give him one hundred thousand lire I cease to be part of his game. If I let him shoot me there'll be chaos, as the experiment would be shattered to fragments and might then assume vast proportions, involving all sorts of other people and factors: newspaper reports, hordes of policemen, courts of law, prison ... the graveyard.

CALOGERO Yet all of them archetypal images?

OTTO Naturally.

CALOGERO What a splendid performance! (*To* ROBERTO) Sir, would you be kind enough to shoot the Professor?

ROBERTO What the hell is going on here?

OTTO Just a moment. I must warn you that if he shoots me ...

CALOGERO You won't die, of course. Didn't you say it was all part of the game?

OTTO I'm afraid you haven't quite understood. If he shoots me I die: this is part of the game. I die and my world with it. Now no one has the right to destroy a whole world. My world, incidentally, is linked to yours. If mine is destroyed, yours will be plunged headlong into heaven knows what abyss. We're but the links in a chain ... We cannot refuse to take part in the game. Now he is to be made to vanish. That, I assure you, is not going to be difficult. (*Begins to revert to his typical patter, as if about to carry out a trick before an audience*) May I have your attention, please. As you know an illusionist often turns to the spectators before a particular number and asks one of them to lend him a ring, a handkerchief, a watch. However, for this particular deception I require one hundred thousand lire. Who among you, ladies and gentlemen, is prepared to give me one hundred thousand lire for this most interesting experiment? (*Points his forefinger at an imaginary audience asking the spectators one by one*) You? You? You? (*Then as if summoned by a spontaneous offer, he turns to* CALOGERO) You, sir! Thank you!

CALOGERO (*perplexed*) But I really ...

OTTO It's a game, just a game. Hand over the money. There's no need to worry.

CALOGERO I don't think I've got it on me. (*Fumbles in his pockets*) I could give you a cheque, but perhaps that won't be acceptable ...

OTTO It'll be perfectly in order. Why not? As long as the figure is clearly written out.

CALOGERO (*produces his chequebook and a fountain*

pen) Here we are. (*Writes out the cheque, tears it off and hands it to* OTTO)

OTTO   Thank you. (*Reads the name of the payee*) Made out in my name, I see. Lend me your pen. (CALOGERO *does so*) All I need do now is endorse it in his favour ... (*Endorses the cheque*) One, two, three! (*Takes the cheque up to* ROBERTO) Here you are, and now scarper!

ROBERTO   (*pockets the cheque after looking at it carefully*) You bet. (*Leaves the room rapidly, without a word*)

OTTO   Et voilà! Le jeu est fait. Roberto Magliano has vanished. (*Hums The Skaters' Waltz*)

CALOGERO   How extraordinary! But ... Professor, what about my money?

OTTO   What money?

CALOGERO   What money? My cheque!

OTTO   (*correcting him*) The image of your cheque, you mean! You thought you were giving me a cheque, but that wasn't so. It's a deception, an illusion, don't you see? If you had seriously thought it was a real cheque you were giving me, with all its financial implications— bank clearing, stock exchange operations, advances, interest, due dates and what have you—why, you would never have given it to me. But for the sake of the game you had no hesitation: you just handed it over. What's a hundred thousand lire for such a superb experiment? It'll find its way back to you, by other avenues and byways, in a different guise ... But when, you may well ask? That is of no importance. Any experiment unfolds according to its own individual rules. There are experiments which have been going on for thousands and thousands of years and are nowhere near their conclusion ...

(Confused voices are raised in the next room. ARTURO'S *voice is then heard more distinctly)*

ZAIRA   *(off)* Amelia!

ARTURO   *(off)* Amelia, speak to me!

ZAIRA   *(off)* She'll be all right presently ... Amelia! Amelia ...

ARTURO   *(enters and in utter despair turns to* OTTO*)* I knew it ... It was bound to happen sooner or later ...

OTTO   What's happened?

ARTURO   Amelia's just passed out ... She's as white as a sheet ... She can't talk ... (OTTO *puts an arm round* ARTURO *to comfort him)* I've spent what little I had to get her the very best medical attention ... They all said the same thing: Her heart's so weak she'll never live to see her twentieth birthday ... No one's been able to help her ... Why? What harm has she ever done anybody? What have I done to deserve this?

OTTO   Calm down ... She'll be all right in no time at all, you'll see ...

ARTURO   No, she won't ... But why, I ask you, why?

ZAIRA   *(off)* *(softly)* Amelia ... Amelia ... *(Louder)* Amelia!

*(*ARTURO *stands still and listens in dismay. A sinister pause follows. Eventually* ZAIRA *appears at the door and stops there. She is too upset to speak)*

ARTURO   *(as if stating a fact)* She's dead. (ZAIRA *does not answer and he rushes into the next room. He is heard sobbing)*

OTTO   *(to* ZAIRA*)* Is she really ...

ZAIRA   *(in tears)* Yes, she's dead. Poor Amelia ... *(Goes out left)*

CALOGERO   *(has been standing aside, frozen and ap-*

palled at the scene, and asks shyly) What's all this,
Professor?

(ARTURO's *offstage sobs are more subdued*)

OTTO (*sadly and bitterly*) Another experiment, that's
all ... (*Collapses on to a chair, as if utterly exhausted*)

CALOGERO Another game ... But ... forgive me, didn't
the lady say: She's dead?

OTTO That's right. Just another game ...

CALOGERO (*after a pause*) But why do we take part in
these experiments? What's in it for us?

OTTO (*struck by* CALOGERO's *question, stares at him
sadly, and puts on a frank expression*) The answer is:
I don't know. It's part of a trick totally unknown to me.
I, a practising illusionist, have to take part in experiments unleashed by another illusionist, far greater and
more important than me ... and so on and so on till
perfection is reached ... This is the prodigious world
of the illusionist! Look ... (*Shows him the cage containing the canaries*) You see those birds? The moment
they see me they sing away happily ... Come and have
a closer look. (*Goes up to the cage with* CALOGERO)
Do you hear? (*The petulant chirping of the canaries is
heard*) They know me. They know me and love me. It
stands to reason—I look after them, I feed them every
morning. I give them millet, cress, cuttlefish bone and
seed. You see? They're waiting for me.

CALOGERO They're so beautiful.

OTTO Then do you know what I do? I put a hand
inside the cage and take one of them out for a vanishing
trick of mine. (*Picks up a smaller cage, the one he used
in ACT ONE*) I put it into this little cage and show it
to the audience. Here you are, ladies and gentlemen. I
cover it with some black material, step back four paces
and bang! goes my pistol. I can hear the audience

whisper: It's gone! How did he do it? He's a wizard! But you see, the bird hasn't vanished at all. It's dead. It died crushed between the bottom of the cage and a false bottom. The pistol shot conceals the noise made by the spring mechanism of the cage. When it comes to tidying it up what do I find? A mushy mess of bones and blood and feathers. (*Points to the birds*) Look at them, see how blissfully ignorant they are! Not for them the world of illusion. It's harsh reality for them. But it is given to man to soar into the realm of illusion, that's his great privilege ... (*Notices* CALOGERO's *downcast expression and switches mood, resuming his bright frivolous attitude*) Come, cheer up. Wake up! We must get on with the game—our game. Look, over there is the public, hanging on our every move. It'll seem like a century to you, but only a few seconds are needed to bring things to a close. (*Points to the auditorium*) Look at the sea, how smooth it is this evening! Are you looking at this splendid sea?

CALOGERO (*would like to give himself up to the game entirely, but attempts to put up some token resistance*) But that's a wall. That's a wall in your house!

OTTO   That's what you think, but can't you perceive the sea through and beyond this imaginary wall? Give me your hand. Walk with me. (*Slowly pulls him beyond the edge of the footlights*) Done. Had there been a wall we'd have come up against it, we'd have felt it, but we've walked and met no barrier. What is the meaning of a wall? What is a wall if not a premeditated trick? Consequently you must agree with me that the wall doesn't exist. There is only one stone. And that is the sea!

(*While* CALOGERO *endeavours to catch a glimpse of the sea,* OTTO *takes advantage of his inattention, snatches up the plastic switch and begins to work it, putting into operation the radiogram with the 'applause' record off-stage. As if from a distance, the ovation heard earlier is repeated. Gradually the mixture of applause and cheering turns into a noise not unlike the sound of waves breaking against the shore. ZAIRA enters, goes up to the window and takes out of the vase the few carnations she had given AMELIA. At the same time GERVASIO enters from the main door, followed by one or two neighbours. One of them carries two candles. They discuss recent events in hushed tones, then quietly file out of the room)*

CALOGERO I can hear it! I can hear it! (*The enthusiastic cheering and clapping increases in volume, merging more and more into the sound of a turbulent sea. CALOGERO, under the spell of the experiment and no longer conscious of reality, gripped by the fascination of the unreal, takes a chair and sits down, looking at the auditorium as if enjoying a view of the sea. OTTO goes out left. Alone, CALOGERO murmurs with utter conviction*) It's the sea! It's the sea!

THE CURTAIN FALLS

ACT THREE

(Four years later.

CALOGERO DI SPELTA's *luxurious apartment. A large room. Upstage, right and left, two windows through which concave wrought-iron bars are visible. Between the two windows, a large English mahogany wardrobe. There are other pieces of furniture and matching leather-covered chairs. Left and right, doors in the baroque style. As the curtain rises the set is in semi-darkness as the inner shutters of the two windows are all but closed. After a short pause* OTTO *enters, followed by* GREGORIO DI SPELTA *and* GENNARINO)

OTTO Let's have some light. Open the shutters. It's half-past nine. Let in the light and some fresh air ...

GENNARINO (*looking extremely smart in his livery*) That's all very well, but the master won't have it. If he finds a window open there'll be no end of trouble.

OTTO Open up. I'll be responsible.

GENNARINO (*proceeds to open the windows*) I wish you were always on the premises, Professor. There's only peace when you are around. You've no idea the things he gets up to. I'm just staying on because I'm fond of him and the job is good, but there are times when (*To* GREGORIO) your brother goes too far. Look here, Professor, is his wife coming back or not?

OTTO   That's no business of yours. You're paid to do your
   work.

GENNARINO   Paid? (*Opens his eyes wide*) Who do you
   think pays me? When I mention my wages he says they're
   not due to me yet because the experiment isn't over,
   that I'm under the impression that time has passed,
   but that it isn't true. Professor, I'm owed nearly four
   years' wages ...

OTTO   You'll be paid to the last penny, don't worry.
   Besides, this gentleman (*Pointing at* GREGORIO) has
   given you the odd advance.

GENNARINO   (*worried*) I'm afraid things are taking a
   turn for the worse. You haven't been here for a week and
   you don't know the latest news. The master hasn't eaten
   for four days.

OTTO   He refuses food?

GENNARINO   And drink as well. He says when he's
   hungry that it's just a delusion. He says he'll start eating
   again once the game is over. This is not funny. He's
   even refusing to go to the lavatory! Four days, I tell
   you: he'll blow up! I heard him moan during the
   night ... no wonder, four days without food. I took him
   some sandwiches; no sir, he didn't want to know. Even
   I have to eat in secret. He said that if he catches me
   eating he'll give me the sack.

OTTO   Wake him up and I'll have a word with him.
   Then order a steak for him in the kitchen.

GENNARINO   Be careful, Professor. If he as much as
   sees a steak he'll go off the deep end.

OTTO   Don't argue. Do as you're told.

GENNARINO   Very good, sir. (*Goes out*)

GREGORIO   (*he is* CALOGERO's *younger brother, and
   dresses with patrician elegance*) You still insist that
   we're dealing with a normal, sane man?

OTTO   I do indeed.

GREGORIO   But didn't you hear what Gennarino said just now?

OTTO   I did. So what?

GREGORIO   I tell you my brother is mad. And you contributed to his going mad.

OTTO   You're barking up the wrong tree. The only connection between me and your brother is an innocent experiment, a game spun as fine as a cobweb and older than the world itself. Would you have us destroy it? How can I explain it to you? It's too difficult. He does not believe the things I tell him, therefore he's sane. But at the same time he keeps questioning me, hoping to trip me into contradiction. In fact it's all I can do to parry some of his more insidious questions so as not to fall into his trap.

GREGORIO   But all the same he won't open the box. Why?

OTTO   Because he is afraid of proving me wrong.

GREGORIO   Why don't you admit he's insane?

OTTO   I get the impression you'd be glad if I admitted it.

GREGORIO   Why should that be?

OTTO   Look here, I'm telling you your brother is not mad. He is just a man who, aware as he is that he has been hurt, clutches at the most absurd straws for the sake of not admitting it—not even to himself: and you still insist! What am I to think? That it suits you, of course.

GREGORIO   I didn't ask your opinion. Whether it suits me or not is my affair. My impression is a different one, and I'll tell you quite bluntly what it is. You're taking advantage of his state of mind, you've made yourself indispensable to him and are slowly bleeding all his money out of him. But this won't go on, let me tell you. I've got the family together and I have decided to . . .

OTTO   Take care. One wrong move and your brother could really go over the edge ...

GREGORIO   I don't need your advice. Another few days and I assure you you won't be allowed to set foot in this house. (*Goes out*)

(CALOGERO, *after a short pause, comes in from the left. He has changed. He has aged and is much paler. His face is deeply lined with suffering; this lends his expression a noble, venerable touch. He speaks more slowly, following each word with a smile which is a mixture of benevolence and absent-mindedness. His hair and moustache are untidy and have gone grey. Now and then he shuts his eyes tight and opens them immediately after, his gaze lost in a pleasant imaginary vision. He is wearing a dressing-gown over his nightshirt. His feet are naked in a pair of bedroom slippers. Under his left arm he is jealously clutching the Japanese box, from which he is now inseparable. When he sees* OTTO *he stops and nods courteously*)

OTTO   Good morning, Mr Di Spelta. (CALOGERO *does not respond, but sits in an armchair by a table, looking at the minute mirrors with which the box is inlaid, regarding his own image*) Good morning, I said. Won't you answer me?

CALOGERO   (*kindly*) No, I won't answer. Why should I utter useless words, conventional clichés? You are making fun of me, and I hate you. You see, I can smile at you in the most friendly manner and hate you at the same time. And I am resisting. Oh yes, I've decided to resist, my dear fellow. You have made me take part in your experiment but you won't tell me its central mystery. Very well. I'll put up the stoutest resistance from now on. I'm on a hunger strike ... I don't drink anything and I'm not even going to the lavatory ...

(*Twists and bends over with discomfort in the armchair*) Time is not passing ... the game will only last a few seconds. But why am I hungry? Why am I thirsty? Why ... (*Twists about in the armchair as before. Then in a fit of excitement becomes aggressive*) Damn you, stop it! Can't you see I'm suffering? Can't you see I can't bear to go on with this diabolical game? (*On the verge of tears*) Help me. Have pity on me. Make the experiment end. Look at me ... I've grown old ... I've gone grey. I have this feeling that years have gone by, and you tell me it isn't true. I'll kill you, you know ... (*Resumes his kindly tone*) I did think of killing you, but it's out of the question, of course. If I do, pop goes your world and heaven knows what would happen to mine then.

OTTO Why do you let yourself go like this? I've told you so many times not to give in to despair. Just behave normally. You are the only one who is refusing to let the game run its course. Why won't you open the box?

CALOGERO (*again on the verge of tears*) Because I can't.

OTTO Because you lack faith, that's all. Then ... all this resistance. What are you resisting? Who are you opposing?

CALOGERO (*looking at himself in the mirrors*) I've gone grey. Can't you see I've gone grey?

OTTO But of course: the game is perfect in every detail. All the sensations you experience must be lifelike. Yet I must warn you that if you try to resist my powers, the experiment will never be over. Two opposing forces neutralise each other. If, on the other hand, you let yourself go and yield to your instinct you will facilitate the progress of the experiment and speed it towards its conclusion.

GENNARINO (*enters nervously from upstage right*

carrying a silver tray with the steak) The steak, sir.

OTTO Come in, come in, Gennarino. (*Enticingly, to* CALOGERO) Look ... a most appetising, juicy steak. I can smell it from here. If you're hungry go on, eat it, it's perfectly all right.

CALOGERO (*downcast*) But for four years now I've been hungry and I've eaten, I've been thirsty and I've drunk, I got sleepy and went to bed. What sort of stupid game is this? (*At a gesture from* OTTO, GENNARINO *approaches* CALOGERO *and encouragingly shows him the dish*) Mm ... what a delicious smell!

GENNARINO Wait till you taste it, sir! I've done it just the way you like it.

CALOGERO (*to* OTTO, *but without averting his eyes from the steak, which is making his mouth water*) You say that in order to hasten the end of the experiment I should yield to my instinct?

OTTO In every possible way, however animal. Whatever your brain orders you, however unreasonable it may seem, go ahead and do it. Act, indulge yourself! Otherwise the game will go on for ever.

CALOGERO (*after a moment's reflection*) Do you know, there are times when I think of the melody of a song, an aria from an opera, and I am tempted to whistle it, or hum it. It seems to happen to me on the strangest occasions. I remember once, at the funeral of a close friend, I suddenly felt like singing a comic song. But I didn't do it, of course. I'd have been too ashamed.

OTTO That's bad. No need to feel ashamed. If you feel like singing, sing. The brain is independent.

CALOGERO (*convinced*) Yes. That's true. At this particular moment, for example, I am extremely hungry. I'd also like to hum something. (*Hums an aria from* Tosca) Ta-ta-ta-ta-ta-tata ... (*To* GENNARINO) Let's sample that steak then. (GENNARINO *puts it down*)

Ta-ta-ta-ta-ta-tata ... (*Begins to eat, then bends over as if in pain. Looks shamefacedly at* OTTO) No need to explain when ... instinct calls! (*To* GENNARINO) Mind you keep that steak warm for me. I'll be back in no time. (*Rises and goes out left, pressing his hands on his stomach*) Ta-ta-ta-ta-ta-tata ...

ZAIRA (*enters right, out of breath as if she had been running. She is carrying a suitcase. To* OTTO) Thank God I've found you. I was afraid you might not be here.

OTTO What's the matter?

ZAIRA Come over here. (*Takes him aside and whispers in his ear*)

OTTO (*registering surprise*) Really?

ZAIRA I've brought your clothes and mine. They're in there. (*Points to the suitcase*) She says she hasn't got the dress she wore that night, but she'll put on one that looks almost exactly like it.

OTTO Good. (*To* GENNARINO) Where can we put this suitcase? I don't want Mr Di Spelta to see it.

GENNARINO (*pointing to the first door on the right*) Over there. Give it to me. (*Relieves* ZAIRA *of the suitcase*) I'll see to it. (*Goes out right*)

OTTO (*with interest*) Where is she?

ZAIRA At our place.

OTTO Go and fetch her. Take a taxi. (*Rushes out right.* ZAIRA *goes out through the main door*)

(GENNARINO *comes back and covers the steak in accordance with* CALOGERO's *instructions*)

CALOGERO (*offstage*) Gennarino!

GENNARINO Sir!

CALOGERO You're a stupid idiot.

GENNARINO (*put out*) But ... why, sir?

CALOGERO It just occurred to me, it crossed my mind,

and I've said it. The brain is an independent free agent. Unless I give way to instinct, unless I speak my mind the game will never end.

GENNARINO *(resigned)* Say whatever you like, dear sir. I shan't mind, especially if it's for the good of your health. Say anything at all ...

(GREGORIO, MATILDE, ORESTE and ROSA enter from the right. GREGORIO is talking with great animation)

GREGORIO Now that I think of it, mother, and I hope you'll forgive my saying so, I'm afraid you've always been weak. Very weak. Father always said so.

MATILDE *(she is about sixty-five years old, with the pinched look of someone who has suffered a great deal, pale as death, her eyes swollen and reddened by tears, yet always ready to defend what she considers a blameless record)* He wasn't being fair, Gregorio. He quite undeservedly accused me of being weak. But he himself, alas, was unable to put a brake on his foolish ideas, which as time went on contributed to the break-up of our family. I have been crying for forty years. My tear ducts are like worn out gutters, battered by the fury of a permanent storm! *(Breaks into tears and sobs. Nobody registers surprise)*

ROSA *(exasperated)* In forty years you should have realised that tears never solve anything.

GREGORIO Well, today we face complete disaster. My brother is insane, no doubt about that. Calogero has gone mad. What are we waiting for? People are laughing their heads off, our family provides the only topic of discussion and gossip in town. What are we waiting for? That charlatan Professor Marvuglia has got Calogero in his clutches. Our assets are being frittered away. We must take immediate and decisive action! I'm afraid, mother, that you're not strong enough to take charge of things. Let me handle it. First of all Calogero is to divorce that whore of a wife of his. She's made our name mud. Secondly we must have him committed for an unlimited period on the grounds of diminished responsibility and insanity. Thirdly, mother is to go into a pleasant, comfortable nursing home where she can rest. I must be given power of attorney ...

ORESTE (ROSA's husband) What about my wife? Isn't she your sister and therefore entitled ...

GREGORIO (who had been expecting this) I'm afraid your wife is not a Di Spelta. She bears your name.

ORESTE I see, but you want her to confirm your brother's insanity and give you full powers of attorney! Our decision, I tell you ...

GREGORIO (cuts him short) It's my mother who will decide what's to be done!

ROSA (resentfully) I'll sign nothing.

MATILDE (intervenes with quiet petulance) Stop it, stop it everybody. I've been crying for forty years ... (Breaks into tears)

CALOGERO (offstage) Gennarino! (Those present gather upstage) Where is my steak? (CALOGERO enters)

GENNARINO Here it is, sir.

CALOGERO (sits down left, prepares to eat and a little later spots his relations) Good morning mother, good morning all! (Regarding them much as one would look at statuary in a museum) You haven't changed a bit. I can see you as if you were real in every detail. Perfect archetypal images of my racial memory. My mother in tears as usual, my brother green with envy, my sister ... sitting on the fence. And my brother-in-law with that greedy look still in his eyes. Perfect. I'm not offering you anything to eat as I'd hate to waste your time unnecessarily. All I'm concerned with is that the game should end. (*Olympically serene, he helps himself liberally to the steak*)

GREGORIO (*places himself on the right, facing* CALOGERO. MATILDE, ROSA *and* ORESTE *follow him and stand behind him*) Listen to me, Calogero. You've been living like this for the past four years. Now we've come to make a last attempt.

CALOGERO Whatever for?

GREGORIO I'm afraid the time has come to tell you the truth. Your wife . . .

CALOGERO How dare you talk of my wife? You've always criticised her, always made the wildest accusations against her, just to drag me down to your own level.

GREGORIO (*hypocritically*) Me?

CALOGERO (*mercilessly*) Yes, you. Today you think I'm finished, in a position of inferiority, so to speak. You talk to me and try to make believe that you want to help me as my dear brother . . . while all you're after is the fulfilment of your insatiable greed!

GREGORIO (*as if stung and faced with a patently unjust accusation*) You must be joking . . .

CALOGERO No, my dear little brother. I've never been more serious. And in order to achieve your dirty little scheming objects, you're even trying to bamboozle our dotty old mother . . . and the more she cries, the more useless she becomes.

MATILDE (*sadly and deeply offended*) Calogero! How can you say that? Of your own mother, too!

CALOGERO I didn't want to say it, mother. But unless I speak my mind the experiment will never end.

GREGORIO So you actually knew what you were saying?

CALOGERO (*simply*) But of course! I've always thought it, only I didn't come out with it before as I used to hold my brain in check.

ROSA You mean you've always lied to us?

CALOGERO   Yes. About the way I felt about you, that is.

GREGORIO   (*as if swallowing bile*) Very well. In that case I'll tell you. Your wife ran away with another man, her lover, and you've been wasting away here like a fool, for four years.

ROSA   (*bitingly*) That's right. Tell him, tell him. And she was doing it even before she left you. (*To* ORESTE) Isn't it true?

ORESTE   Yes it is.

GREGORIO   (*to* MATILDE) You knew it too, didn't you, mother?

MATILDE   (*sobbing*) I've been crying for forty years ...

CALOGERO   You may think it's forty years. But you've been crying for centuries ... for thousands of years ... (*To his mother*) You are part of another experiment! As for you, Gregorio, yes, you are yet another one. And so are you Rosa, and you, Oreste ... Even poor Gennarino is part of one, admittedly a more idiotic experiment, but he's still part of it. You were saying that my wife ran away with some man four years ago, and that she was unfaithful to me even before she left me. Why didn't you warn me at the time? Why didn't you tell me when my wife and I were still together? Because it suited you. That's why. And that is why you now appear before me as real and living beings, although you are actually no more than the flickering images of my racial memory.

ORESTE   That's the sort of nonsense Professor Marvuglia has planted into your mind. And every day he sponges more and more money off you.

GREGORIO   That's enough talk! You are insane. Can't you see, mother, that there's nothing more we can do? Apart from ruining us, apart from damaging irretrievably our good name, this man dares to insult us to our face, disregarding all that we consider most holy in our family.

CALOGERO (*with a superior smile*) Silly fool!

GREGORIO (*angrily*) What's that?

CALOGERO Well, it crossed my mind and I just had to blurt it out. (*Goes on eating*)

GREGORIO I think you are not only insane, but criminally insane!

ROSA You'll come to a bad end!

CALOGERO (*calls out*) Professor! Where is the Professor?

OTTO (*enters right*) Here I am. What do you want?

CALOGERO (*pointing to his relations*) Are you particularly interested in these images?

OTTO No. Why?

CALOGERO Because unless they're particularly relevant to the game, I'd be obliged if you'd make them disappear. I'd like to finish my steak in peace.

OTTO No, they're not particularly relevant to the experiment. I'll have them vanish straightaway. (*Goes up to the others and takes them aside*) His wife has come back!

GREGORIO (*astonished*) When?

ROSA Where is she?

OTTO In the room next door. (*CALOGERO's relations consult briefly and decide to leave. They go out in silence in Indian file*) Done. Vanished!

CALOGERO Thank you so much.

OTTO Do you need anything else?

CALOGERO Would you call my man?

OTTO (*calling out*) Gennarino! Your master wants you. (*Goes out right*)

GENNARINO (*enters*) Yes sir. Would you like something else?

CALOGERO Yes. I'd like the image of some cheese.

GENNARINO (*feigning disappointment*) I'm afraid we're out of cheese. This morning I gave in to my instinct,

and in order to play the game I had the impression of
having it for breakfast.

CALOGERO (*understandingly*) You did well. But is
there not even a semblance of it left?

GENNARINO I'm afraid not, sir. Not even an after-
image.

CALOGERO All right. Be kind enough to have the impression of bringing me a glass of wine.

GENNARINO I'm sorry, but last night I yielded to the
illusion of taking the last four bottles home with me, and
had the impression I drank them over supper with my
wife. It was such an uncannily natural vision!

CALOGERO I see. Is there anything left in the kitchen?

GENNARINO (*promptly*) Nothing at all, sir. Just the
image of an empty larder.

CALOGERO In that case, I want you to believe firmly
that you're on your way to the shops, where you are to
buy archetypal images of groceries.

GENNARINO Very good, sir. But I think I'll have to
imagine I'm going to take the image of some money
from the drawer, sir. Unless shopkeepers' images are
presented with the image of money I'm afraid they won't
play the game.

CALOGERO Go ahead, go ahead ...

GENNARINO (*is about to go, then comes back*) Did you
like the snapshot of that steak?

CALOGERO (*clicking his tongue appreciatively*) A
superb example of photography!

GENNARINO Good. Go on developing it. I'll be off then.
(*Goes out hurriedly*)

CALOGERO (*now alone, smiles placidly. After a while
he walks to the centre of the stage and begins to hum*)
Ta-ta-ta-ta-ta-tata ... It's extraordinary, you know! The
tune crosses my mind and I simply must hum it, I can't
and won't resist the temptation! (*Looks at himself in the*

mirrors inlaid in the box) My hair is still grey. The experiment isn't over yet. (*Amused*) God knows how I'll feel when the game is over and my hair goes dark again! And yet ... When I think about it it's enough to drive me mad. Yes, because this deception could go on long enough to bring about the impression of old age. Wrinkles, rheumy eyes ... One fine day I'll look in the mirror and find all my teeth have dropped out ... There's one that's hurting already ... I may even receive an impression of death. I wonder whether I'll be afraid? (*Excluding this possibility*) Never! Why should I be afraid? Of the end of the deception? The end of the game? Not likely. Besides, it's up to me. If I want the game to end all I need to do is yield to instinct. If my brain thinks anything, anything at all, I must say it outright. That's all very well ... How can I say it all? Hypotheses, desires, thoughts ... (*Works himself up to a frenzy and opens his eyes wide. Staring out into space he lifts up his arm and rapidly moves his hand, articulating all his fingers, as if to penetrate and rummage into the point in space at which he is staring. All of a sudden, joyfully, he closes his fist as though he had caught something*) Here we are: a thermometer! (*Dejectedly*) Why a thermometer? Oh, I suppose I must have thought of one. (*Repeats his gesture*) Man! Yes, man. Man, on average, lives about seventy years, perhaps less. It's not enough, not enough. All experiments and games are based on that conventional life-span. But if only man could live four hundred years, say, all the tricks in the book would have to be revised and produced all over again. Politics ... take politics for example. The way it's handled now, why ... it just wouldn't work as a game if man could live that long. Yes, because then young people would be on average ... about one hundred and fifty years old, and politicians' speeches would be utterly discredited. They'd have to keep their promises, too, since old boys aged about three hundred and sixty-five would say: Come on, come on, friend tell us another! You told us that rubbish three hundred and twenty years ago! (*Hums*) Ta-ta-ta-ta-ta-tata ... How beautiful that cage full of birds was! (*Offstage the twittering of birds is heard.* CALOGERO *sadly recalls* OTTO's *words at the end of ACT TWO*) ... I put a hand inside the cage and take one out for one of my numbers. I put it into this little cage and show it to the audience. Here you are, ladies and gentlemen. I cover it with some black material, step back four paces and bang! goes my pistol. But the bird hasn't vanished at all. It's dead. It died crushed between the bottom of the cage and a false bottom. The pistol shot conceals the noise made by the spring mechanism of the cage. (*Now completely in the grip of hallucinatory fantasies*) Oh dear, oh dear, there have been too many pistol shots, too many big bangs, too many explosions ... And God, the blood, and crushed bones ... but no feathers ... (*He is close to tears. Pause*) Let yourself go, obey your instinct ... (*As if faced with a sudden revelation*) ... and that will lead you to faith. (*Recalls* OTTO's *pronouncement at the start of the experiment*) If you open the box in good faith you will see your wife again. If you open it in bad faith you will never set eyes on her again. I have faith now. I am in good faith. (*Holds up the box*) My wife is inside. And it was I who locked her into this box. I'd become unbearable, selfish, indifferent: I'd become ... a husband. (*Suddenly rises and rapidly goes up to the wardrobe. He opens it and takes out objects at random: dresses, underwear, hats and ladies' shoes. Takes the bundle into the centre of the room and drops the lot on the floor. Then lies down on the floor, among the garments, and looks at them, handling them with nostalgic fondness*) Her dresses! Her hats! Her shoes! (*Takes one of the dresses and drops it softly on his arm, talking to it as one would to a person*) I remember when you first wore this dress. And I even tried not to look at you so as not to have to tell you how much I liked it. I wonder why? Pride, I suppose. Or shyness. But I should have said instead: You're more attractive than ever! I like you like that! (*From the right, dressed in his frock-coat etc. as in ACT ONE,* OTTO *enters followed by* MARTA *and* ZAIRA. *The latter is wearing her theatrical costume, while* MARTA *wears a dress similar to the one she wore on the evening of her disappearance.* MARTA *looks tired and defeated. A few threads of silver in her hair and a deep line across her forehead add to her mild, understanding expression. The three stop still and listen, as yet unseen by* CALOGERO) There was this icy barrier between us. I never spoke. Neither did she. I no longer paid her compliments. I never said a tender word. We couldn't be frank and ... innocent with one another. We were no longer lovers! But now I believe ... I have faith ... (*In a dull undertone, as though afraid of the happiness bestowed on him by his newly-found faith, which he still doubts*) And I can open it ... If I open the box I shall see you, because I am in good faith now! And my hair will grow dark again. I'll be as young as I was a moment ago, at the start of the experiment! (*Stretches out a hand and places it on the box, then moves his hand over it attempting to find the catch*) Now I'll open it. Here we go. (*As if about to perform the most important act in his life*) One, two ...

OTTO ... three! (*With the classic gesture with which conjurers conclude a trick he points to* MARTA) The game is over!

(MARTA *looks at* CALOGERO *tenderly, while* ZAIRA

assumes the stance and stereotyped smile of an illusionist's partner)

CALOGERO (*turns to the others, without a glance at the box, which is still unopened. He dares not speak. Long pause. Then, hardly audibly and tentatively*) Marta ...

OTTO The experiment is over. Here is your wife!

CALOGERO (*as if asking for confirmation*) Speak to me, Marta: speak to me!

MARTA (*moved*) It's me all right!

CALOGERO It's you ... (*Looks around as if trying to establish his surroundings*) But why am I in my flat? If the experiment is over and hasn't lasted more than a few moments why aren't we all in the garden at the Metropole?

OTTO I'm afraid when the experiment was over you fainted with shock. We brought you home by taxi.

CALOGERO (*not altogether convinced, picks up the box and looks at himself in the mirrors*) But my hair is still grey. Why isn't it black?

OTTO The shock made your hair go grey.

CALOGERO Just like that, from one moment to the next?

OTTO Just like that. Here is your wife.

CALOGERO Marta!

MARTA (*though upset by having to act out a fantasy in front of* CALOGERO, *she cannot help going along with the deception*) Yes, here I am!

CALOGERO You've suffered, too! The game was hard, inexorable on you as well. Your hair is turning grey. Say something. Speak to me.

MARTA (*changes her mind*) No! Let's stop this. And don't you two try to interfere. What should I say? You know everything only too well. Why should I continue this charade which is so humiliating for us both? Four years have passed; four real, genuine years. And you have gone grey because time does age us. Time destroys all of us! All this has happened because of our obstinacy and lack of communication and a misguided hankering after freedom. Yes, there's been another man in my life. And you must face up to this if we are to save ourselves from this maddening deception.

CALOGERO (*in an outburst of bitter sincerity*) What have you done? (*His expression now registers in turn rancour, hatred, jealousy, contempt. He controls himself and resumes his former abstracted tone*) Who is this woman? What is she talking about? I can't understand a word she's saying.

(*The Skaters' Waltz is heard in the distance*)

OTTO She's your wife. It's not an illusion. The game is over.

CALOGERO What game?

OTTO The experiment I started a moment ago in the garden at the Metropole.

CALOGERO That's a lie for a start. It was I who started it. You said so yourself. I pushed the experiment to the limit. I am the only one who can make my wife reappear! Mine, and mine alone is the responsibility. You have betrayed yourself. You made a mistake at a most crucial moment. You came in an instant before I opened the box. What a pity.

OTTO But I tell you the box is empty!

CALOGERO Who says so? How can you demonstrate it? All my faith, my good faith, is in that box. How can you possibly hope to see that? I do not know this woman. Perhaps she's part of an experiment which does not concern me. Tell her that her world is linked to countless other worlds, and that she has no choice but to play the game; she can't opt out. Having done that, please do away with this archetypal image of the returning wife. I couldn't stand the thought of having to cope with two experiments.

OTTO But it really is your wife I've brought back!

CALOGERO You imagine you've brought her back. You even think you're in my flat: but you're wrong. It's a cumulative manifestation of your archetypal images. Now I am the one to make you experience racial memories ... She (*Pointing to* MARTA) plays the part of an adulterous wife, but in reality she doesn't really exist. You, a celebrated conjurer, are but an archetypal image yourself. I am the only illusionist now! Let's get on with the experiment, Professor. Time is within us, don't let's look at it as a petty accountant would, day in day out. Try to see things through my third eye. (*Points upstage*) There's the public, watching. (*Points to the auditorium*) There is the sea ... It'll seem like a century to us, but then we'll realise the trick lasted no longer than a few seconds! (*Calls out*) Gennarino!

GENNARINO (*enters*) Yes, sir.

CALOGERO These images must be made to vanish. I'd like you to have the impression of opening the front door. I want you firmly to imagine they are going out. Once you're absolutely convinced they've all gone, close the door. In fact slam it after them.

GENNARINO But ...

CALOGERO (*imperiously*) Do as I say! (GENNARINO *shrugs his shoulders and motions the others to leave.* MARTA *is quietly crying and is comforted by* OTTO *and* ZAIRA. *They leave.* GENNARINO *leads the way. After a while the sound of the door being noisily slammed is heard.* The Skaters' Waltz *stops.* CALOGERO, *after a pause and in absolute silence, feels utterly alone in the world. Manically he clutches the box to his heart*) It's closed! It's closed! Don't look inside! The third eye watches over you ... and perhaps you'll find a crock of gold at the end of the rainbow, provided you carry it with you, shut tight, for ever! (*Stands riveted to the spot, firmly believing in the illusion which is now his reality*)

THE CURTAIN FALLS

Filumena Marturano

translated by Carlo Ardito

CHARACTERS

Filumena Marturano
Domenico Soriano
Alfredo Amoroso
Rosalia Solimene
Diana
Lucia *the maid*
Umberto
Riccardo
Michele
Nocella *a solicitor*
Teresina *a dressmaker*
First Waiter
Second Waiter

This version was first produced in Great Britain on BBC Radio 4 on 9 May 1988 with the following cast:

Domenico	*Robert Stephens*
Filumena	*Billie Whitelaw*
Alfredo	*Peter Sallis*
Rosalia	*Patricia Hayes*
Diana	*Joanna Mackie*
Lucia	*Joan Walker*
Nocella	*Laurence Payne*
Umberto	*Ian Michie*
Riccardo	*Mark Straker*
Michele	*Ken Cumberlidge*

Directed by *Glyn Dearman*

ACT ONE

(The Soriano household.

A spacious dining-room, lavishly furnished in a definite 1920s style, which nevertheless suggests fairly moderate taste. A few paintings and ornaments dating back to the turn of the century, once part of the furniture in DOMENICO's *childhood home, are carefully arranged about the walls and furniture and clash harshly with everything else in the room. Downstage left a door leads to the bedroom. Upstage left, beyond a wide window, a large terrace covered in flowers and shaded by a brightly striped awning can be seen. On the right the room extends back a long way, and beyond an open space and a half-drawn silk curtain is* DOMENICO's *study, which he has also furnished in the peculiarly Italian 1920s style. A glass showcase displays a great many trophies of all shapes and sizes won by his racehorses. Two crossed pennants on the front wall, above a writing table, testify to his victories at the Montevergine race meetings. No books, newspapers or letters. The study is clean and tidy, but utterly characterless. The table in the middle of the dining-room is carefully laid for two, down to freshly picked roses in the middle of the table. Late spring: nearly summer. Dusk. The last traces of daylight are vanishing from the terrace.*

FILUMENA *is standing by the bedroom door, her arms*

folded defiantly. She is wearing a long white nightdress. Her hair is dishevelled and hastily rearranged. She is wearing a pair of bedroom slippers on her naked feet. Her troubled features bear the marks of past struggles. Traces of her working-class background show through and she makes no attempt to conceal this. Her manner is open, her voice always frank and decisive. She is the sort of woman who prefers to face up to life in her own independent way. She is a youthful forty-eight, and only the occasional grey hair betrays her age. Her eyes, in particular, have retained a youthful vigour: they are dark in a typically Neapolitan way. She is pale, deadly pale, partly as a result of the dramatic events that have just taken place, partly because of the storm which is about to break around her. She shows no fear, however, but like a wounded animal looks ready to spring on her opponent.

DOMENICO is standing in the opposite corner downstage right. He looks offended and outraged by recent events. He is a well built man in his early fifties. His wealth and the easy life that goes with it have contributed to his preserving an animated, youthful countenance. His doting father, Raimondo Soriano, was one of the wealthiest and shrewdest confectioners in Naples, with factories at Vergini and Forcella, not to mention elegant shops in Toledo and Foria. DOMENICO's youthful pranks, when he was known as Don Mimi' Soriano, were so extravagant that they are still talked about in Naples. He is passionately interested in racehorses, and has been known to spend days on end reminiscing with his cronies on the racing prowess of his horses. He is wearing a pyjama jacket over hastily pulled on trousers, hurriedly buttoned up. He is standing, pale and upset, opposite FILUMENA, *who now has him in her power.*

ROSALIA *is standing on the left of the room, in the corner next to the terrace. She is meek and humble, about seventy-five years old: Her hair is neither white nor grey, though the former colour predominates. She is wearing a dark rather mournful dress. She is slightly hunched but still full of life. She used to live in a basement in the Vico San Liborio, opposite where the Marturanos used to live. She has known* FILUMENA *since she was a young girl, and was always on hand to give her a word of comfort and understanding as only our working-class women know how. Motionless, she is following* DOMENICO's *every move with some apprehension, never for a moment taking her eyes off him. She knows from bitter experience the effects of* DOMENICO's *rages.*

ALFREDO *stands in the fourth corner of the room. He is an agreeable man of sixty, solidly built and vigorous in appearance. His friends nicknamed him 'The Jockey'. In fact he enjoyed some fame in his day as a jockey and trotter. When* DOMENICO *gave him a job he became his right-hand man, his functions so varied as to include those of scapegoat, pimp and confidant. He is totally loyal to his master. He is wearing a partly threadbare grey jacket and trousers of a different colour, and a beret which sits crooked on his head. He wears a gold chain on his waistcoat.*

As the curtain rises the four characters are standing each in a corner of the room, as if about to engage in an innocent game, but in fact life itself has cast them into mutually hostile positions.)

DOMENICO (*slapping his own face angrily*) I'm a fool. a fool, a bloody fool!

ALFREDO   (*mildly*) What's the matter now?

(ROSALIA *picks up a shawl from a chair and wraps it round* FILUMENA's *shoulders*)

DOMENICO   I'm just a nonentity! I ought to stand in front of the mirror and keep spitting at myself! (*Darting a look charged with hatred at* FILUMENA) I've given you, wasted on you, twenty-five years of my life, my health, strength and brains. What more do you want from Domenico Soriano? Isn't the fact that you've bled me white enough for you? (*Accusingly to the world at large, and beside himself with rage*) You've all done as you pleased with me! (*With self-contempt*) And while I thought I was Jesus Christ himself you all made a monkey out of me! You, you and you, this very street, this district, Naples, the world, you've all taken me for a ride! (*The memory of the trick* FILUMENA *has played on him makes him angrier still*) The thought of it alone is enough to drive me mad! It was only to be expected though. Only a woman like you could have done what you have done. The leopard doesn't change its spots. Even twenty-five years couldn't change a woman of your sort. But don't think for a moment that you've got away with it. You haven't, not by a long chalk. I'm going to kill you! And all those who were in it with you, the doctor, the priest ... (*Points at* ROSALIA, *who gives a start, and at* ALFREDO, *who seems very much at ease*) and these two scoundrels I've been feeding for years ... I'm going to kill the lot of you! My gun ... give me my gun!

ALFREDO   (*calmly*) I've taken it to the gunsmith's for cleaning, like you said.

DOMENICO   Oh yes, I've said a great many things and I'm supposed to have said even more! Right—it's all over now. I've got the picture. (*To* FILUMENA) You get out of this house ... and unless you go quietly they'll carry you out feet first. Nothing on earth, not God Almighty himself is going to change my mind. I'll have the lot of you charged with fraud and false pretences! I'll have you slung in jail! Oh yes, I've got the money, I pay the piper and I'm going to call the tune. Filume': you're going to dance to my tune, you mark my words. When I tell everybody the sort of place I picked you up in they'll all be on my side. I'm going to break you, Filume', so help me I'll finish you!

(Pause)

FILUMENA *(unruffled and sure of herself)* Have you finished? Nothing more to say?

DOMENICO *(vehemently)* Keep quiet. Don't say a word ... I can't trust myself to listen to you. *(The sound of her voice alone is enough to enrage him)*

FILUMENA When I've finished telling you all I've got bottled up inside me *(Points to her stomach)*—right here, then I'll keep quiet!

DOMENICO *(with contempt)* You're just a tart, and always will be!

FILUMENA What's the point of bringing that up? That's no news. Don't you think everybody knows what I was and where you found me? As for the house I worked in, let me tell you that you were a frequent caller. You and the others. And I treated you like everyone else, what else do you expect? After all, men are all alike, aren't they? What I was and what I have done is something between me and my conscience. Now, however, I'm your wife. And not even the police will make me budge an inch from this house!

DOMENICO Wife? Whose wife? Filume': are you going clean out of your mind? Who do you think you're married to?

FILUMENA   (*coldly*) To you!

DOMENICO   You really are mad. It was all a transparent deception, nothing but a low trick. And I have witnesses to prove it! (*Points to* ALFREDO *and* ROSALIA)

ROSALIA   (*without hesitation*) I know nothing. (*She obviously does not wish to be involved in so grave a matter*) All I know is that Donna Filumena got sick, took to her bed, got worse and started breathing her last.

DOMENICO   (*to* ALFREDO) What about you? Didn't you know that the death rattle was a put-up job?

ALFREDO   Don Dummi', for the love of God! Donna Filumena can't stand the sight of me. Do you think she'd let me into her secrets?

ROSALIA   (*to* DOMENICO) What about the priest? Wasn't it you yourself who asked me to fetch him?

DOMENICO   Only because she ... (*Pointing to* FILUMENA) asked for him. I just wanted her to feel ... comfortable ...

FILUMENA   You just couldn't help rejoicing at the thought I was about to peg out! I bet you were glad at the thought you were going to be rid of me!

DOMENICO   (*spitefully*) Right! At last you've got the message! And when the priest, after a word with you, said to me: Marry this poor woman *in extremis*, go on, it's her dying wish, regularise this bond with the Lord's blessing, I said ...

FILUMENA   ... you said to yourself: 'What have I got to lose? She's dying anyway. Another couple of hours and she'll be out of the way.' (*Mockingly*) You were taken aback, weren't you, Dummi', when the moment the priest left I jumped out of bed and said: And the best of luck to you, Dummi', we're now man and wife!

ROSALIA   Gave me quite a turn! I laughed till I cried! (*Laughing at the memory*) Split my sides I did!

ALFREDO (*laughs too*) ... and what about the death rattle?

DOMENICO Quiet you two or I'll give you the death rattle! (*Pause*) It's not happening. It's just not possible. (*Suddenly as if remembering someone else who to his mind could alone be responsible*) Hmm ... of course: the doctor. That's right, the doctor ... what's become of science, I ask you. There's a doctor who can't tell whether a woman is dying or pulling the wool over his eyes ...

ALFREDO It's my opinion he made a mistake.

DOMENICO Shut up, Alfre'. (*Decisively*) That doctor is going to pay for this. He's going to pay for it, I promise you! I bet you he was in it with you! (*To* FILUMENA, *maliciously*) You bribed him, didn't you ...

FILUMENA (*thoroughly disgusted*) Money. That's all you understand! It's money that bought you all you ever wanted! Why, you bought me with money! They used to call you Don Mimi' Soriano ... only the best tailors, the best shirtmakers ... your horses were running and you made them run ... but as for you, mark this, I held your reins and made you run! Why, you ran my kind of race without realising it. And you'll go on doing so, you've still got a long way to go! (*Pause*) The doctor didn't know a thing. He fell for it too—and why shouldn't he! Any woman after twenty-five years at your side is entitled to be at death's door! I've been a slave to you, that's what I've been. (*To* ROSALIA *and* ALFREDO) A wretched slave to him, for twenty-five years, and you both know it. He used to go away for a bit of fun: London, Paris, race meetings ... and I looked after things for him at this end. The factory at Forcella, the one over at Vergini, the shops at Toledo and Foria. If I hadn't taken care of things his employees would have robbed him right, left and centre. (*Impersonating*

DOMENICO) What would I do without you ... Filume':
you're some woman!—I used to spoil him all the time.
I used to lick his boots! Not now, but when I was
a slip of a girl. Yet he never once made me feel appre-
ciated. Never! Always used to push me around like a
servant you can kick out from one minute to the
next!

DOMENICO Did you ever give me a sign of understanding, of how things really stood between us? You
were always cross, scowling. I used to ask myself: Could
I be in the wrong? Could it be that I've done something
to upset her? No. Always cold and hard. All the years
I've known you I've never seen you cry once, like other
human beings.

FILUMENA Now why should I cry over you?

DOMENICO There's something peculiar about you, you
know. I've never seen you shed a tear. You might as
well be a woman who never eats or drinks or sleeps.
Now that I think of it I've never seen you sleep, either.
You're some kind of creature from another planet ...

FILUMENA You rarely gave yourself a chance of seeing
me asleep. More often than not you couldn't find your
way home. God knows how many Christmasses and
Easters I've spent on my own. And as for crying, do you
want to know when it is that people cry? When they
know what happiness is and it's denied them. I've never
even known the meaning of happiness, and no one can
cry who has only known misery. No, Filumena Marturano has never cried, you're quite right. You've always
treated me like dirt and that's the truth! (*To* ROSALIA
and ALFREDO, *the only witnesses of the truth she is
voicing*) I'm not talking of the days when he was young,
at least then one could have said that he had money and
looks. But now, at his time of life—and he's fifty-two if
he's a day—he comes home with his handkerchiefs

smeared with lipstick, the filthy pig ... (*To* ROSALIA)
Where are they?

ROSALIA In my safekeeping.

FILUMENA Now you'd think he'd be careful, that he'd
say: Shouldn't I get rid of them? What if she finds
them? But no: Let her find them. What's she going to
do about it anyway ... Who is she, what rights has she
over me?—and goes on lusting after that ... whatsher-
name!

DOMENICO (*as if caught out, angrily*) What do you
mean?

FILUMENA (*not at all put out and matching* DOMEN-
ICO's *tone*) Lusting after that bitch! Do you think I
didn't know what you were up to? The trouble with you
is you're no good at lying. You're fifty-two years of age
and you want to shack up with a girl of twenty-two!
Aren't you ashamed of yourself? You even brought her
into the house, passing her off as a nurse—of course you
thought I was going to kick the bucket any minute,
didn't you ... (*As if telling an incredible story*) And
just an hour ago, before the priest arrived and you
thought I was about to give up the ghost ... and was blind
into the bargain, why, you were cuddling and kissing
at the foot of my bed! (*Disgusted*) God, what filth! And
if I'd really died what would you have done next?
There—(*Points to the table*) the table is laid for two.
For you and that ... that Angel of Death! Sure, you'd
have had dinner the moment I was dead.

DOMENICO So just because of that I was to starve myself,
put an end to all nourishment, I suppose.

FILUMENA ... and roses on the table ...

DOMENICO So what?

FILUMENA Red roses?

DOMENICO (*angrily*) Red, green, purple—who's to stop
me putting them there? Who's to stop me feeling

delighted at the thought you were going to be out of the way?

FILUMENA But I'm not dead, you see? (*Maliciously*) I've no intention of dying for the time being, Dummi'.

DOMENICO That's the snag. (*Pause*) I can't quite understand. If, as you say, you've always treated me like all the others, because according to you all men are alike, why set so much store on marrying me? And if I happen to fall in love with a girl and I want to marry her—and marry Diana I shall—what's it to you if she is twenty-two or whatever?

FILUMENA (*ironically*) You really make me laugh! I do feel sorry for you. Do you think I care about you, about the girl you've lost your head over, that I give a tinker's curse about all you've just said? Don't think for a moment that I've done all this on *your* account. A woman like me, you've said it yourself, and you've been saying it all these years, is nothing if not calculating, and now you're useful to me. And get it out of your mind that after twenty-five years' forced labour I'm just going to pack up and go quietly.

DOMENICO (*triumphantly, as though suddenly understanding the reason for the trick she has played on him*) It's money then! But surely you know I'd have looked after that. You must know that Domenico Soriano, son of Raimondo Soriano, one of the largest and most respected confectioners in Naples, wouldn't have left you in the lurch. I'd have set you up in a flat somewhere, made all the necessary financial arrangements ...

FILUMENA (*disheartened by his obtuseness*) Oh be quiet. You don't understand a thing. Money, you say. You can keep your money. What I want from you is something else, and you're going to give it to me. Listen to this, Dummi': I have three sons.

(DOMENICO and ALFREDO go pale with astonishment.
ROSALIA *on the other hand is her usual impassive self)*

DOMENICO   Three sons? Filume', what are you saying?

FILUMENA   I have three sons.

DOMENICO   *(at a loss)* Well ... whose sons are they?

FILUMENA   *(coldly and aware of* DOMENICO's *fears)*
Oh, the sons of men like you.

DOMENICO   Filume', you're playing with fire, take care.
What exactly do you mean by 'The sons of men like
you?'

FILUMENA   Because you're all alike.

DOMENICO   *(to* ROSALIA*)* Did you know about this?

ROSALIA   Yes sir, I knew about it.

DOMENICO   *(to* ALFREDO*)* What about you?

ALFREDO   *(ready as always to justify himself)* How could
I possibly know ... Donna Filumena hates my guts, you
know that.

DOMENICO   *(as yet unconvinced, to himself)* Three
sons! *(To* FILUMENA*)* How old are they?

FILUMENA   The eldest is twenty-six.

DOMENICO   Twenty-six ...

FILUMENA   Don't look so scared: have no fear, they're
not yours!

DOMENICO   *(somewhat relieved)* But ... do they know
you? Do you ever see them? Do they know you're their
mother?

FILUMENA   No. They don't know I'm their mother.
But I see them now and then. I even have an occasional
chat with them.

DOMENICO   Where do they live? What do they do for
a living?

FILUMENA   Your money took care of that.

DOMENICO   *(surprised)* My money?

FILUMENA   That's right. Your money. You see, I stole

from you. I took money out of your wallet, under your very nose!

DOMENICO (*contemptuously*) Thief!

FILUMENA (*unperturbed*) Yes, I stole from you. And another thing, I used to sell your suits, your shoes ... and you never noticed. Can you remember that diamond ring you thought you'd lost? Well, you didn't lose it: I sold it. And it was your money that helped me provide for my children.

DOMENICO (*with distaste*) So I've been harbouring a thief in my house. (*Pause*) What sort of creature are you?

FILUMENA (*as though uninterrupted by his last remark*) One of them has a shop just round the corner: he's the local tinker.

ROSALIA (*corrects her*) He's a plumber.

DOMENICO What?

ROSALIA He's a plumber: mends taps, replaces washers, even services municipal fountains. (*Referring to the second son*) Now the other one ... what's his name ... oh yes, Riccardo. What a good-looking boy! There's a handsome lad for you. He's got a shop in the Via Chiaia. He's a shirtmaker, that is, he makes shirts to measure. And what a clientele he's got! As for Umberto ...

FILUMENA Oh, he's the bookish one. Always been keen on his studies. He's an accountant, and writes for the newspapers.

DOMENICO (*sardonically*) We've even got a writer in the family!

ROSALIA (*extolling* FILUMENA's *maternal exploits*) What a wonderful mother she's been to them! How well she looked after those kids! She always provided for them ... why should an old woman like me tell anything but the truth? Those children had everything money could buy!

DOMENICO ... my money could buy!

ROSALIA (*impatiently drops her guard*) You were always such a big spender!

DOMENICO That was my business.

FILUMENA Take no notice, Rosalia.

DOMENICO (*endeavouring to control his temper*) Filume': you're pushing me too far. You're driving me round the bend! Do you think I'm a man of straw? Look here: these three gentlemen—and I don't know them from Adam, I've no idea where they've come from —these three gentlemen at this very moment might well be thinking: Never mind, we'll get by with Don Domenico's money.

ROSALIA (*butting in*) No sir. Not that. They don't know anything. Donna Filumena always handled things like the sensible woman she is. Carefully, discreetly. She got a solicitor to give the plumber some money when he put up shop. He said a lady who wished to remain anonymous wanted to help. She did the same for the shirtmaker. And what's more the lawyer paid Umberto his allowance to see him through college. You are completely out of it.

DOMENICO (*bitterly*) All I do is pay!

FILUMENA (*in a flash*) Would you sooner I'd got rid of them, before they were born? No doubt that's what you'd have liked me to do. I suppose you think I should never have had them, like so many women. That's right: be sensible, Filumena, do the wise thing, get rid of them, have an abortion. Answer me: is that what you'd have had me do? Because that was certainly the advice I got from the girls at work. (*She is referring to the brothel*) 'What are you wasting time for, solve the problem once and for all!' On the contrary, I'd have set myself a problem: I couldn't have survived that kind of remorse. And then, thank heaven, I talked with Our Lady ...

(*To* ROSALIA) Our Lady of the Roses—do you remember?

ROSALIA Do I remember! Our Lady of the Roses dispenses a special grace every day!

FILUMENA (*recalling her mystical encounter*) It was three in the morning. I was walking along the street, on my own. I'd left home six months before. (*Referring to her awareness of her first pregnancy*) It was my first time. What was I to do, I kept asking myself, who was I to tell? I kept hearing the girls' advice: What are you waiting for—solve the problem once and for all. We know a very good man ... I kept on walking, walking. Then suddenly I found myself right by the street shrine of Our Lady of the Roses. I challenged her. (*Puts her hands on her hips defiantly and looks up at an imaginary shrine, as if about to address the Virgin Mary in a woman-to-woman fashion*) What am I to do? You know it all. You also know why I'm in this pickle. What am I to do then?—There was no answer. (*Excitedly*) Come on, tell us what to do. I get you now: the more you keep mum, the more people believe in you! It's you I'm talking to! (*Arrogantly*) Answer me! (*Pause. Impersonating a disembodied voice*) 'Our children are our children'—I just stood there, petrified. (*Looking up at the imaginary shrine*) Perhaps if I'd bothered to turn round I'd have seen where the voice had come from: out of an open window, from up the street or round the corner. Yet I said to myself: if it's not Our Lady, then why just now, why did I hear those words just now? Nobody round here knows my situation ... It was Our Lady then. I'd gone up to her and put it to her straight, and she spoke out. I suppose she uses one of us to speak through. When the girls said to me: Solve the problem—it was Our Lady who'd really said it, through them, to test me. Well, to this day I don't know whether it was me

or Our Lady of the Roses who nodded just like this.
(*Nods as if to say 'Yes, you've understood'*) Our children
are our children. I made a vow then ... (*To* DOMENICO,
vehemently) That's why I stuck to you all these years.
It was for their sake I put up with you and the way
you treated me. Remember the young man who wanted
to marry me? You and I had been together five years:
you were safely married, in your own home, and I was
at the flat at San Putito, the first place you set me up in.
It took you five years to take me away from you-know-
where. That poor boy fell for me and wanted to marry me
so badly! But you went all jealous. I can still hear you:
I'm married already ... I can't marry you. And if he
marries you ... And you started crying. Quite the opposite to me: can you cry! I just said to myself: All right.
I suppose that's the way it's got to be. Dummi' in his
own way is fond of me, and with all the good will in
the world can't marry me as he's already lumbered with
a wife ... So we carried on, in the flat at San Putito.
But then, two years later, your wife died. Still I thought:
He's young, he's not keen to tie himself for life to one
woman. Perhaps one day he'll settle down and come to
his senses. He'll realise how much I've done for him.
Do you remember when I used to say to you: Dummi',
have you heard who's just got married? The girl that
lives opposite ... You just laughed, that mocking laugh
I used to hear when you and your pals were halfway up
the stairs of the house you used to patronise. That
mocking scoffing cackle that starts halfway up the
brothel's stairs and I've never forgotten. It's always the
same, that laugh, whoever laughs it. I could have
murdered you when I heard that snigger! (*More
patiently*) And I waited. I waited twenty-five years. We
have you, Dummi', to thank for this long wait. And now
he's fifty-two years old: he's an old man. Is he though!

Why he thinks he's still a young rooster! Still runs after every bit of skirt he can find, makes a bloody fool of himself, brings home handkerchiefs smeared with lipstick ... brings the bitch right into this house! (*Threateningly*) Just you try to bring her into my home now I'm your wife! I'll kick you both out. Get it into your head that you and I are married. The priest married us. This is my home!

(*The doorbell rings.* ALFREDO *goes out upstage right*)

DOMENICO Your home? (*Laughs, with forced irony*) Now that's really funny!

FILUMENA Laugh away ... you know, it does me good to hear you laugh like that ... because when I'm finished with you you'll laugh no more.

(ALFREDO *returns, looks at all of them evidently embarrassed by what he is going to say*)

DOMENICO (*roughly to* ALFREDO) What do you want?
ALFREDO They've ... they've brought dinner.
DOMENICO All right, all right: aren't I entitled to eat?
ALFREDO (*as if to imply it's not his fault*) Please, Don Dummi' ... (*Shouts towards the front door*) Come on in ...

(*Two waiters from a nearby restaurant enter carrying covered dishes and a hamper*)

FIRST WAITER (*servile and cringing*) Here's dinner, sir. (*To the* SECOND WAITER) Put it down here. (*They put down the hamper and dishes on the spot indicated by the* FIRST WAITER) Sir, there's only one chicken, but quite a big one, enough for four people. Everything you ordered is absolutely first class. (*Is about to get busy with the food*)
DOMENICO (*stops the waiter with a gesture*) Shall I tell

you what I want you to do? I want you to get out! That's what I want you to do!

FIRST WAITER Sir? (*Takes a pudding out of the hamper and puts it on the table*) This is the sweet the young lady's so keen on ... (*Takes out a bottle*) And this is the wine. (*The waiter's words are received in complete silence. The waiter, unaware of the prevailing atmosphere, chatters on, this time in his fawning voice*) You ... haven't forgotten?

DOMENICO Forgotten what?

FIRST WAITER You know, what you said when you came to order dinner, do you remember? I asked you whether you had an old pair of trousers you wanted to chuck away. You said: When you come tonight I'll tell you whether or not I've had a good piece of news. If what I'm praying for happens, I'll tell you what I'll do: I've got a new suit, well—I'll give it to you as a present! (*The others listen in gloomy silence. Pause. The waiter looks genuinely concerned*) You haven't had the piece of good news?

DOMENICO (*aggressively*) Clear out I tell you!

FIRST WAITER (*surprised at* DOMENICO'*s outburst*) All right, we'll go. (*Looks at* DOMENICO, *then, sadly*) Let's go, Carlu', he hasn't had his piece of good news after all. Just my luck! (*Sighs*) Good night everybody. (*Goes out upstage right followed by the* SECOND WAITER)

FILUMENA (*after a pause, to* DOMENICO, *sarcastically*) Eat then. Go on, eat! Have you lost your appetite?

DOMENICO (*embarrassed and angry*) I'll eat when I'm good and ready! All in good time.

FILUMENA (*referring to the young woman mentioned earlier*) Yes: just as soon as the Angel of Death gets back.

(DIANA *enters from the main door. She is a good-looking*

*girl of twenty-two, or rather she tries to pass herself off
as twenty-two but is in fact twenty-seven. She is affectedly
elegant and rather a snob, and looks down her nose at
everybody. As she walks in she is addressing no one in
particular, conscious of her superiority over the assembled company. She is not aware, moreover, that*
FILUMENA *is present. She is carrying small parcels
of medicines and drugs which she places languidly on
the table. She picks up a white nurse's overall from a
chair and puts it on)*

DIANA   Oh dear oh dear, what a crowd at the chemist's!
(*As if issuing a command*) Rosalia, run me a bath, will
you? (*Notices the roses on the table*) Oh ... red roses!
Thank you, Domenico. What a heavenly smell: I'm a
little hungry. (*Picks up a box of phials from the table*)
I've managed to get camphor and adrenalin, but they
were out of oxygen. (DOMENICO *stands as if riveted to
the floor.* FILUMENA *doesn't bat an eyelid: she is waiting.* ROSALIA *and* ALFREDO *register some amusement.* DIANA *sits by the table facing the audience and
lights a cigarette*) It's just crossed my mind that ... God
forbid ... I hate to say the word but ... if she were to
die tonight, I'll leave first thing in the morning. A girl
I know has offered me a lift in her car. I'd only be in
the way if I stayed here. I've got a number of things to
see to in Bologna, a few little matters that need settling.
I'll be back in ten days. Then I'll come to see you. How
is she? Still sinking? Has the priest been sent for?
FILUMENA   (*restraining herself with difficulty walks
slowly towards* DIANA. *With studied courtesy*) The
priest was indeed sent for ... (DIANA, *astonished, takes
a few steps backwards*) ... and having established the
gravity of my condition ... (*Savagely*) Take that off!
DIANA   (*off balance*) What?

FILUMENA   Take off that overall! (*More patiently*) Go
on, take it off.

(DIANA *in some alarm slips out of the overall*)

FILUMENA   (*who has been following* DIANA's *every
movement*) Now put it on that chair. On that chair.

(DIANA *does as she is told*)

FILUMENA   (*again with studied courtesy*) ... and the
priest, as I said, taking into account the gravity of my
condition advised Don Domenico Soriano to regularise
our union ... how do you say it ... *in extremis*. (DIANA,
*uncertain as to what to do next, takes a rose from the
bowl in the middle of the table and sniffs it*. FILUMENA
casts a malevolent look at her) Put it back!

(DIANA *as if obeying a military order puts it back in the
bowl*)

FILUMENA   (*with mock courtesy, as before*) Needless to
say Don Domenico saw the fairness of the suggestion.
He must have said to himself: It's only right. This poor
soul has been at my side for twenty-five years ... And so
on and so forth, I won't bore you with details, which are
none of your business anyway. The priest came to my
bedside and Domenico and I were duly married with
witnesses in attendance and the blessing of Holy Mother
Church. (*Pause*) It could be that marriage ceremonies
have healing, health-giving properties, because the
minute we were pronounced man and wife I was fighting fit again! I got out of bed and postponed my death
indefinitely. It follows that there's no longer any need
for nurses in a place without sick or dying patients ...
and as for mucky, filthy, (*With the forefinger of her
right hand she administers light measured taps to*

DIANA's chin, *which seem to compel the latter to shake her head at each tap as if saying 'No'*) disgusting practices (*goes on tapping her chin*) in front of a dying woman, because as far as you knew I was dying ... go and do that sort of thing somewhere else! (DIANA *smiles ineptly as if to say 'What's all this about?'*) Off you go ... You're not wanted here.

DIANA (*still with a grin on her face walks backwards up to the entrance door*) As you wish ...

FILUMENA Now if you really want to fix yourself up properly, go and work in the house I was once in.

DIANA Where?

FILUMENA (*pointing to* DOMENICO) Ask him: he'll tell you. Why, he used to be an honoured and frequent customer at that sort of establishment. Still is to this day! Off with you then!

DIANA (*suddenly registers panic*) Thank you! (*Retreats upstage right*)

FILUMENA Don't mention it!

DIANA Good night. (*Goes out*)

DOMENICO (*who up till that moment appears to have been lost in thought, absorbed by who knows what strange speculations, turns to* FILUMENA) Was that the way to speak to her?

FILUMENA She got no more than she deserved. (*Makes a spiteful gesture*)

DOMENICO You know, you're like some poisonous insect: one's got to keep one's eyes open when you're around. Everything you say has got to be taken down in evidence, noted and carefully weighed. I should know, make no mistake about it. You're like a poisonous insect; whatever you touch you destroy. You were saying something to me earlier, and I was thinking about it just now. You said 'What I want from you is something else, and you're going to give it to me!' (*Pause*) Well, it can't be money, you know I'd have given it to you. (*Shouting, like a man possessed*) What else can you possibly want? What's got hold of you? Answer me!

FILUMENA (*quietly*) You know the song, Dummi', the one that goes 'I'm teaching a little goldfinch—lots and lots of things ...'

ROSALIA (*looks up, forlorn*) Oh my God!

DOMENICO (*on his guard, suspicious and fearful*) Meaning what?

FILUMENA You are the goldfinch.

DOMENICO For heavens' sake don't talk in riddles, woman! Don't push me too far!

FILUMENA (*in earnest*) Our children are our children.

DOMENICO And what's that supposed to mean, for Christ's sake!

FILUMENA They must be told who their mother is. They must come to know all I've done for them. They should love me. (*Fervently*) They're not to feel ashamed when they go and ask for documents or show their birth certificates ... they're not to be regarded as bastards! They too must have a family to fall back on and rely on for advice, so they can let their hair down or let off steam. (*Pause*) They're to bear my name.

DOMENICO And your name is ...

FILUMENA My name? My name! We're married, aren't we? My name is Soriano!

DOMENICO (*passionately*) I knew it! I wanted to hear it from you though, from your blasphemous tongue: this alone would justify my kicking you out, doing away with you altogether, as one squashes a snake underfoot if only to protect others from its fangs! So. So you'd give them my name, bring them into my house ... Those sons of a ...

FILUMENA (*aggressively*) Sons of a ...?

DOMENICO Yours anyway. Yes, if you ask me: whose

sons? I can honestly answer: yours. If you ask me again:
and who else's? Then I can't answer, because I don't
know it. And I dare say you don't know it either. I know,
you thought you could square everything, set your conscience at rest, by bringing these strangers into my house.
Over my dead body! They're not going to set foot in
this house! (*Solemnly*) I swear it on my father's grave!

FILUMENA (*attempts to stop him making the vow*)
Don't swear, Dummi'! It's on account of a vow that
I've been like a soul in torment all these years ... don't
make a vow you might not be able to keep! One day
you might want to come begging to me on your knees ...

DOMENICO (*as if hypnotised by* FILUMENA'*s words,
yet beside himself with impotent rage*) What else are
you cooking up? You're a witch! But I'm not afraid of
you! You don't scare me at all!

FILUMENA (*challenging him*) Oh no?

DOMENICO Shut up! (*To* ALFREDO, *taking off his
pyjama jacket*) Fetch me my jacket! (ALFREDO *goes
silently into the study to fetch it*) Tomorrow out you go.
I'll get hold of my solicitor and lodge a complaint. I've
got witnesses. And in the unlikely event of the law
finding in your favour, why, I'll kill you, I'll kill you,
Filume'! How I wish I could bring myself to pick you
up and sling you ...

FILUMENA (*ironically*) Where?

DOMENICO ... back in the place I found you in, where
you belong. (*He is now deliberately offensive.* ALFREDO
comes back with his master's jacket. DOMENICO
snatches it from him and puts it on*) Tomorrow you're
to get my solicitor, is that clear? (ALFREDO *nods*) Then
we'll talk, Filume'.

FILUMENA Right, we'll talk.

DOMENICO I'll show you who you're dealing with!
(*Starts walking upstage on his way to the main entrance*)

FILUMENA *(pointing to the table)* Rosali', let's have something to eat. I'm sure you must be hungry too. *(Sits at the table facing the audience)*

DOMENICO   And the best of luck to you, Filume'.

FILUMENA   *(sings)* I'm teaching a little goldfinch ...

DOMENICO   *(on hearing* FILUMENA *sing, guffaws and sniggers, as if to insult and wound her)* Remember this laugh, eh, Filumena Marturano? *(Goes out followed by* ALFREDO *as*

THE CURTAIN FALLS

ACT TWO

(The following day. The same room. In order to scrub the floor LUCIA *has pushed the chairs out of the way: some she has put out on the terrace and others upside down on the table. The remainder she has moved into* DOMENICO's *study. The rug, in the middle of which stands the dining-table, is folded over itself. It is a sunny morning.* LUCIA *is the maid-of-all-work, a jolly healthy girl of twenty-three or thereabouts. She has nearly finished her chores and is wringing a rag for the last time over a pail of water. She then stores away her cleaning things on the terrace)*

ALFREDO *(evidently tired out and still sleepy comes in from the main entrance, while* LUCIA *straightens out the rug)* Good morning, Luci'.

LUCIA *(stopping him in his tracks with a gesture)* Don't you come walking all over with your big feet!

ALFREDO Shall I walk on my hands?

LUCIA I've just this minute finished cleaning ... *(Points to the floor which is still damp)* and you walk all over the place with those big flat feet of yours!

ALFREDO Watch your tongue, girl, and not so much talk of flat feet. I'm worn out. *(Sits by the table)* Do you know the meaning of worn out? I've been keeping watch over Don Domenico all night. There he sat, the whole night through, on a bench by the seafront. It was freezing.

Whatever made me work for him in the first place!
Not that by and large I've any complaints: no. He's
always been very fair. May he live to be a hundred but let
it be a quiet, peaceful life. I'm not so young as I was.
I'm sixty. I can't spend the whole night out in the open.
Luci', bring me a cup of coffee, there's a good girl.

LUCIA *(while* ALFREDO *is talking replaces all the
chairs, without paying much attention to him)* There's
no coffee.

ALFREDO *(disappointed)* No coffee?

LUCIA No, apart from what's left over from yesterday.
I had a cup, Donna Rosalia didn't want hers and gave it
to Donna Filumena instead, and I've kept the last cup for
Don Domenico, in case he comes back.

ALFREDO *(unconvinced)* In case he comes back?

LUCIA Yes. Donna Rosalia, you see, hasn't made any
fresh coffee.

ALFREDO Couldn't you make some?

LUCIA I can't make coffee. No one ever taught me.

ALFREDO *(scornfully)* You can't even make coffee. Why
didn't Rosalia see to it?

LUCIA She went out early this morning. She said she
had to deliver three urgent letters for Donna Filumena.

ALFREDO *(pricks up his ears)* ... for Donna Filumena?
Three letters, did you say?

LUCIA Yes, three: one, two, three.

ALFREDO *(reverting to his exhausted condition)* I've
simply got to have some coffee. Shall I tell you what
we'll do, Luci'? Take half the coffee out of Don
Domenico's cup, let me have it, and top up his cup with
water.

LUCIA What if he finds out?

ALFREDO I doubt whether he'll come back, for the
moment at any rate. He looked as if he was going to
take up residence in the middle of the Via Caracciolo.

And whether he comes back or not, my need is greater than his as I'm the older man. What on earth made him spend the whole night in the open?

LUCIA   Very good. I'll heat it up and bring it to you. (*Starts walking towards the door on the left, but when she sees* ROSALIA *entering from the right, stops and warns* ALFREDO) It's Donna Rosalia ... (ALFREDO *looks at* LUCIA *silently*) What'll I do then? Bring you the coffee all the same?

ALFREDO   Why of course! Now Rosalia is back she can make a fresh lot for Don Domenico. (LUCIA *goes out.* ROSALIA *enters and spots* ALFREDO. *She behaves as if she hadn't seen him, filled as she is with the importance of the errand she has just run for* FILUMENA, *and makes for the latter's bedroom. Her subterfuge, however, does not escape* ALFREDO, *who addresses her sardonically as she reaches the bedroom door*) Have you lost your tongue, Rosali'?

ROSALIA   (*unconcerned*) I didn't see you.

ALFREDO   You didn't see me. So I'm the invisible man now. Where have you been?

ROSALIA   To mass.

ALFREDO   (*sceptically*) To mass? In that case you couldn't deliver Donna Filumena's letters.

ROSALIA   (*caught out, tries to control herself*) Why ask me then if you knew it all along?

ALFREDO   (*simulating indifference*) Well, just to pass the time of day. Where did you take the letters?

ROSALIA   (*implying he can't keep a secret*) You blab too much. You're a gossip, and what's more you spy on people.

ALFREDO   Gossip? Me? Spy? When have I ever spied on you?

ROSALIA   Who would ever want to spy on me? My life is an open book, I tell you. (*In a monotonous drone, as if repeating a piece she knows by heart*) I was born in 1870: I'll leave you to calculate my age. My parents were poor but respectable. My mother, Sofia Trombetta, was a washerwoman, and my father, Procopio Solimene, was a blacksmith by trade. Rosalia Solimene—that's me— and Vincenzo Bagliore, a casket-maker—and umbrella mender on the side—were duly joined in holy matrimony on the 2nd November 1887. Our union was blessed by three children, triplets as it happened. When the midwife went round to my husband's workshop to notify him of the happy event, she found him with his head in the sink ...

ALFREDO He was having a wash ...

ROSALIA (*repeats the latter part of her sentence with deliberate formality, as if to suggest his quip was in bad taste*) ... found him with his head in the sink, the poor man having been struck down moments earlier by a fatal stroke, which snatched him away in the prime of life from the bosom of his family. Both children were orphaned at a stroke, and I found myself ...

ALFREDO I thought you said three ...

ROSALIA (*undeterred*) ... in the unhappy position of having to bring up three children on my own. I got fixed up at number 80, Vico San Liborio and sold flyswats, remembrance candles for the dead and paper hats for festive occasions. I used to make the fly-swats myself, and the little I earned enabled me to bring up my children. It was in the Vico San Liborio that I first met Donna Filumena, who as a little girl used to play with my children. By the age of twenty-one, my sons still couldn't find work, so one went to Australia and two to America. I haven't heard from them since. I was left on my own with my fly-swats and candles and paper hats. When Donna Filumena set herself up with Don Domenico she took me in and I can truly say that without her I might have ended up a beggar on the steps of some church. Thank you very much and come again soon. The film is over.

ALFREDO (*smiling*) No trailer for the next show? Go on ... tell me where you took the three letters.

ROSALIA I cannot divulge the details of a confidential errand. Especially to a blabbermouth like you.

ALFREDO (*disappointed and with sudden venom*) What a nasty piece of work you are! Your malice even shows through your ugly mug. And by God you're ugly. You've got a face I wouldn't chop wood on!

ROSALIA So who's looking for a husband ...

ALFREDO (*as though the outburst had not taken place, resumes his habitually friendly tone*) I've got a button missing on this jacket ... will you sew it on for me?

ROSALIA (*starts walking towards the bedroom*) To-morrow, if I find the time.

ALFREDO And I've got a hole in my pants which needs patching up.

ROSALIA Go out and buy a woollen patch and I'll do it for you. (*Mockingly*) And now, if you'll excuse me ... (*Goes out*)

(LUCIA *enters upstage left carrying a cup half filled with coffee. The doorbell rings. She had been walking towards* ALFREDO, *but on hearing the doorbell doubles back to open the front door*)

DOMENICO (*enters after a pause. He looks pale and fatigued. He is followed by* LUCIA, *still carrying the coffee cup, which he now spots*) Is that coffee?

LUCIA (*looks helplessly at* ALFREDO *who has risen on* DOMENICO's *appearance*) Yes sir.

DOMENICO Give it here. (LUCIA *hands the cup to* DOMENICO, *who drains it greedily*) I needed that coffee.

ALFREDO (*disconsolately*) So did I.

DOMENICO (*to* LUCIA) Bring him some coffee then. (*Sits at the table, his face in his hands in gloomy meditation*)

(LUCIA *attempts to convey to* ALFREDO *by silent mimicry that the cup of coffee she is about to bring him is the one that has been watered down*)

ALFREDO (*impatiently*) Bring it all the same.

(LUCIA *goes out upstage left.*)

DOMENICO What was that all about?

ALFREDO (*with a forced smile*) She said the coffee's cold, and I told her to bring it anyway.

DOMENICO She can warm it up for you. (*Resumes his former train of thought*) Did you get hold of my solicitor?

ALFREDO Yes.

DOMENICO When is he coming?

ALFREDO The moment he is free. Within the day at any rate.

(LUCIA *enters upstage carrying the cup of coffee. She hands it to* ALFREDO *in some amusement, then goes out again giggling.* ALFREDO, *a resigned look in his eyes, prepares to face the ordeal of drinking it*)

DOMENICO (*voicing the end of a mental sentence*) ... yes, but what if it turns out a filthy mess?

ALFREDO (*resignedly, in the belief that* DOMENICO *is referring to the coffee*) I won't make an issue of it: I'll pop downstairs and have a quick cup at the corner cafe.

DOMENICO To hell with your coffee! What I am saying is that if the solicitor tells me I haven't a hope of winning, that there isn't a hope of an annulment, that I'm in the wrong ...

ALFREDO (*having tasted the coffee makes a grimace of*

disgust) Impossible! *(Puts down the cup on a piece of furniture upstage)*

DOMENICO   How can you tell?

ALFREDO   *(with the air of a connoisseur)* How can I tell? Why it's revolting!

DOMENICO   You've said it. The whole thing is revolting. *(Pause)* ... may well say: Not a hope. Can't make it! ...

ALFREDO   Don Dummi': she's never been able to make it!

DOMENICO   Have no fear. I'll resort to the law of the land! I shall appeal. I'll go right up to the Supreme Court!

ALFREDO   *(stunned)* Take it easy now. Is it worth it for the sake of a cup of coffee?

DOMENICO   Oh shut up about your coffee! I'm talking of my own affairs.

ALFREDO   *(looks puzzled, as the penny hasn't quite dropped)* Well ... *(Smiles as he realises the misunderstanding)* Oh, I see ... *(Laughs)* Well ... *(Fearing* DOMENICO*'s displeasure immediately assumes a serious mien in an attempt to identify with his master's predicament)* Ah, well ...—By God!

DOMENICO   *(who has not failed to notice* ALFREDO*'s changes of expression, gives up trying to discuss his problems with him)* Why do I bother to talk to you about these things ... what can I talk to you about? The past, I suppose. Certainly not the present. *(Looks at* ALFREDO *as though he had just met him. His voice is benevolent)* Look at you, see what's become of you, Alfredo Amoroso. You're full of wrinkles, your hair is white, your sight is failing, and you've gone gaga into the bargain!

ALFREDO   *(as if agreeing emphatically with everything* DOMENICO *has been saying, partly because he would never dare contradict his master)*—By God!

DOMENICO (*realising that he himself is older, and that time has wrought change in him as well*) The years go by, and that applies to all of us. (*Reminiscing*) Do you remember Don Mimi' Soriano?

ALFREDO (*was thinking of something else, but feigns immediate interest*) No. I can't say I do. Is he dead?

DOMENICO (*bitterly*) Yes, he's dead all right. Don Mimi' Soriano is dead.

ALFREDO (*realises his blunder*) Oh, I see ... that's what you were talking about ... (*Gravely*)—By God!

DOMENICO (*sees himself again as a young man in his mind's eye*) There I was: small black moustache, straight as a rod. I used to turn night into day! Never slept a wink.

ALFREDO (*yawning*) You're telling me!

DOMENICO Do you remember that gorgeous girl up in the hills? What a splendid creature! And what about the vet's wife, eh, what about her?

ALFREDO Yes, it's all coming back to me. Now, the vet's wife had a sister-in-law ... I was after her ... But somehow I couldn't get in there.

DOMENICO It was even better in town. Riding in the park ...

ALFREDO You were the smartest horseman ...

DOMENICO That I certainly was. My favourite colours were grey or nut brown ... Silk hats, silver spurs ... To think that I owned the best horses. Remember 'Silver Eyes'?

ALFREDO 'Silver Eyes'! The grey mare! (*Nostalgically*) What a horse! She had a rump like a harvest moon. When one was face to face with her behind, why it was like looking at the gates of Paradise! I fell in love with that mare, and I was broken-hearted when you sold her.

DOMENICO (*giving rein to his memories*) Paris, London ... and racing. I was on top of the world. I felt

I could do everything and anything I chose to do. (*As if inspired*) No one ever told *me* what to do. I could move mountains, drain the seas ... I was the master of my fate! Look at me now: finished, broken, utterly indifferent. But it's up to me to prove to myself I'm still the man I used to be. (*With determination*) I've got to fight. Domenico Soriano will not concede defeat! (*Quietly, to* ALFREDO) What's been going on here while I was out?

ALFREDO   (*reticently*) Couldn't find out. They keep me in the dark ... you know as well as I do that Donna Filumena hates me. All I know, and I found out through Lucia, is that Rosalia delivered three urgent letters for Donna Filumena.

DOMENICO   (*as if his suspicions were being confirmed*) Who to?

(ALFREDO *is about to say something but stops when he sees* FILUMENA *enter left*)

FILUMENA   (*is wearing a housecoat and looks a trifle dishevelled. She acts as if the two men were not there. She is followed by* ROSALIA *who is carrying bedclothes. Calls out*) Luci'! (*To* ROSALIA) Give me the keys.

ROSALIA   (*hands over the keys*) Here you are.

FILUMENA   (*pockets them and waits impatiently for* LUCIA) Will she never come? Luci'!

LUCIA   (*enters, full of solicitude*) Here I am.

FILUMENA   (*cuts her short*) Take these sheets. (ROSALIA *hands over the sheets*) You know the sofa in the small room next to the study ... make up a bed there.

LUCIA   (*surprised*) Very good. (*Makes as if to leave*)

FILUMENA   Wait. I need your bedroom, too. (LUCIA *registers astonishment*) Here's some clean sheets and two blankets. You can sleep on a camp bed in the kitchen.

LUCIA (*crossly*) What about my things? Have I got to move them out too?

FILUMENA I tell you I need your room.

LUCIA (*raising her voice*) Where shall I put my things?

FILUMENA Use the cupboard in the passage.

LUCIA All right. (*Goes out left*)

FILUMENA (*as if noticing* DOMENICO *for the first time*) Look who's here ...

DOMENICO I live here. (*Coldly*) Will someone tell me what all these changes are in aid of?

FILUMENA Of course. Let there be no secrets between man and wife. I need another two bedrooms, that's all.

DOMENICO Whatever for?

FILUMENA For my boys. I originally wanted three rooms, but as one of them is married with four kids, he'll go on living at his place.

DOMENICO Oh, I see ... We've even got grandchildren ... (*Provocatively*) And what's the surname of this tribe you've been hiding?

FILUMENA (*confidently*) Mine, for the moment. And later, yours.

DOMENICO I don't think that's likely to happen without my consent.

FILUMENA Oh you'll give your consent all right. (*Goes out*)

ROSALIA (*to* DOMENICO, *with ostentatious servility*) If you'll excuse me. (*Follows* FILUMENA *into the bed-room*)

DOMENICO (*with sudden vehemence shouts after* FILUMENA) I'll throw them out! Do you hear? I won't have them in the house!

FILUMENA (*offstage, ironically*) Shut the door, Rosali'.

(*The door shuts in* DOMENICO's *face*)

LUCIA (*enters upstage*) Miss Diana has just called, with a gentleman.

DOMENICO (*interested*) Show them in.

LUCIA She doesn't seem to want to. I asked them in, but she said would you please see her on the landing. She's scared of Donna Filumena.

DOMENICO (*exasperated, to* LUCIA) So now I've saddled myself with a terrorist! Tell them not to worry and to come right in. Say I'm here.

(LUCIA *goes out*)

ALFREDO If Donna Filumena catches her, I wouldn't guarantee her safety.

DOMENICO (*raising his voice to ensure he is heard beyond the closed bedroom door*) Don't talk rot, Alfre'. I am the master in this house. She (*Alluding to* FILUMENA) doesn't count!

LUCIA (*enters upstage. To* DOMENICO) She won't come in. She says her nerves are playing her up.

DOMENICO But didn't you say she had someone with her?

LUCIA Yes sir. It's a solicitor friend of hers. (*After consideration*) He seems a bit scared too.

DOMENICO Come now. That's three men altogether.

ALFREDO You'd better count me out. The way I'm feeling this morning I'd be no use to you. (*His mind made up*) I'm not needed here. I need a wash and I'll just wander off into the kitchen to have one ... call me if you need me. (*Goes out upstage without waiting for an answer*)

LUCIA Well, sir. What do you want me to do?

DOMENICO Leave it to me. (LUCIA *goes out upstage left and* DOMENICO *goes out upstage right. The latter re-emerges immediately with* DIANA *and* NOCELLA) Don't even say it in jest. This is my house.

DIANA *(hesitates on the threshold, somewhat agitated, her back to* NOCELLA) I'm sorry, Domenico, but after yesterday's scene I don't feel like facing that woman again.

DOMENICO *(reassuringly)* Diana: please! Don't make me feel like a fool. Come in, don't be afraid!

DIANA I'm not afraid. Not in the least. But I'd prefer to avoid trouble.

DOMENICO I tell you I'm here.

DIANA You were here last night, too.

DOMENICO That was different. That was like a bolt out of the blue. I assure you there's nothing to be afraid of. Come in, Mr Nocella, make yourself at home.

DIANA *(steps forward cautiously)* Where is she?

DOMENICO Don't worry. Please sit down. *(Pulls out chairs. The three sit round the table;* NOCELLA *in the middle,* DOMENICO *to his right,* DIANA *to his left. She keeps an anxious eye on the bedroom door)* Well, then?

*(*NOCELLA *is a very ordinary man in his forties. He is soberly dressed and appears to have been dragged reluctantly into the Soriano case by* DIANA. *His attitude hints at a certain lack of interest in the whole matter)*

NOCELLA I'm a neighbour of Miss Diana's. We live in the same boarding house. That's where we met.

DIANA Mr Nocella, I'm sure, can vouch for me and tell you the sort of person I am.

NOCELLA *(unwilling to become involved)* Well, we only meet in the evening, over dinner. That is, when I happen to be in. I'm always out late with clients. I normally keep myself very much to myself.

DIANA *(controlling her anxiety with difficulty, takes yet another look at the bedroom door, whence she fears* FILUMENA *might spring from one moment to the next*) Forgive me, Domenico: I'd rather like to sit where you are sitting. Do you mind?

DOMENICO Not at all.

(They swap places)

DIANA It was over dinner last night that I told Mr Nocella about your problems.

NOCELLA That's right. We had a good laugh.

(DOMENICO looks at DIANA in reproof)

DIANA I beg your pardon: I didn't laugh at all.

(NOCELLA looks quizzically at DIANA)

DOMENICO If you must know, Diana was here to impersonate a nurse.

DIANA *(petulantly)* But I am a nurse! I've a diploma to prove it! Didn't I ever tell you, Domenico?

DOMENICO *(taken aback)* No ...

DIANA After all, why should I have bothered to tell you? As I was saying, I described your state of mind to Mr Nocella, your reluctance to be tied to a woman you have nothing in common with ...

(The doorbell rings)

DOMENICO *(worried)* Look, would you mind coming into my study? There's someone at the door ...

(LUCIA crosses the room upstage right to left)

DIANA *(rising)* Yes, perhaps it would be as well.

(NOCELLA also rises)

DOMENICO *(shows them into the study)* After you.

NOCELLA Thank you. *(Is the first into the study)*

DOMENICO *(to DIANA)* Any news?

DIANA *(conspiratorially)* Hm. I'll tell you later. Oh dear, you're a little pale. (DIANA *caresses* DOMENICO's *cheek and goes into the study, followed by* DOMENICO)

LUCIA (*escorting* UMBERTO *into the room*) Come in, please.

(UMBERTO *is a tall, well set up young man. He dresses quietly. He seems a studious, bookish man. The way he talks and his keen sense of observation tend to make others uneasy*)

UMBERTO (*enters*) Thank you.

LUCIA Sit down, won't you. I'm not sure how long Donna Filumena is going to be.

UMBERTO I'd like to. Thank you.

(UMBERTO *sits left near the terrace. Begins scribbling in a notebook he has taken out of his pocket.* LUCIA *is on her way to the door on the left but stops in her tracks on hearing the doorbell. She retraces her steps and goes out upstage right. A little later she comes back with* RICCARDO)

LUCIA Come in.

RICCARDO (*he seems charming and wears rather showy clothes. As he enters he is looking at his watch*) Let's hope we get a move on. I'd like to make a quick getaway. (LUCIA *has nearly reached the door on the left.* RICCARDO *has been looking at her appreciatively and tries to detain her*) Listen, love. How long have you been in this job?

LUCIA A year and a half.

RICCARDO You're a nice-looking little thing.

LUCIA (*flattered*) Why, thank you.

RICCARDO Come and look me up at my shop sometime.

LUCIA You've got a shop?

RICCARDO In the Via Chiaia. Number 74—just inside the main door of the building. I'll make you a nice shirt.

LUCIA   Oh yes? What am I going to look like in a man's shirt I'd like to know? Get away with you.

RICCARDO   But I cater for both men and women. That is, I clothe men, and undress pretty girls like you! (*As he completes the sentence he makes a grab at* LUCIA)

LUCIA   (*in a huff, tries to push him away*) Leave me alone, do you hear? (*Breaks free*) Are you mad? What do you take me for? I'll tell the mistress, I will. (*Refers to* UMBERTO *who has just been looking on impassively*) With him watching too!

(*The doorbell rings again*)

RICCARDO   (*sees* UMBERTO *and grins*) Well I never ... I didn't see him. I thought we were alone.

LUCIA   (*resentfully*) You should leave respectable girls alone!

RICCARDO   (*invitingly*) Well, will you look me up at the shop? Go on ...

LUCIA   (*won over by* RICCARDO) 74 ...?

RICCARDO   (*implying 'I'll expect you'*) ... Via Chiaia.

LUCIA   Oh ... all right. (*Goes out upstage right to open the door and smiles her agreement to* RICCARDO)

RICCARDO   (*walks up and down the room, notices that* UMBERTO *is looking at him, and feels the need to justify his recent behaviour with* LUCIA) Not bad, eh?

UMBERTO   It's a matter of the utmost indifference to me.

RICCARDO   (*resentfully*) What are you, some sort of monk?

(UMBERTO *does not answer and continues to make notes*)

LUCIA   (*comes in with* MICHELE) This way, Miche'.

(MICHELE, *in plumber's blue overalls and carrying his toolbox enters. He is a healthy, stoutish young fellow.*

He is uncomplicated and jovial)

MICHELE *(takes his cap off)* What's gone wrong this time, Luci'? Don't tell me the bath-tub is leaking again. I soldered it only the other day.

LUCIA Nothing wrong with the bath.

MICHELE What else has sprung a leak then?

LUCIA No leaks anywhere. Just a minute, I'll call Donna Filumena. *(Goes out left)*

MICHELE *(to RICCARDO)* Your servant, sir. (RIC-CARDO *acknowledges the greeting with a slight nod)* I've left my shop unattended ... *(Pulls a half-smoked cigarette out of his pocket)* Got a light?

RICCARDO *(haughtily)* No, I haven't.

MICHELE I'll forget about the smoke then. *(Pause)* Are you a relation?

RICCARDO What's this, an official interrogation?

MICHELE Would you mind explaining that?

RICCARDO What I mean is you're a bit of a chatterbox, and I'm not.

MICHELE You could be a little more polite. Who the hell do you think you are?

UMBERTO *(butting in)* He's a practising rapist.

RICCARDO Say that again?

UMBERTO You walked in here, and without so much as by your leave, in somebody else's house you started molesting the maid. Then you started bothering me. Now this poor devil comes in and you start pushing him around too.

MICHELE *(crossly, to UMBERTO)* According to you I'm easy to push around, is that what you mean? *(To RICCARDO)* Charming class of person one gets to meet around here!

RICCARDO You're really beginning to annoy me. I feel like teaching you a lesson.

MICHELE *(angrily, drops his toolbox and walks slowly towards* RICCARDO) Go ahead! Teach me a lesson then!

RICCARDO *(starts towards* MICHELE) Do you think I'm afraid of you?

(UMBERTO goes up to them in order to prevent what looks like an imminent fight)

MICHELE You bloody ... *(With a rapid gesture is about to land a punch on* RICCARDO, *but the latter parries, aided by* UMBERTO's *efforts in his attempt to part them. To* UMBERTO) You mind your own bloody business!

(There is a fight between MICHELE *and* RICCARDO, *in which* UMBERTO *is involved. Kicks and punches and slaps fly, but somehow never seem to reach their target. The three shout insults at each other)*

FILUMENA *(enters from the left and puts an end to the mêlée in a no-nonsense tone of voice)* Stop it! *(*ROSALIA *has followed her into the room and is standing right behind* FILUMENA) Where do you think you are?

UMBERTO *(touching his aching nose)* I was trying to part them ...

RICCARDO So was I.

MICHELE Me too.

FILUMENA Who was doing the actual fighting then?

THE THREE *(in unison)* Not me ...

FILUMENA You ought to be ashamed of yourselves. Just like hooligans. One against the other. *(Pause)* Well, boys ... *(Doesn't quite know how to begin)* How is business?

MICHELE Not too bad, thank God.

FILUMENA *(to* MICHELE) Are the kids well?

MICHELE They're all right now, but last week one of

them ran a temperature. He'd eaten four pounds of grapes behind his mother's back. His poor little tummy went as tight as a drum. With four kids, one or the other's always up to something. Luckily they all enjoy castor oil. Would you believe it, if one is given a dose of castor oil the others demand their dose too, and there's no end of howls and screams till they get their share of the stuff. Then they all sit down happily on their potties alongside each other, in perfect formation. That's kids for you.

UMBERTO Madam, when I received your note I'm afraid your name meant little to me. However from the address at the top of the letter I recalled seeing you nearly every evening in the street when I'm on my way to the newspaper offices, and that I once had the pleasure of helping you home when one of your feet was hurting. I've therefore reconstructed ...

FILUMENA Yes, I was limping badly that day.

RICCARDO (*to the point*) I don't want to rush you, but could you tell us why we're here?

FILUMENA (*to* RICCARDO) Is the shop doing well?

RICCARDO Tolerably. Fortunately not all my customers are like you. With customers like you, who needs enemies? If they were all like you I'd go bankrupt inside a month. Whenever you come, it's as if someone hit me with a blunt instrument. You make me take down from the shelves my entire stock of material: This pattern isn't quite what I want, this is nice but I'll have to give it some thought ... By the time you leave it's as if a tornado had hit my shop. And when at last you leave I feel like engaging extra staff to tidy up.

FILUMENA (*maternally*) I'll try not to cause you any more trouble.

RICCARDO It's not that. The customer is always right. It's just that every time you come I shake in my boots.

FILUMENA (*with some amusement*) Now listen: I sent for you because I've something quite important to tell you. If you'll kindly step this way (*Points to the first door on the left*) we'll be able to talk quietly.

DOMENICO (*enters from the study, followed by* NOCELLA. *He appears to have got his nerve back, and sounds sure of himself. To* FILUMENA, *with good-natured decisiveness*) Leave well alone, Filume', there's no need for you to make matters worse for yourself. (*To* NOCELLA) I knew it all long before you appeared on the scene. It was as clear as daylight. (*FILUMENA looks at him doubtfully*) Let me introduce you to Mr Nocella, who is a solicitor and can give you chapter and verse. (*To* UMBERTO, RICCARDO *and* MICHELE) I'm afraid Donna Filumena has made a mistake and troubled you unnecessarily. Please forgive us and ... don't let us detain you.

FILUMENA (*as the three are about to leave*) Wait a moment. I've made no mistake. I sent for them. (*To* DOMENICO) It's got nothing to do with you.

DOMENICO (*firmly*) Do you want to wash our dirty linen in public?

FILUMENA (*aware that something unexpected has taken place and that matters have taken a turn for the worse as far as she is concerned.* DOMENICO's *calm and determined manner confirms her in this view. To* RICCARDO, UMBERTO *and* MICHELE) Would you mind stepping out on the terrace for a few minutes?

(UMBERTO *and* MICHELE *make for the terrace in some confusion*)

RICCARDO (*consulting his watch*) I'm sorry but there's such a thing as taking advantage of other people's patience. I've a lot of things to attend to.

FILUMENA (*imperiously*) You do as you're told and

wait out there! That's where the others are going to wait
and that's where you'll wait.

RICCARDO (*disconcerted by* FILUMENA'*s peremptory
tone*) All right then. (*Joins the others reluctantly*)

FILUMENA (*to* ROSALIA) Give them a cup of coffee.

ROSALIA Immediately. (*To* UMBERTO, RICCARDO
and MICHELE) Go out there then. On the far side, it's
nicer. (*Points the way*) I'll bring you a nice cup of coffee
in a moment. (*Goes out upstage left as the three go out
on the terrace*)

FILUMENA (*to* DOMENICO) Well?

DOMENICO There's a solicitor right here. Have a word
with him.

FILUMENA I've no time for lawyers. But let's hear what
you've got to say.

NOCELLA Perhaps I'd better say, madam, that I'm not
really concerned in all this.

FILUMENA You're not? What are you doing here then?

NOCELLA That is, I'm not involved in the sense that
this gentleman is not my client, and indeed never applied
for my services.

FILUMENA But you came all the same.

NOCELLA No. That is, yes ...

FILUMENA (*ironically*) Did someone else get you to
come?

NOCELLA In a sense ... though I never act on instructions by third parties.

DOMENICO (*to* FILUMENA) Will you let him say his
piece?

NOCELLA As a matter of fact it was the young lady who
brought the matter to my attention. (*Turns round and is
surprised not to see her standing there. He casts a glance
in the direction of the study*) Where is she?

DOMENICO (*impatiently*) Never mind who brought it
to your attention. Get to the point please.

FILUMENA (*with savage sarcasm*) She's in there, isn't she? Hasn't the guts to come out here! (*To* NOCELLA) Go on then.

NOCELLA Well, the case as put to me by him ... I mean by her ... anyway, there's Article 101, which I've jotted down here (*Pulls out a piece of paper and shows it round*) ... now Article 101 is quite clear. Under the heading 'Marriage when one of the contracting parties is in mortal danger, either pending or real.' 'Should one of the contracting parties be about to ...' etcetera etcetera. Then it sets out the clauses. It seems to me that in this particular case there's been no mortal danger whatsoever, neither pending nor real, as according to the gentleman here present the whole thing was a sham.

DOMENICO (*quickly*) I have witnesses: Alfredo, Lucia, the porter, Rosalia ...

FILUMENA The nurse ...

DOMENICO The nurse as well! All of them! The minute the priest left, she jumped out of bed like a jack-in-the-box: Dummi', we're man and wife!

NOCELLA (*to* FILUMENA) In this case Article 122 is clearly in his favour. (*Reads*) 'The validity of the marriage may be challenged by those of the contracting parties whose consent has been obtained under duress or by deliberate deception.' The deception is obvious, therefore according to Article 122 the validity of the marriage is duly challengeable in law.

FILUMENA I didn't understand a thing.

DOMENICO (*though all at sea himself, tries to give* FILUMENA *what he thinks is the correct interpretation of the letter of the law, partly to put an end to any further arguments on her part*) It means I was going to marry you provided you died.

NOCELLA I beg your pardon: that's not quite correct. A marriage cannot be subjected to terms or conditions.

According to Article ... I can't quite remember which article just now ... however, it unequivocally states 'If the parties concerned attach terms and conditions to the contract, the registrar in charge, or the officiating priest as the case may be, cannot proceed with the ceremony.'

DOMENICO But you said just now there was no question of mortal danger ...

FILUMENA (*brusquely*) Shut up. It's all Greek to you as well. (*To* NOCELLA) Put it all in plain language for us.

NOCELLA (*hands the sheet of paper to* FILUMENA) Here is the document. Read it yourself.

FILUMENA (*tears up the paper without even looking at it*) I can't read and I don't accept papers from strangers!

NOCELLA (*offended*) Let me put it this way. As you were not about to die, it's just as if the marriage had not taken place. It was invalid.

FILUMENA What about the priest?

NOCELLA He could only confirm what I've told you. Moreover he'd tell you you'd committed sacrilege. Utterly invalid.

FILUMENA Invalid ... but if I'd died ...

NOCELLA Ah, then ...

FILUMENA So if I'd died ...

NOCELLA In that case it would have been perfectly in order.

FILUMENA (*pointing to* DOMENICO, *who has been looking on with a wooden expression*) In that case he could have married again immediately after my death, he could have had children ...

NOCELLA That is correct. He could have married, as a widower of course. This other person would have been marrying the widower of the late Mrs Filumena Soriano.

DOMENICO (*pointing to* FILUMENA) She'd have been

Mrs Soriano? ... ah, but mercifully only if she'd died.

FILUMENA *(with bitter irony)* That would have suited you down to the ground. Is that justice, I ask you? You spend your whole life trying to get a family together and the law won't allow it.

NOCELLA The law cannot uphold a principle, however distressing the circumstances, by becoming an accomplice to a trick perpetrated at the expense of others. Domenico Soriano had and has no intention of marrying you.

DOMENICO And you'd better believe that! Should you entertain any doubts on that score I'd advise you to appoint a lawyer of your choice. He'll tell you the same thing.

FILUMENA No need for that. I believe you. Not just because you're saying it, or the solicitor is saying it. I can tell by the look on your face. I know you, and you're quite yourself again. If you'd been lying you'd have done it without looking me in the eye. You've never been able to lie. It's true enough all right ...

DOMENICO Mr Nocella, please proceed.

NOCELLA Thank you.

FILUMENA *(after a moment's reflection answers the last part of the sentence* NOCELLA *addressed to her)* Nor I him! *(To* DOMENICO*)* I don't want to marry you either, do you hear! *(To* NOCELLA*)* Do 'proceed' if you must. I don't want him. It's not true I was on the point of death, I admit it. It was all a trick. I just wanted his name. *(Calls out to the terrace)* You out there, step inside!

DOMENICO *(accommodatingly)* Please don't ...

FILUMENA Be quiet! (RICCARDO, UMBERTO *and* MICHELE *come in from the terrace.* ROSALIA *enters upstage right at the same time carrying a tray with three cups of coffee, but sensing the awkwardness of the situation puts down the tray and settles down to listen.*

Addresses RICCARDO, UMBERTO *and* MICHELE)
These gentlemen are men of the world. The world with
all its laws and rights, the sort of world that fends off
trouble and inconvenience with scraps of paper. (*Points
to herself*) Here on the other hand am I: Filumena
Marturano, the freak that can't even cry. Dummi': isn't
this what people have been saying about me?—'Have
you ever seen a tear in her eyes?' Well, I'm running true
to form, and without so much as a sob—you can see my
eyes are as dry as dust—(*Stares at the three young men*)
I am your mother!

DOMENICO Filume' ...

FILUMENA (*firmly*) Who are you to stop me saying, in
front of my sons, that I am their mother? (*To* NOCELLA)
Is there a law to prevent it? (*Aggressively*) Yes, you are
my sons. And I am Filumena Marturano—need I say
more? You are grown men and I suppose you've heard
people talk about me. (*The three stand as if petrified.*
UMBERTO *has gone pale.* RICCARDO *looks at his shoes
in embarrassment,* MICHELE *looks astonished and
moved*) I became what I became when I was seventeen.
(*Pause*) Mr Nocella, do you know about slums? The
ones at San Giovanni, at Vergini, at Forcella, Tribunale
or Pallunnetto? Black, smoky hovels ... there's so many
people to a room that in summer it's so hot you can't
stand it, and so cold in winter that your teeth chatter.
That's where I come from, from one such slum in the
Vico San Liborio. As for my family there were so many of
us I lost count. I don't know what's happened to them
and frankly I'm not interested. All I can recall are sad,
hungry faces, always at odds with each other. You would
go to sleep at night and nobody ever said goodnight.
We'd wake up the following day and no one ever said
good morning. The only 'kind' word that was ever said
to me came from my father ... and I still shudder at

the memory of it. I was thirteen at the time. He said:
You're getting to be a big girl, and there isn't much to
eat in this house, you know ... And the heat. At night,
with the door shut, you couldn't breathe. We'd sit around
the table ... there was just one big dish and heaven
knows how many forks. I may have imagined it, but I
felt that every time I dipped my fork into the dish they
were looking at me disapprovingly, as though I were
stealing that food. When I was seventeen I began to
notice how well dressed some people were. Young women
with pretty shoes walking past ... I just stared. One
evening I came across a girl I knew: she was so well
turned out I hardly recognised her. In those days I
attached more importance than I do now to that sort
of thing. She said to me: (*Articulates the words with
care*) You just do this ... this ... and this ... I couldn't
sleep all night. God, and that heat. (*To* DOMENICO)
That's when we met. (DOMENICO *gives a start*) In that
'house' which to my eyes was like a palace at first. My
heart beat so fast the evening I went back to the Vico
San Liborio! I thought: They'll throw me out, shut the
door in my face! But nobody said a word. On the contrary: one gave me a chair, another stroked my cheek ...
they all stared at me as though I was in some way superior
to them. They were ill at ease in my presence. It was
only my mother ... when I went up to her to say
goodbye, who looked away from me, sobbing. I never
went back there again. (*Loud*) I haven't killed my sons!
I've looked after *my* family for twenty-five years! (*To*
RICCARDO, UMBERTO *and* MICHELE) I've brought
you up, made men out of you. I stole from him so you'd
be well looked after!

MICHELE (*goes up to her affectionately*) All right, but
calm yourself now. You couldn't have done more.

UMBERTO (*goes up to her*) There's so much I'd like to

say to you, but I'm not much of a talker ... I'll write you a letter.

FILUMENA   I can't read.

UMBERTO   In that case I'll read it to you myself.

(Pause. FILUMENA *looks at* RICCARDO, *expecting him to say something. He goes out upstage without a word)*

FILUMENA   He's gone ...

UMBERTO   *(sympathetically)* It's just his way. He hasn't quite understood. I'll drop in at his shop tomorrow and have a talk with him.

MICHELE   *(to* FILUMENA*)* You can come and stay with me. Our place is small but we'll fit you in. There's even a small balcony. *(With happy anticipation)* To think that the kids kept asking: Grandma ... haven't we got a grandma? Where is she?—and I had to put them off with silly excuses. The first thing I'll shout when we get home is going to be: Here's grandma then!—why, they'll be all over you! *(Enticingly)* Come on, let's go ...

FILUMENA   *(has made up her mind)* All right. I'll come with you.

MICHELE   Let's go then.

FILUMENA   Give me a moment. Wait for me downstairs. *(To* UMBERTO*)* Why don't you go out together? I'll only be five minutes. I've got something to say to Don Domenico.

MICHELE   *(joyfully)* Right you are then. But hurry up, mind you. *(To* UMBERTO*)* Shall we go?

UMBERTO   Very well.

MICHELE   Goodbye, everybody. *(He begins to walk out upstage)* I knew something was going to happen ... that's why I was so talkative ... something inside me ... *(Goes out with* UMBERTO*)*

FILUMENA   *(to* NOCELLA*)* Would you mind leaving

us alone for a couple of minutes? (*Points to the study*)

NOCELLA Not at all. I must be going anyway.

FILUMENA Please don't. I'd sooner you stayed. In fact I'd like you to be here after I've had my talk with Don Domenico. (NOCELLA *goes into the study with some reluctance.* ROSALIA, *of her own accord, goes out upstage left.* FILUMENA *puts her keys on the table*) I'm going, Dummi'. Tell the lawyer to take his legal steps. I deny nothing and I'll give you your freedom.

DOMENICO You've no choice! Why didn't you settle for a sum of money in the first place, instead of going through all this ...

FILUMENA (*undeterred*) Tomorrow I'll send for my things.

DOMENICO (*perturbed*) You're quite mad. Why upset those poor lads' peace of mind? Why tell them at all?

FILUMENA (*coldly*) Because one of them is your son.

DOMENICO (*stunned by what* FILUMENA *has just said, struggles to overcome his inner agitation*) I don't believe a word of it!

FILUMENA One of them is your son.

DOMENICO (*quietly*) It's not true ...

FILUMENA I could so easily have said they were all yours. And I could have made you believe it.

DOMENICO It isn't true.

FILUMENA It is true, Dummi', it is true. You can't remember. You used to go away so often, to London, Paris, women, horses ... One night, one of many, you were just about to go off on one of those jaunts. Do you remember that before going away you always used to give me a one hundred lire note? Well, that night you said to me: Filume' let's pretend we really love each other!—and you switched off the light. That night I really loved you. But you didn't. And when you switched on the light again, you gave me the usual hundred lire note. On one corner of that note I wrote down the day and the date: I can't write in the ordinary way, but I can jot down figures. Then off you went, and I waited patiently for you to return: You don't remember when that was. I kept it all from you. I told you there'd been no changes in my life. As a matter of fact when I realised you hadn't understood, there was little point in changing my ways.

DOMENICO (*roughly, in an attempt to mask his growing anxiety*) Which one is it?

FILUMENA (*firmly*) Oh, no! That you'll never know.

DOMENICO (*after a moment's hesitation, as if obeying an impulse*) It's not true. It cannot be true. You'd have told me at the time, to tie me down. A child would have been your only weapon, and one which you, Filume', wouldn't have hesitated to use.

FILUMENA If I'd told you you'd have made me get rid of it. I couldn't possibly have told you: especially the way you used to think in those days. And even now. You haven't changed a bit in that respect. Oh yes, you'd have made me get rid of it. You have me to thank if your son is alive today.

DOMENICO Which one is it?

FILUMENA I'm not going to tell you. They've all got to be treated the same.

DOMENICO (*viciously*) Let them be all the same, then! They're yours anyway. I'll have nothing to do with them! I don't know them ... or him! Get out of my sight!

FILUMENA Yesterday, I said to you: Don't make a vow you may not be able to keep. Remember? When I said you might come begging to me on your knees ... Look here, Dummi': mind you keep what I've just told you about the children to yourself. If ever you tell them, so help me I'll kill you. That's not just the sort of empty threat I've been hearing from you all these years. When

I say I'll kill you that's exactly what I'll do. Is that understood? (*Calls out*) Mr Nocella! Come back in ... (*Calling* DIANA) You come too, I won't harm you. You've won, and I'm going. (*Calls out again*) Rosali', come here a minute. (ROSALIA *enters and* FILUMENA *embraces her*) I'm just going. Tomorrow I'll send for my things. (NOCELLA *emerges from the study, followed by* DIANA. ALFREDO *enters quietly upstage*) All the best, and goodbye everybody! Mr Nocella, I'm sorry you've been dragged into all this. (LUCIA *also enters*) I hope I've made myself clear, Dummi', (*With forced joviality*) I'm telling you in front of all these people: don't you dare breathe a word of what I've told you. Not to a soul. Keep it to yourself. (*Opens a locket she is wearing round her neck and takes out a soiled hundred lire note, folded over many times. She opens it out, tears off a small piece at the corner and turns to* DOMENICO) I'm keeping the bit where I've written down an old account of mine. The rest is yours. (*Places the money on the table and with mock cheerfulness tempered with contempt adds*) There are things money can't buy! (*Goes out*)

THE CURTAIN FALLS

ACT THREE

(The same room. Ten months later. Late afternoon.

Flowers everywhere, including elegant bouquets and sprays with the sender's card pinned to each. The flowers are of a delicate colouring, not red or white. An air of festivity hangs about the room. The curtain which divides the room from the study is drawn across the entrance to the latter. ROSALIA, *in her best clothes, enters upstage right. At the same time* DOMENICO *comes in from the study. He is a changed man. Gone is his brusque, bullying manner. He now seems milder, almost a paragon of humility. His hair has turned a shade whiter)*

DOMENICO *(to* ROSALIA) Have you been out?

ROSALIA Yes. On an errand for Donna Filumena.

DOMENICO What kind of errand?

ROSALIA *(teasingly)* Don't tell me you're jealous ... I went over to the Vico San Liborio.

DOMENICO Whatever for?

ROSALIA *(giggles)* Well I never ... you are jealous!

DOMENICO Jealous my foot!

ROSALIA I was pulling your leg. *(With a glance at* FILUMENA's *bedroom door)* I'm going to tell you, but don't let on to Donna Filumena I've said anything. She doesn't want you to know.

DOMENICO Don't tell me then.

ROSALIA You may as well know, because it's to her
credit. Donna Filumena got me to take one thousand
lire and fifty candles to the shrine of Our Lady of the
Roses in the Vico San Liborio. She made me ask an old
woman who lives in the street and usually looks after
the shrine to light the candles at six o'clock on the dot.
Shall I tell you why? Because the wedding is at six. At
the very moment you get married here, the candles will
be lit in front of Our Lady of the Roses.

DOMENICO I see.

ROSALIA You're marrying a saint, that's who you're
marrying. She seems younger, too: she's looking so
pretty! I said to her, I said: Don Domenico won't ever
give you up! He's just had the marriage annulled on a
point of principle ... he'll go back to you ...

DOMENICO (a trifle bored by ROSALIA's chatter) Yes,
yes, Rosali'. Why don't you go and give Donna Filumena
a hand?

ROSALIA I'm on my way. (Makes no move however) But
for her, heaven knows what would have happened to me!
She took me in with her, the blessed woman. Here I am,
and here I'll stay till I die.

DOMENICO Suit yourself.

ROSALIA I've got everything ready: cap, a white gown
with lace trimmings, drawers, white stockings. All neatly
laid out in my wardrobe: Donna Filumena knows where
everything is. She'll have to dress me. Who else have I
got? If only my sons came back ... one lives in hope. I'm
going now. (Goes out left)

DOMENICO (now alone in the room, glances at the
flowers, reads some of the cards, and completes a mental
sentence out loud) ... so be it!

(The voices of UMBERTO, RICCARDO and MICHELE
are heard offstage)

MICHELE *(offstage)* All right, all right, but the wedding isn't till six anyway!

RICCARDO *(offstage)* That's all very well, but our appointment was at five!

UMBERTO *(offstage)* I was punctual at any rate.

(They enter talking)

MICHELE We said five, I know, but I was only three quarters of an hour late ...

RICCARDO That's nothing according to you.

MICHELE Look: one always allows half an hour, give or take a minute. It's the done thing. If you fix an appointment for five, it means half-past, or even a quarter to six ...

RICCARDO *(ironically)* ... or the following day, or the next month.

MICHELE What's more I have four destructive kids and I daren't keep a watch: they took my last one to pieces.

UMBERTO *(notices DOMENICO and greets him respectfully)* Good evening, Don Domenico.

RICCARDO *(respectfully too)* Good evening, Don Domenico.

MICHELE Good evening, Don Domenico.

(They line up in front of DOMENICO in silence)

DOMENICO Good evening. *(Long pause)* Why so quiet all of a sudden? You were chatting away earlier on.

UMBERTO *(in some confusion)* Yes, we were talking but ...

MICHELE ... the conversation came to an end ...

DOMENICO ... the moment you saw me. *(To MICHELE)* So you kept the others waiting.

MICHELE That's right sir.

DOMENICO *(to RICCARDO)* But you were there on time.

RICCARDO Yes sir.

DOMENICO (*to* UMBERTO) And you?

UMBERTO   I was there on the dot, sir.

DOMENICO (*soliloquising*) On the dot sir ... yes sir ...
(*Pause. To* RICCARDO, UMBERTO *and* MICHELE)
Sit down, won't you ... (*They sit*) There's plenty of time.
The priest isn't due till six. Meanwhile we're the only
ones here. Filumena didn't want to ask anyone, apart
from the two witnesses. What I'm driving at is this ...
I believe I've brought this up before ... the fact is I'm
not too happy about your calling me 'sir'.

UMBERTO   (*timidly*) Quite so.

RICCARDO   (*as above*) Quite so.

MICHELE   (*as above*) Quite so.

UMBERTO   You haven't told us, though, what you would
like us to call you.

DOMENICO If I haven't it's because I was hoping you'd
have worked it out by yourselves. Tonight I am going
to marry your mother, and as you know I've made an
appointment with my solicitor for the arrangements
concerning you. Tomorrow you'll bear my name,
Soriano ...

(*The three look at one another, at a loss for an answer.
Each hesitates in the hope another will speak first*)

UMBERTO   (*summoning up courage*) Well, I'll try to
answer for the three of us, as I think we all feel the
same way. Somehow we find we cannot in all honesty
call you what you, quite rightly and generously, would
like us to call you. One has to feel these things instinctively ...

DOMENICO (*anxiously*) And I take it that you don't
feel this instinctive ... let us call it ... need to call
one ... call me, for example, dad?

UMBERTO   It would be unfair to you if I said other than
... no. At least for the moment.

DOMENICO (*to* RICCARDO) What about you?

RICCARDO I'm sorry, but I feel the same way.

DOMENICO (*to* MICHELE) And you?

MICHELE I go along with them, Don Domenico.

DOMENICO It doesn't matter, perhaps you'll change your mind in time. (*Pause*) Let me tell you how glad I am you're all here. You're my kind of people. You all work hard, in your different fields, and I'm sure you do so with good will and perseverance. Good boys. (*To* UMBERTO) You work in an office, and I hear that you also write.

UMBERTO The odd short story ...

DOMENICO I suppose you'd like to become a great writer.

UMBERTO I'm not that ambitious.

DOMENICO Why not? You're young. I know that in order to succeed in that profession you need dedication. You've got to be born to it ...

UMBERTO I don't think I've got that kind of native gift. If only you knew how many times, in a moment of depression, I've said to myself: Umberto, you've made a mistake, you're barking up the wrong tree ... do something else.

DOMENICO (*interested*) What else would you have liked to do?

UMBERTO I don't know. Young people are full of so many aspirations ...

RICCARDO Come to that, so much is due to chance in life! How do you think I got my shop in the Via Chiaia? It all began when I started making love to a pretty shirtmaker.

DOMENICO (*on the scent*) Have you made love to lots of girls then?

RICCARDO A fair number, I daresay. (DOMENICO *rises, and examining* RICCARDO *closely, endeavouring to detect in him a gesture, phrase or mannerism he can*

link to his own youth) You know what? I can't seem to
find my type. I see a girl, I like her and think: She's
the one for me. A moment later: I'll marry her. Then I
spot another pretty face, I fancy her even more than the
previous one. I never seem to be able to settle to one:
there's always another just round the corner who's an
improvement on whoever came before!

DOMENICO *(to* UMBERTO*)* I take it you're not quite
so volatile, that where women are concerned you give the
matter some thought.

UMBERTO Well, up to a point. Nowadays girls hardly
give you a chance to give it much thought. Wherever
you turn you see nothing but pretty girls, all of them
ready and willing. It's difficult to choose. What is one
to do? I'll go on ringing the changes till I find the right
one.

*(*DOMENICO *is disappointed at finding the same tenden-
cies in both* UMBERTO *and* RICCARDO*)*

DOMENICO *(to* MICHELE*)* I suppose you're a woman-
iser too ...

MICHELE I got married young. I met my wife, and that
was that. She keeps me on a short rein: if you knew my
wife you'd agree there's little chance of messing around
on the side. So I toe the line. Not that I wouldn't fancy
a bit of the other occasionally, but frankly I'm too scared.

DOMENICO *(discouraged)* Yes, you like women all right.
(Pause. Then, on another tack) In my young days I was
keen on singing. There was a group of us, seven or eight
fellows. We'd have dinner out in the open, and end up
with a singsong. Guitars, mandolins ... Do any of you
sing?

UMBERTO I don't.

RICCARDO I don't either.

MICHELE *(brightly)* I do.

DOMENICO (*delighted*) You do?

MICHELE I couldn't carry on working without singing.
I'm always singing away in the shop.

DOMENICO (*hopefully*) Let's hear you sing.

MICHELE (*suddenly bashful*) Me? What do you want
to hear?

DOMENICO Anything you like.

MICHELE I'm not sure ... I'm shy ...

DOMENICO But you just said you spend the whole day
singing.

MICHELE That's different ... all right. Do you know
Core 'ngrato? That's a smashing song. (*Begins to sing,
hopelessly out of tune and in a reedy colourless voice*)
Core, Core 'ngrato—t'hai pigliato 'a vita mia—tutto e'
passato—io non ce pienzo cchiu' ...

RICCARDO (*breaks in*) I can sing like that. Do you call
that a voice?

MICHELE (*slightly offended*) What do you mean?

UMBERTO Even I can do better than that.

DOMENICO Anyone can do better than that. (*To*
RICCARDO) Let's hear you sing.

RICCARDO I hardly like to. I'm not as brazen as he is.
Still, here goes. Core, core 'ngrato—t'hai pigliato 'a
vita mia—(UMBERTO *joins in*) tutto e' passato—
(MICHELE *joins in too*) io non ce pienzo cchiu'.

(*The resulting discordant and inhuman noise is painful
to the ear*)

DOMENICO (*interrupting them*) That's enough, thank
you. (*They stop*) No need to go on. You're not quite
yourselves today ... (*Aside*) It's not possible ... three
Neapolitans who can't sing!

(FILUMENA *enters from the left in a magnificent new
dress. She wears her hair 'up' in the Neapolitan fashion,*

two strings of pearls and clip earrings. She looks younger.
She is arguing with TERESINA, *the dressmaker, who*
follows her in with ROSALIA *and* LUCIA)

FILUMENA   I tell you I know there's something wrong
with it. It doesn't quite fit.

(TERESINA *is one of those Neapolitan dressmakers*
who are completely impervious to their clients' tantrums
and insults. Her imperturbability is almost irritating)

TERESINA   You're imagining things, Donna Filumena.
It fits you perfectly. I've been making dresses for you
for donkey's years. I should know.

FILUMENA   You're impudent, that's what you are. If I
say it doesn't fit, it doesn't fit.

TERESINA   Tell me where it doesn't fit then.

MICHELE   Good evening, mum.

RICCARDO   Good evening, and congratulations!

UMBERTO   Good evening.

FILUMENA   (*pleasantly surprised*) You're here already!
Good evening. (*To* TERESINA, *with obstinacy*) I'll
tell you why it doesn't fit. Because whenever you get your
hands on a customer's length of material, you cut off a
piece to run up a dress for your little girl!

TERESINA   Really ... I never ...

FILUMENA   It's happened before. I saw your daughter
once in a dress you made up from one of my lengths of
material. You then made my dress with what was left
over!

TERESINA   Don't talk like that or you'll make me
angry. Naturally, if there's something left over ...
(FILUMENA *looks at her reproachfully*) But never at
the expense of the customer. That would be dishonest.

ROSALIA   (*admiringly*) Donna Filume': you're beautiful. You really look like a bride!

TERESINA How was I meant to make that dress?

FILUMENA (*angrily*) Without stealing my material, that's how!

TERESINA (*a little hurt*) You're not to call me a thief. And if you think there was any material left over, I've got news for you. (*Makes a gesture to indicate how little material has in fact been left over*)

DOMENICO (*up to this moment has been watching rather impatiently, his mind on something else*) Filume' I'd like a word with you.

FILUMENA (*limps towards* DOMENICO. *Her new shoes are pinching*) God, these shoes!

DOMENICO Are they hurting you? Take them off and put on another pair.

FILUMENA What do you want to talk to me about?

DOMENICO Teresi', I wonder if you'd mind leaving us alone.

TERESINA Not at all. I'm off. (*Folds a black cloth she has been carrying and puts it on her arm*) Congratulations and good luck! (*To* LUCIA, *as she goes out*) I ask you: what kind of dress did she want me to make her? (*Goes out followed by* LUCIA)

DOMENICO (*to* RICCARDO, UMBERTO *and* MICHELE) Go into the study and look after the witnesses. Give them a drink. You go with them, Rosali'.

ROSALIA (*nods*) Yes sir. (*To* RICCARDO, UMBERTO *and* MICHELE) Come. (*Goes into the study*)

MICHELE (*to his brothers*) Come on then.

RICCARDO (*poking fun at him*) With a voice like yours, you're in the wrong job. Proper little Caruso you are ...

(*The three go laughing into the study*)

DOMENICO (*looks admiringly at* FILUMENA) How

lovely you look, Filume'. You're like a young girl all
over again. And if I were calm and collected I'd even
say that you're still capable of turning a man's head.

FILUMENA (*evasively, bent on avoiding the subject
which* DOMENICO *wishes to pursue*) Everything seems
to be ready. I'm quite pleased.

DOMENICO I, on the other hand, am worried and
anxious.

FILUMENA (*misunderstands him intentionally*) There's
nothing to worry about. You may rely on Lucia. Alfredo
and Rosalia are getting on, it's true, but ...

DOMENICO You know what I'm talking about, Filume'.
Keep to the point. You know what's going through my
mind. (*Pause*) You could, if you wished, remove the
cause of my worry and anxiety.

FILUMENA Me?

DOMENICO You should be satisfied that I have done
what you wanted me to do. When the marriage was
annulled I called on you ... not just once, but many
times. You always got them to say you weren't in. It was
I who persisted and came to you and begged you:
Filume', let's get married!

FILUMENA Well, tonight we are getting married.

DOMENICO Are you glad we are? Just a little?

FILUMENA Of course I am.

DOMENICO Why then not make me happy too? Sit
down and listen to me. (FILUMENA *sits down*) If only
you knew how many times I've tried to talk to you these
last few months. I tried with all my strength to overcome
my reluctance, and I failed. You see, the whole matter is
so delicate that I hesitate to cause you the embarrassment
of answering certain questions. But we are getting
married, and that makes all the difference. In a little
while you and I will kneel down before God, not like
two young things who get married in the belief that

love is an urge that can be fulfilled and gratified in the simplest and most natural way. Filume': you and I have been through all that. I am over fifty-two years old, and you are forty-eight. We are old enough to know it's our duty to understand and face up to the step we're about to take, with all the responsibilities that go with it. Now you know why you're marrying me. I don't. I only know that I'm marrying you because you told me that one of those boys is my son.

FILUMENA   Is that the only reason?

DOMENICO   No. I'm marrying you because I love you, too; we've been together twenty-five years, and that's a lifetime, with all its memories and shared experiences. I know I'd be lost without you ... and also because I believe in it. There are things that one feels deeply. I know you well enough, and that's why I can talk to you this way. (*Gravely and sadly*) I can't sleep at night any more. It's been like this for ten months, since that evening ... do you remember? I can't sleep, I can't eat, I can find no peace! You don't know how much I'm suffering. It's like something that stops me from breathing. I do this (*As if to inhale a lungful of air*) and it stops here. (*Touches his throat*) You can't let me go on living like this! You are a kind, mature woman, you understand me and perhaps even care for me a little. You once said to me: Don't swear ... and I didn't swear. You were right, Filume': here I am, I've come begging on my knees. Just as you said it would happen: on my knees, kissing your hands, your feet ... tell me, tell me which one is my son, my own flesh and blood! You've got to tell me, out of fairness to yourself, so as not to make me feel you're blackmailing me ... I'll marry you all the same, I swear it!

FILUMENA   (*after a long pause, during which she has been looking at* DOMENICO) You really want to know?

Very well. I'll tell you. But the moment I say to you:
It's that one—do you know what you'll do? You'll make
him your favourite, take him with you everywhere,
make plans for him, and, naturally, you'll think of a
way of giving him more money than the other two.

DOMENICO   Well?

FILUMENA   All right. Give him all the help you want
then. He needs it: he's got four kids to support.

DOMENICO   The tinker?

FILUMENA   (*nods*) The plumber, as Rosalia calls him.

DOMENICO   (*aside, his enthusiasm gathering pace as he
plans ahead*) He's a good boy, handsome in his way, and
healthy enough. Granted, he married a bit early in
life ... He can't earn all that much with such a small
shop. He needs a helping hand. With a little capital he
could add a workshop and get some staff. He'd be his
own boss. The shop could be enlarged and stocked up
with modern appliances. (*With a sudden glance at
FILUMENA and a hint of suspicion*) Oh yes ... it would
be the tinker ... the plumber ... Of course, he's got a
wife and four kids, and needs more help than the others.

FILUMENA   (*feigning disappointment*) What is a mother
to do if not try to help the weakest? All right—you saw
through that. You're clever, I'll grant you. Very well
then: it's Riccardo, the businessman.

DOMENICO   The shirtmaker?

FILUMENA   No—it's Umberto, the writer.

DOMENICO   (*at the end of his tether*) Even now, at the
eleventh hour, you're trying to push me over the edge!

FILUMENA   (*touched by DOMENICO's evident distress,
endeavours in her simple way to give him an explanation
that will satisfy him*) Listen to me carefully, Dummi',
and there'll be no need to go over the same ground again.
(*With an upsurge of love she has long repressed*) I have
loved you all my life with all my heart! You were every-

thing in my eyes ... and I still love you, perhaps more and better than ever ... (*Aware for a moment of her naivety and his astonishment*) What have you done, Dummi'! You've brought all this suffering on yourself. You had everything a man could ever want: health, looks, money ... you even had me, and so as not to worry you I'd have kept quiet about the children, I wouldn't have said a word, even on my death bed ... and you ... you'd be a generous man who'd given a helping hand to three poor devils. (*Pause*) Don't ask me again because I'm not going to tell you. I can't tell you. You must be enough of a gentleman not to press me, because I love you so much I might come out with it in a weak moment, and that would ruin everything. Can't you see, the minute I said the plumber was the one, you were off ... you mentioned money ... capital sums ... a bigger shop. Fair enough, you feel it's the right thing to do, after all it's your money. Then you'd go even further and think: Why not tell him I'm his father?—Whose sons are the other two I'd like to know? What rights have they ... Worse still could happen. The very idea of money might set one against the other. They're men now. Why, it could drive them to murder. Don't think of yourself, don't think of me—think of them. Dummi': it's too late now for us to enjoy our children at their best. The best years are when they're babies, when they're small enough to cuddle, when they're sick and can't tell you where it hurts. Or when they run up to you with their tiny arms wide open and shout 'Daddy!' They're like the kids you see coming home from school with cold little hands and red noses asking you for a sweetie. But when they're older, when they're grown men it's a different matter. (*Pause*) You're still in time: I bear you no grudge. Let's leave things as they are and go our own separate ways!

(The sound of a harmonium rehearsing is heard offstage)

ROSALIA *(comes in from the study followed by*
MICHELE, RICCARDO *and* UMBERTO*)* He's here ...
the reverend priest is here!

MICHELE   Mum ...

DOMENICO   *(rises and looks at everyone present. Then,*
as though he has just made a decision) ... Let's leave
things as they are and go our own separate ways. *(To*
the boys) I've got something to say to you. *(They wait*
in some suspense) I am a gentleman and I've no intention
of deceiving you. Now listen ...

RICCARDO ⎫
MICHELE ⎬   Yes, dad ...
UMBERTO ⎭

DOMENICO   *(touched, and with a glance at* FILUMENA,
makes up his mind) Thank you. I am very grateful. *(In*
a businesslike manner) Now, when two people get
married it's usually the father who gives the bride away.
As no parents are with us tonight we'll have to make
do with the children. Two of you will give the bride
away, and one'll be best man.

MICHELE   We'll go with you, mother. *(Goes up to*
FILUMENA *and beckons* RICCARDO *to do the same)*

FILUMENA   *(suddenly remembers something)* What's
the time?

RICCARDO   Five to six.

FILUMENA   *(to* ROSALIA*)* Rosali' ...

ROSALIA   Have no fear. At six on the dot the candles
will be lit in the appointed place.

FILUMENA   *(leaning on* MICHELE'*s and* RICCARDO'*s*
arms) In we go.

(They go into the study)

DOMENICO (*to* UMBERTO) You come with me.

(*They form into a procession and step into the study.* ROSALIA *stays put, clapping her hands. Offstage, the organ strikes up the wedding march.* ROSALIA *weeps.* ALFREDO *joins her and they follow the others into the study.* LUCIA *goes in after them. The lights dim and gradually complete darkness ensues. Slowly through the terrace first a moonbeam, then the chandelier light up the room again. Some time has elapsed*)

FILUMENA (*followed by* UMBERTO, MICHELE *and* ROSALIA *enters from the study and walks towards the left of the stage*) Oh dear, I'm so tired!

MICHELE Rest now. We'll soon be going. I've got to be up early in the morning.

ROSALIA (*carrying a tray with empty glasses*) Congratulations and good wishes! What a perfect wedding! May you live to be a hundred. You've been like a daughter to me.

RICCARDO (*offstage from the study*) It all went off very well.

FILUMENA (*to* ROSALIA) Bring me a glass of water please.

ROSALIA Immediately, Mrs Soriano. (*Goes out upstage*)

DOMENICO (*comes in from the study with a bottle of 'special reserve' wine, the cork liberally smothered with sealing-wax*) No guests, no reception ... but surely we can drink a bottle among ourselves. (*Picks up a corkscrew from a table upstage*) This'll lull us to sleep.

ROSALIA (*comes back with a glass of water on a saucer*) Here is the water.

DOMENICO Water?

ROSALIA (*as if to say 'Donna Filumena sent for it'*) For the mistress.

DOMENICO Tell Donna Filumena that tonight of all nights water is not fit for drinking. And give Lucia a shout ... oh dear, I nearly forgot: send also for Alfredo Amoroso, the well known jockey, trotter and connoisseur of racing horses.

ROSALIA (*calls out upstage right*) Alfre', Alfre', come and have a glass of wine with the master. Luci', you come too.

ALFREDO (*comes in with* LUCIA) Sir!

DOMENICO (*has filled the glasses and hands them round*) Here you are, Filume'. Drink up. (*To the others*) Drink up.

ALFREDO (*drinks*) Happy days!

DOMENICO (*looks at his faithful retainer with affection*) Remember the time when our horses were running, Alfre'?

ALFREDO I do.—By God!

DOMENICO They've stopped running, you know. They stopped long ago. I refused to believe it; in my imagination I saw them running all the time, into eternity. But it's clear to me now that they came to a halt a long time ago. (*Points to the young men*) They're in the running now. They're the ones about to be put through their paces. They're young, they're thoroughbred colts! We couldn't compete with them, we'd be laughed off the course!

ALFREDO So we would.—By God!

DOMENICO Drink up, Alfre'. (*They drink*) Our children are our children ... and when you get three or four of them in a family, it often happens that the father singles one out as his favourite, sometimes for the strangest reasons: either because he's weaker, or uglier or more headstrong than the others. And the others don't take it amiss. They realise it's almost a father's right. In our case, our family got together a little late in the day.

Maybe it's for the best. It means that the love I might have had the right to lavish on one will be shared equally by all three. (*Drinks*) Good health! (FILUMENA *does not comment. She has taken, from her bosom, a bunch of orange blossom and smells it now and again.* DOMENICO *turns to* MICHELE, RICCARDO *and* UMBERTO) Boys: you're coming to dinner tomorrow.

THE THREE   Thank you.

RICCARDO   (*to* FILUMENA) We must be going now. (*Kisses her*) Good night.

UMBERTO   (*also kisses her*) Good night, mum.

MICHELE   (*kisses her*) Good night.

UMBERTO   (*to* DOMENICO) Good night, dad.

RICCARDO and MICHELE   } Good night, dad.

DOMENICO   (*gratefully*) Till tomorrow then.

(UMBERTO, RICCARDO *and* MICHELE *go out, followed by* ALFREDO, ROSALIA *and* LUCIA. DOMENICO *looks at them pensively as they leave. He goes up to the table and pours himself a drink.* FILUMENA *slumps into an armchair and takes off her shoes*)

FILUMENA   I'm so tired. I'm really finished. It's all caught up with me.

DOMENICO   (*tenderly*) You've had a hard day. Think of all the things you've had to cope with these past few days. Relax. Just sit there quietly. (*Takes his glass and walks towards the terrace*) What a beautiful night!

(FILUMENA *feels a lump in her throat and utters a soft moan. She stares vacantly into space as if waiting for something to happen. Her face moistens with tears*)

DOMENICO   (*concerned*) Filume', what's the matter?

FILUMENA   (*happily*) I'm crying, Dummi' ... God how wonderful it is to cry!

DOMENICO (*hugs her fondly*) There, there, it's all right.
You've been running ... running. Then you had a fright
and fell. But you got up, you picked yourself up again.
You've had a lot on your mind and now you're tired.
You've no more running to do. Stop worrying. Have a
good rest. (*Goes back to the table and helps himself to
more wine*) Our children are our children ... and they've
all got to be treated the same. You're right, Filume',
you're so right! (*Gulps down the wine as*

THE CURTAIN FALLS

Napoli Milionaria

adapted by Peter Tinniswood

NOTE ON ADAPTATION

When I was a small boy in Liverpool and got into mischief, my Uncle Fred would say: 'Hey, buggerlugs, if you don't start behaving yourself, we'll get Icky the Firebobby onto you'.

What a perfect threat. Instantly I would stop trying to eat my cousin's Meccano set and guilt would tingle in my armpits as I applied pubic hair to pictures of Titty in the books of Arthur Ransome.

Icky the Firebobby! No one ever told me who he was, but he's still a potent image to me. I see a stoop-shouldered figure with concave shins, long, lank hair, a greying, straggling beard and eyes like aniseed balls. Totally terrifying. In fact, he looks just like I do now.

I've done this adaptation of Eduardo's play in the accents of my native city. Not its dialect.

I'm not keen on dialect writing in English. It relies too much on a heavily-coated treacled ear and too little on love and sympathy and affection.

My idea of utter despair is to find myself on a half-day closing Thursday in a blunt-thumbed hotel in the Yorkshire Dales with grumpy trouser presses in all bedrooms and integral gloom in all public rooms. And it's raining and you can't go outside because of the sheep and the bar's closed owing to essential renovations to the potato crisps and all you have to read are backnumbers of glossy local 'society' magazines packed full of adverts for all-weather finger stalls and jars of home-made wart ointment. And you open it up and all the pages are blank except for one which contains a short story in Yorkshire dialect written by someone with a name like G. Dudley Slakehouse. And it starts thus:

> Owd Ridley were reet cossopped. Well, tha' knows, t'owd 'un 'ad nobbut and garracked 'is wilkins' threep ends wi' a dollop of thriddle fly juice and . . .

So that's why this play hasn't been done in dialect. I've tried to catch the rhythms and rhymes and the lilt and the swagger that reflect the verve and vigour of my native city.

I had thought of having a go at Cardiff, but on reflection we all thought that Liverpool of all British cities most resembled the uniqueness of Naples with its wicked, cruel effervescence, its dark, brooding melancholy, its exuberance and wittiness and, above all, its indomitable spirit.

There's no Icky the Firebobby in this play, but it's loaded with characters whom my old Uncle Fred would instantly recognise and feel free to use as a threat against me.

Peter Tinniswood

CHARACTERS

Gennaro Jovine
Amalia Jovine
Maria Rosaria
Amedeo
Donna Peppenella
Adelaide Schiano
Federico
Errico
Peppe
Riccardo
Sergeant Ciappa
Franco ('o miezo prevete)
Pascalino
Assunta
Teresa
Margherita
Wine Man
Doctor
Two Plain Clothes Policemen
Customer
Voices
A Man

Napoli Milionaria was first performed in this version on the Lyttelton stage of the National Theatre on 27 June 1991, with the following cast:

Gennaro Jovine	*Ian McKellen*
Amalia Jovine	*Clare Higgins*
Maria Rosaria	*Angela Clarke*
Amedeo	*Phil McKee*
Donna Peppenella	*Jennifer McEvoy*
Adelaide Schiano	*Antonia Pemberton*
Federico	*Peter Sullivan*
Errico	*Mark Strong*
Peppe 'the jack'	*Ian Burfield*
Riccardo Spasiano	*Richard Bremmer*
Brigadier Ciappa	*Peter Jeffrey*
Franco	*Derek Hutchinson*
Pascalino	*Alan Perrin*
Assunta	*Geraldine Fitzgerald*
Teresa	*Helene Kvale*
Margherita	*Christabelle Dilks*
Wine Man	*Sam Beazley*
Doctor	*Crispin Redman*
Policemen	*Bruce Purchase*
	Seymour Matthews
Donna Vincenza	*Judith Coke*
Rita (Rituccia)	*Danielle Dobrowolski*
	Laura Moretto
Neighbour	*Alison Johnston*
Baker	*Simon Kunz*

Directed by *Richard Eyre*
Designed by *Anthony Ward*
Lighting by *Mark Henderson*
Musical Director *Dominic Muldowney*

ACT ONE

(Late autumn of 1942. Early morning.

A large, dirty, smoke-blackened room.

Upstage is a door with glass panels and wooden shutters opening straight onto the street. Through it we can see on the wall opposite a shrine to the Madonna del Carmine with, hanging above it, a small votive oil lamp. To the right of the door a partition made out of odds and ends of wood goes across a corner to form a narrow rectangular cubicle. The other doors are on opposite sides of the room.

The one on the left leads to other parts of the house – the rooms of AMALIA; AMEDEO *and* RITUCCIA *for instance.*

The one on the right leads to a scullery where food is prepared and wine bottled. The door is plain except for the crudely-painted sign: 'door to the wine cellar'. This door also leads to the courtyard.

There is an enormous iron double bed with tarnished brass fittings, a chest of drawers, an ornate sideboard with pictures of saints on it, a plain wooden table and some straw-bottomed chairs.

The rest of the room is a clutter of crude nineteenth-century furniture, making the room seem cramped and difficult to move around in when crowded with people.

The table has on it coffee cups of all shapes, sizes and patterns and a large copper bowl with water in it.

As the curtain rises we hear shrill voices raised in argument outside some distance away. Standing by the table, washing coffee cups and placing them neatly on the table, is MARIA ROSARIA. *She is a girl of about nineteen, dressed very plainly and taking no notice whatsoever of the commotion outside, which little by little becomes louder and louder and in which the voice of her mother,* AMALIA, *predominates.*

AMEDEO *enters from door left, scratching and yawning, having obviously just woken up. He is a young man in his early twenties, slim, dark-skinned, pleasant of manner and not too robust. He wears a faded, woollen, well-darned vest and carries a scrap of damp towel)*

AMEDEO   God, I could murder a coffee.

MARIA   It's not ready yet.

AMEDEO   Why not?

MARIA   Because I'm waiting for the water to boil.

AMEDEO   Oh, great. Terrific. You know I sometimes feel that one day – one day quite soon – there's an outside chance that I'll wake up feeling like a genuine, one hundred per cent human being. Is mother around?

MARIA   She's out.

AMEDEO   What about father?

MARIA   He's still asleep.

(From the cubicle room we hear GENNARO's *sleepy voice)*

GENNARO   *(off)* Asleep? Me asleep? Who's asleep? God almighty, when does anyone ever get chance to sleep in this mad house?

(In the alleyway outside the quarrel becomes louder. AMALIA's *voice predominates)*

Listen to it. Will you listen to that din? Struth, it's like a bloody battlefield out there.

AMEDEO *(to* MARIA*)* What's it all about?

MARIA It's mother and Donna Vincenza at it again.

AMEDEO Oh God, say no more. Say no more.

MARIA They're only talking.

GENNARO *(off)* Talking? You call that talking? Ye Gods, they're ripping great hunks out of each other. They're gorging on each other's flesh. You can hear the blood flowing.

AMEDEO *(wearily)* Why do they always have to be having argie-bargies about something that happened weeks and weeks ago?

MARIA Simple. Because Donna Vincenza's a two-faced old bitch.

AMEDEO Aye, you're right there.

MARIA Course I am. Donna Vincenza! Greedy old crone. How many times does she come round here all sweetness and light, and mother makes her a nice cup of coffee and slips her little goodies for her daughter – a couple of eggs here, a drop of cream there, right? And then as soon as she finds out where we get our coffee from the old bitch is tear-arsing off to get some for herself. And then what happens? The punters all go round to her place for their coffee, don't they? Oh yes, it's a longer walk, but her coffee is half a lira cheaper than ours.

GENNARO *(off)* Bloody old ratbag.

MARIA And that's not all she's up to. The old bag's only going round now telling everyone we put chicory in our coffee.

GENNARO *(off)* Oi, hold on. Hold your horses, eh? Not so much of the 'our' if you don't mind. This coffee you and your mother make has got bugger all to do with me. It's out of my province, is that coffee of yours. If the cops come bursting in and catch you red-handed with it, then that's your business. Don't drag me into it.

MARIA   If it was left to you, we'd all be starving.

GENNARO   (*off*) Wrong, missy. Wrong. If it was left to me, we'd all be living like honest people.

MARIA   And what's so dishonest about selling coffee?

AMEDEO   Too bloody true. If we didn't do it, there'd be plenty of others bursting their boilers to jump on the bandwagon. You better believe it, mate. Look at Donna Vincenza.

GENNARO   (*off*) Listen to me, son. Let me tell you something.

AMEDEO   What?

GENNARO   (*off*) Last week – only last week – someone round here threw himself out of a third floor window.

AMEDEO   So what's that got to do with me?

GENNARO   (*off*) Plenty. You want to try doing it yourself some time.

AMEDEO   Ach, there's no point talking to you. You're pots for rags, you are. You don't understand nothing. Not a dicky bird. You're living on a different planet, you are.

(MARIA *motions for him to ignore* GENNARO. *He shrugs his shoulders*)

All right, all right. I suppose he might have a point.

GENNARO   (*off*) Oh, might he? Well, well, you're changing your tune, aren't you? I shouldn't bother. I know your sister's told you to pay no attention to me. And she's right. Well, I'm just a simple old fogey, aren't I? I don't understand nothing. Poor old sod, you've got to feel sorry for him, haven't you? Well, listen to me, my little chucky eggs. You're the ones I feel sorry for. You lot. Dear God above, what a crazy, mixed-up generation. (*Pause*) Tell me something. Just tell me this. You know that coffee you

sell to the punters for three lire a cup? Well, has it
occurred to you where the black marketeers get it from?
I'll tell you. They get it from the clinics and the hospitals
and the infirmaries and the children's wards and the . . .

AMEDEO   Give over, father. Give it a rest. Talk about
getting out of your depth. You're fifteen feet under, mate,
and your mouth's full of shit. You're talking a load of old
cobblers. What clinics? What infirmaries? They don't get
a sniff of coffee. So how can they sell it, if they haven't got
none? You've got to face facts, mate. Who was it came
round here the other day offering mother five kilos of
coffee at seventy lire a kilo? You know perfectly well who
it was. Some big, fat, bloated Fascist high-up. Course it
was. And the only reason mother didn't buy it was
because she didn't know who it was. For all she knew it
could have been a trap – a typical police fit-up. Course it
could. We're talking about facts here. We're talking
about the high-ups who should be setting a good example
to poor, ignorant, starving scum like us. Good example
my backside. All they are is a load of thieves and crooks.
So you look at them in their smart suits and their swanky
cars and you say to yourself – you know, mate, you've got
the right idea. You're on top of the world, aren't you?
You've got a wallet full of dosh and a great big, fat,
groaning belly. And what about me? I'm dying of starvation. So what's the answer? Simple. What's good
enough for you, is good enough for me. Right? Let's all
steal. Right? What's yours is mine. Everyone for himself.
Everyone steal. Right?

GENNARO   (off) Oh no. Oh no, you don't, my son. As
long as you live in this house you do not steal. Understand me? You never ever steal. You don't even think of
stealing. You don't even mention the word.

AMEDEO   All right, all right, keep your wool on. I was

only joking. God, can't we even crack a few measly jokes now? (*The quarrel in the street has all but finished now. He shrugs his shoulders*) Ah, bugger the coffee. I'll get myself some breakfast. (*From the sideboard he takes a large bowl covered with a plate, a large spoon and a chunk of stale bread.* MARIA *gives him an odd look*) What's the matter with you? What are you gawping at? It's only a bit of spaghetti I saved from yesterday.

MARIA   I didn't say a word.

(AMEDEO *crosses to the table and sits down. He tears off a chunk of bread and munches at it hungrily. He uncovers the bowl. It's empty*)

AMEDEO   For Christ's sake, it's empty. What's happened to my spaghetti?

MARIA   How should I know?

AMEDEO   (*furious*) I was saving this for my breakfast. I saved it special. (*Looks across to* GENNARO's *cubicle*) Someone's nicked my spaghetti. Father, have you been at my spaghetti?

GENNARO   (*off*) Oh, wasn't it mine then?

AMEDEO   No, it was not, you bastard. It was . . . You know, it's wonderful living in this house, isn't it? Feed off the fat of the land, we do here. Slap up meals morning, noon and night. Table groaning with grub. Take what you like. Dig in, lads. Plenty more where that came from. (*Savagely to* GENNARO) So where's your spaghetti then? I suppose you guzzled it all back yesterday, didn't you?

GENNARO   (*off*) How am I expected to remember? Yours. Mine. It's everyone for himself these days. You said so yourself.

AMEDEO   It beats me, this does. I'm stumped. How do you do it? Do you get up special in the middle of the night? Snuffle, snuffle like a little mouse, eh? Gobble up all the left-overs, eh? Eat other people's food so you can keep going till morning, eh? What next? I'll tell you. You'll be prowling round at night eating our socks and our kecks.

GENNARO *(off)* What a song and dance to make over a miserable bit of spaghetti.

AMEDEO It was not a miserable bit. It was a large bit. And it was mine.

GENNARO *(off)* Listen to him. Just listen to him. Anyone'd think it was the end of the world. Get up special in the middle of the night, he says. Well, I don't suppose old clever dick there happened to notice the air raid sirens last night, did he? Sirens – you know. *(Mimics them)* I suppose he slept through it all. Well, I didn't. Oh no. Two and a half hours in the shelter I was. And frozen to the bloody marrow when I got back. Frozen stiff. Perished. And I couldn't sleep, could I? And I felt hungry, too. Really really hungry. And then I remembered – there was a bit of spaghetti left over from supper. Fine. Dandy. How the hell was I to know it was yours? You know what you want to do? Next time you want to put your name on it. On the bowl there. Write it large, eh? 'Property of Amedeo – Bugger off.' What a fuss and palaver about nothing.

AMEDEO *(trying to be reasonable)* It is not a fuss about nothing, father. Because of you I have to go to work on an empty belly. *(Suddenly blazing)* Jesus Christ, I want my food left where I put it. Is that too much to ask? I don't go round tampering with other people's property in this house. I don't . . . I will. I swear it. I'll smash this whole bloody place to smithereens.

(GENNARO *lifts up the curtains of his cubicle and steps out in his shirtsleeves with his trousers hastily buttoned up and his braces hanging down. He is a man of about fifty. He's thin and spindly-shanked. He has an open, honest face lined with hardship)*

GENNARO Smash this place up, son? This palace? This wonderland? Come on, calm down. I tell you, I didn't realise that spaghetti was yours. Struth, to hear you carrying on anyone'd think it was the end of the world.

AMEDEO I am not carrying on, father. I am merely stating that because of your predations I am the one who is having to go hungry. I'm bloody well starving here.

GENNARO *(scornfully)* A few bits of spaghetti.

AMEDEO It was a whole flaming plateful. (GENNARO *absent-mindedly picks up the bread and starts to break a piece off.* AMEDEO *angrily snatches it back)* Give it here. It's my bread, is that.

GENNARO Have it. I hope it chokes you. God, what it is to be blessed with a loving son.

AMEDEO And a loving father. A loving father who stuffs himself with my spaghetti so it's pouring out of his ears. See this bread? This bread has got to last me till dinnertime. A miserable bit of stale, stinking bread, and he even begrudges me that. Jees, I'm getting out of here. I've had enough. Right up to here with it, I am. *(Exits to his room)*

GENNARO Ah, maybe he's right. I suppose he's got a belly to feed just like the rest of us. *(He goes back into his cubicle)*

DONNA PEPPENELLA *(offstage)* You did right, Donna Amalia. It's high time someone put that old cow in her place. She's been asking for it for years.

AMALIA *(offstage)* And this time she well and truly got it. Oh yes, Donna Peppene', did she get it. And all the trimmings, too.

(MARIA *goes to the scullery as* AMALIA *comes in from the street followed by* DONNA PEPPENELLA. AMALIA *is still an attractive woman in her late thirties. Her way of speaking, her tone of voice and her gestures are all decisive. She is obviously someone well used to taking charge. She is dressed in workaday clothes. The only concession to vanity is her silk stockings. She has restless eyes which don't miss a thing. She is hard, businesslike and unsentimental*)

AMALIA Two-faced old bitch. How many times has she been round here grovelling and fawning, wheedling and whingeing? (*Mimics her*) 'Oh, Donna Amalia, love, you don't happen to have a fresh egg, do you?' 'Oh dear, oh dear, Donna Amalia, I seem to be right out of spaghetti this morning.' In and out of here all day she is. In and out like a stoker's shovel. There's no end to it. A joint of boiled beef here. A hunk of salami there. And food's not cheap either, Donna Peppene'. And even when you can get your hands on it, half the time it's not fit to sling to the cat. Do you know what I gave her daughter the other week? I gave her a metre and a half of heavy wool. A metre and a half! I'm a bloody fool, me. I'm going right off me beanpole. Honest to God, without a word of a lie, I'm convinced I'm going simple. (*To* MARIA) Have you got that water boiling yet out there?

MARIA (*offstage*) It's just starting.

AMALIA Right, you'd best come and get the coffee then. Now then, Donna Peppene', I'm afraid I'm going to have to ask you to go.

DONNA PEPPENELLA Oh, that's quite all right, my dear. Don't mind me. Pay no attention. You just carry on with what you're doing.

(*Scowling,* AMALIA *goes to the bed, rather furtively lifts the mattress and takes out a packet tied with string*)

AMALIA   I believe this is what you were asking for, isn't it? Flour. Half a kilo.

DONNA PEPPENELLA   Half a kilo! Crikey bobs, Donna Amalia, that's fantastic, love. Thank you very much, I must say. I wasn't expecting that.

AMALIA   Forty lire.

DONNA PEPPENELLA   What?

AMALIA   Forty lire.

DONNA PEPPENELLA   Forty lire? Are you telling me it's gone up ten lire since last week?

AMALIA   Take it or leave it. It's no skin off my nose. I can easy tell my supplier not to bother next time. I'm only doing it as a favour, you know. I don't make nothing out of it for myself. Good God, no. All it is for me is one long pain in the butt. Someone's only got to go to the police, telling a whole pack of fibs and lies, and it's . . . it's . . . No, Donna Peppenella, I am definitely not in this for the money. No way.

(GENNARO's *head appears above the top of his cubicle*)

GENNARO   I don't know why you had to get mixed up with it in the first place. If they want flour, let them go and find their own. (*To* DONNA PEPPENELLA) Don't you people know where to go for it?

DONNA PEPPENELLA   Well, since you ask. Don Gennaro – no, we don't know where to go for it.

GENNARO   So why come here? What do you think this place is, a bloody flour mill? Does it look like a flour mill? Does it make you itch and sneeze like a flour mill? I'm telling you, missus – this place is not a flour mill. (*To* AMALIA) And as for you not being in it for the money. There's only one reason for that – because I will not tolerate that sort of behaviour going on under my roof in my own house. Is that clear? I will not stand for it.

DONNA PEPPENELLA Quite right, Don Gennaro. Quite right. But there's no need to get all het up about it. It's never occurred to your wife to make money out of it. Perish the thought. She does it purely out of the goodness of her heart. We all know that. What all this is about is very simple. Donna Amalia here happened to hear that I could do with some flour, and she couldn't rest till she'd got me some. That's right, isn't it, dear? (*She takes out her purse and hands the money to* AMALIA *with a hard stare*) Forty lire, I think you said, Donna Amalia.

AMALIA (*returning the stare with equal measure*) That's right. Forty lire, dear.

DONNA PEPPENELLA I don't suppose you've got any beans, have you?

AMALIA Beans? No, I'm right out of beans at the moment. He promised faithful he'd bring some around, but you know how it is these days. If they come in, I'll . . .

DONNA PEPPENELLA You'll put some by for me.

AMALIA Naturally. Of course, you realise they'll have gone up.

DONNA PEPPENELLA Oh, naturally. But you're not to worry. I'll manage. Somehow. Right then, I'll say good-bye.

AMALIA Goodbye, Donna Peppenella.

DONNA PEPPENELLA Goodbye, Don Gennaro, I'm just off.

GENNARO Good riddance. And go somewhere else next time.

DONNA PEPPENELLA I will. Don't you bother your arse about that. (*She exits to street, muttering darkly.* MARIA *appears in the doorway of the scullery*)

MARIA Have you got the coffee? (AMALIA *lifts up the*

mattress, takes out a packet of ground coffee and hands it to
MARIA)

AMALIA   There. (MARIA *makes to go, but* AMALIA *calls her
back*) Oi! You! Come here. (MARIA *returns to her and slaps
her hard on the face*) Tonight you'll be tucked up in bed at
the proper time. Understand?

MARIA   (*uncowed*) I only went to the pictures with some
mates. What's the harm in that?

AMALIA   Plenty. There's every harm in the world not
doing as you're told. One o'clock in the morning you got
back last night. What sort of time do you call that? And
in the blackout, too. No wonder people are talking –
nosey load of buggers. You don't find your father and me
gallivanting out all hours. We stayed in all night specifically so we couldn't be caught out late in the blackout.
We don't want people talking about us. This is a respectable house, this, and I intend to keep it that way. I'm
telling you, lady. I'm warning you here and now – watch
your step or there'll be all hell let loose. Understand?
Understand what I'm saying? (MARIA *stares at her coldly*)
Don't you look at me in that tone of voice, my girl. Don't
you flash your eyes at me. Shift yourself and get that
coffee made. Shift yourself before the punters are round
here screaming their bloody heads off.

(MARIA *goes out to the scullery still unbowed.* GENNARO
*comes out of his cubicle, still half-dressed and starts to lather his
face in front of a small mirror attached to the wall of his cubicle*)

GENNARO   There's no need to fly off the handle like that,
Ama. She's only a youngster. She needs proper handling.
All you have to do is keep a careful eye on her. There's no
need to . . . Well, there isn't. There's no need for it.

(AMALIA *ignores him. She goes to the bed and brings out some*

beans from a small sack and puts them in a colander without
GENNARO *noticing. She goes to the scullery door with them*)

AMALIA   Right then. When you've done making the
coffee, you can get cracking with these beans. (*Hands them
to* MARIA)

GENNARO   I thought we didn't have any beans. I said, I
thought we . . . Ach, talk to yourself, Gennaro. Talk to
yourself.

ADELAIDE   (*from outside in the street*) Get the fire going,
will you, Assunta, love? And then you can make a bit of
soup for later. Use a beef cube if you can find one. Use
anything you can lay your hands on. Try dipping the
dog's tail in it, if you can catch him.

(*She enters from the street. She is a talkative, middle-aged woman.
She carries a cheap, torn shopping bag with various packages of
food and green vegetables*)

Donna Ama! Donna Ama, love, what a treat it is taking
your little Rituccia to school these days. Honest to God,
it's a real treat. And good? She was so good today I
couldn't help meself. I could not. I just had to go and buy
her a present. No kidding – I bought her a present. Just
like that. Ah, God bless her and love her, she's such a
dear little mite. And she's got such lovely ways with her,
too. She's as bright as a button, is your little Rituccia.
And so old-fashioned, too. I could eat her. I could,
honest to God. How old is she these days?

AMALIA   Five.

(AMEDEO *has come in from his room in his gas company
uniform. He's gone to the chest of drawers for a brush and is now
using it on his peaked cap*)

ADELAIDE   Well, she will be, Donna Ama. She's forced
to be at her age. Honest to God, she speaks so nice and so

quaint I just want to melt. Bless her little cotton socks. I
could lick her all over. I could. Do you know, just now,
just this moment I ses to her, I ses: 'Rituccia, darling, tell
me something. Who do you like the most – your mama or
your papa?' And do you know what she said? I swear to
God she said without a word of prompting: 'Mama.' Just
like that she said it – 'Mama.'

GENNARO   Rituccia's always been one for her mama.

ADELAIDE   Oh, I wouldn't go as far as to say that, Don
Gennaro. I did give her a second chance, you know. Oh
yes, I looked her straight in the eyes and I said: 'But
what about papa? What do you think about him?' And,
God bless her and love her, she pursed them lovely little
lips of hers and out it come: 'Papa's a bloody idiot,' she
said. Just like that.'Papa's a bloody idiot.' It was so
sweet.

GENNARO   I'm not rising to it, you know. Oh no. She's
five years old. She doesn't know what she's saying. Bad
language means nothing to her. (*To* AMEDEO) Not like
some people I could mention.

AMEDEO   Hey, don't look at me like that. It's nothing to
do with me. If she picks up bad language, she gets it from
the street outside.

GENNARO   Bollocks. You're the one she gets it from. She
hears you using it, and she comes out with it herself. Poor
little sod.

AMEDEO   Have you gone completely round the twist?
Have you gone totally ga-ga?

GENNARO   No, I have not. You know perfectly well what
I'm talking about. You're the one who . . .

ADELAIDE   Don Genna. Don Genna, there's no need to
get all aereated, love. It's not doing her no harm, isn't the
foul language. She's a sweet little girl, is your Rituccia.

And she's got the most beautiful voice. Such a lovely lilt to it. Such an angelic tone.

GENNARO   And such angelic language, too, eh?

ADELAIDE   It's just her way, love. There's no malice in it. God bless her and love her, if only you could have seen her. There she was, prancing through the school gates, holding her skirt out like this and singing at the top of her voice: (*Sings it*) 'Papa's a bloody idiot. Papa's a bloody idiot.'

GENNARO   Maybe it *is* something she's picked up in the street. Or maybe it's something she's picked up from her mother. (AMALIA *shrugs without bothering to reply*) Listen to me – papa may be a bit absent-minded, but he's certainly not gone doodle alley. Oh no. The old brain might not be as sharp as it was, I grant you. But don't blame me for that. Blame the last war. It did something to me up here, did the last war. Oh yes. It's my mind, you see. It wanders. I start to do something, and two minutes later I've completely forgotten what it was I was going to do. Just like with the spaghetti. I saw it there and immediately I thought it was mine.

AMEDEO   And so I've had to go without. Great. Terrific. (*Enter* FEDERICO *from the street. He works with* AMEDEO. *He is in his uniform and carrying his lunch under his arm*)

FEDERICO   (*to* AMEDEO) All set then?

AMEDEO   When I've had my coffee.

FEDERICO   Oh, I've already had mine. I had it at Donna Vincenza's. Do you know, Donna Amalia, it's half a lira cheaper there than it is at your place.

AMALIA   Then you'd be better off drinking at Donna Vicenza's permanently, wouldn't you?

FEDERICO   Oh no. Her coffee's rubbish. Gnat's piss, it is. Nothing like yours. I told her so. Oh aye, I did. I said: 'This coffee's not a patch on Donna Amalia's.' And it isn't. I mean to say, it's . . . it's . . . (*Silence. He changes the subject*) Having a shave, are you, Don Gennaro?

GENNARO   Having a shave? Me? Good God, no. I'm having a crap, aren't I?

FEDERICO   Sorry. I seem to have said the wrong thing.

GENNARO   Look, mate, instead of asking bloody stupid questions, why not save your breath and speak when you're spoken to?

FEDERICO   Yes. Right. (*Pause*) What do you think of the war then, Don Gennaro? How do you think things are going?

GENNARO   Don't try that on with me, son. I know what you're up to. You're trying to take a rise out of me, aren't you?

FEDERICO   No, I'm not.

GENNARO   Yes, you are. Well, you just pin back your lugholes and listen to me. All I'll say about the war is this – as far as I'm concerned, if it was left to me and I was the Minister of Whatshisname in charge, I'd have the whole bloody lot sorted out tomorrow.

FEDERICO   (*leading him on*) Course you would, Don Gennaro. No doubt about it. I mean, look at all these shortages. You'd soon get shut of them, wouldn't you?

GENNARO   Shortages, shortages? What shortages? There aren't any shortages. There's an ample sufficiency for everyone. Flour, oil, butter, cheese, clothes and sundry clobber like that – it's the same old story all over again ad infinitum.

FEDERICO   What old story, Don Gennaro?

GENNARO   (*continuing to shave*) Ach, you're too young to remember. But we had exactly the same set up in the last war. Exactly the same – things in short supply, prices going through the roof, everything disappearing under

the counter. And why? Why do you think people start
wars in the first place?

FEDERICO   I don't know.

GENNARO   To make everything disappear, cloth ears.

(*They laugh, half in agreement, half in mockery.* GENNARO
stops shaving as he gets carried away by his argument)

It's true, it's true. They make everything disappear, and
then what do they do? They slap on your price control.
Sounds simple, doesn't it? Blindingly obvious. 'Price
control – that's the answer, lads,' they say. Bollocks.
Price control always has been, always will be the ruin of
mankind. It's easy to talk about it. Course it is. 'I know
what we'll do,' they say. 'We'll slap on price control, and
we're home and dry.' Well, just you listen to me, my
friends, price control is the root of all evil. The minute
you bring it in, what do you do? You play straight into
the hands of the shopkeepers and wholesalers. Oh yes,
right into their sticky, greedy, grasping hands. It's an
open invitation for them to line their pockets. It's like a
conjuring trick. Now you see it, now you don't. So what's
the ordinary man in the street left with? I'll tell you. He's
got three choices – die of starvation, go on the parish or
end up in prison. Do you know what I'd do, if I had any
say in the matter? I'd bring in an edict. That's right. I'd
bring in an edict with immediate – and I do mean
immediate – an edict with immediate effect.

(*He is interrupted by the arrival from the street of* ERRICO *and*
PEPPE. *They are taxi drivers who are out of work because of
traffic restrictions.* ERRICO *is strikingly handsome in a Neapolitan sort of way. He is in his mid thirties, dark-skinned and
wavy-haired. He is strong and well-built with alert eyes. He's a
likeable wide boy, good-humoured and rather patronisingly self-*

confident especially with women. PEPPE *is cruder and slower and none too bright. He is very powerfully built. His huge chest and bull-like neck suggest the strength of someone who can lift cars with his shoulders, an ability which has earned him the nickname, 'The Jack'. He's used this talent to go into partnership with crooks stealing tyres. He seems to be permanently in a bit of a daze)*

ERRICO Good morning, good morning, one and all. Now then, Don Gennaro, what's all this about your immediate edict?

GENNARO If you've come here for a coffee, have it quick and then bugger off.

PEPPE I don't want to bugger off. I want to hear about your edict.

AMALIA *(calling to* MARIA) Is that coffee ready yet?

MARIA *(offstage)* Give it another minute.

ERRICO Come on, Don Gennaro, don't be shy. That's not like you, my old chum. Tell us all about this edict of yours. *(Nudges* PEPPE) We're all ears, aren't we, Peppe? We're dying to know about this edict.

PEPPE Oh yes. Course we are. What edict?

GENNARO Well, it's a proposal of mine, you see. A sort of proposition. We were talking about shortages. And I say there aren't any. I maintain that if it weren't for price control, there'd be ample sufficiency for everyone. Look at it this way round. How can I put it? Well, it's hard to explain in a couple of sentences. It's bloody impossible, in fact. I'd be at it till Kingdom come.

ERRICO Well, couldn't you kind of sum it up in a nutshell?

PEPPE Yes, put it in a nutshell. I'm not much good if it goes on too long. It slips in one ear and out the other, you see. And then I start to nod off.

GENNARO No one's asking you to listen, pillock. Why
  don't you bugger off?

ERRICO Yes, belt up. (*To* GENNARO) Carry on, Don
  Gennaro. Just ignore him.

GENNARO Right. Well, as I was saying, it'd take a
  lifetime to go into it all properly. I mean to say, I've not
  had all that much schooling and not being in politics sort
  of thing, well, it's . . . you know, it's . . . What I'm trying
  to do is give you the experience of a lifetime. I've seen it
  all, you see. I've had my ups and downs. My God, have I
  had my ups and downs. I served all through the last war
  and if anyone doubts it, I'll show you my discharge
  papers. It's all written down on my discharge papers.
  You can see it in writing. 'Served his country honour-
  ably,' it says. You don't believe me? Right. I'll go and
  fetch them.

ALL We believe you . . . There's no need to bother . . .
  Everyone knows you're an old soldier . . . No, you stay
  where you are . . . etc, etc, etc.

GENNARO All right, all right, there's no need to make a
  meal out of it. Now then, what was I saying? Ah yes,
  price control. (*Warming to his subject*) The thing is, price
  control was brought in for one reason and one reason
  only – to benefit a specific strata of people. What strata
  of people you ask? I'll tell you – the people who know
  how to hold a pen.

ERRICO What people?

GENNARO The professors, of course. The intellectuals.
  The bastards who know how to work things out to their
  advantage and to our disadvantage. Well, don't look so
  gormless. It's perfectly simple. What they're saying
  about price control is this: 'Listen here, you silly twats,
  you don't know how to manage on what you've got, so
  we'll take it off you and manage it on your behalf.' And so

what they're doing ipso facto is to make out that ordinary
people, folk like you and me, are too thick, lazy and pig
ignorant to take responsibility for anything. So what do
they do then? They go on and on about it so that by the
time they've finished, everyone is so confused they
believe them, and so they end up being in the cat bird
seat. They are in control. And who are we talking about?
I'll tell you. The Fascists. (*He's said this last word much
louder than he intended to and he pulls himself up short*) I say,
why don't one of you have a swift shuftie outside? If
anyone hears me talking like this, it's . . . (*Mimics firing
squad*) . . . well, you know what I mean.

(FEDERICO *goes to the door and looks down the street both
ways*)

ERRICO   Don't worry, Don Gennaro. No problem. Carry
on, old son. The professors are still in bed this time of
day.

GENNARO   The college porters aren't.

FEDERICO   (*from door*) It's all right out here. The coast's
clear. Not a sinner in sight. Carry on, Don Gennaro. You
carry on, mate.

PEPPE   What about Our Lady in the street out there?
Madonnas have ears, you know.

GENNARO   I'll have him. I swear I'll . . . What was I
saying? Ah yes, the professors, the intellectuals. What it
is is this, my friends. They get the upper hand and then
they begin to call the tune. It's all very clever. Oh yes.
They do it bit by bit, you see. They make it seem as
though they're doing it solely for your benefit – just you
and you alone. And so they get the people under their
thumb. First come the speeches and the manifestos. And
then come the threats and the decrees and the emergency
measures. And then finally, ultimately – the firing squad.

And then every single one of us is so shit scared we daren't even open our mouths.

(*They all agree without smiling*)

ADELAIDE   I wish you'd keep your voice down, Don Gennaro. I'm not saying it's not a very nice voice with a lovely lilt to it, but, Mother of God, if the police . . .

GENNARO   I know, Donna Adelaide. I know. (*Sighs*) Look at us now. The people and the professors are at logger-heads. And so what's happened? Little by little we've got to the point where nothing belongs to us any more. Nothing. Streets, buildings, houses, gardens – nothing is ours. It's all been appropriated. They do what they like and we, my friends, dare not say one single word against it. And then? The war. 'Who wanted to go to war?' we all say. 'The people,' say the professors. But, my friends, who was it who declared war? 'The professors,' say the people. 'The bloody professors.' And so, if the war's lost, it's the people's fault. If the war's won, the professors take all the credit. Now I know what you're going to say to me.

PEPPE   What?

GENNARO   You're going to say: 'What's all this got to do with price control?' Well, I'll tell you. Price control is one of the ways they use to humiliate people, keep them in their place, forever in a state of abject inferiority. So what am I going to do about it, you ask? I'll tell you. I'll bring in an edict with immediate – and I do mean immediate – an edict with immediate effect that will give each person his own little bit of responsibility. And all these little bits of responsibility added together become one single responsibility shared out equally – joy, pain, wealth, poverty, life and death. And so there's no person, no person on earth, who can stand up and say: 'Look at me. I'm a responsible citizen and you are not.'

PEPPE   I didn't understand a single word of that.

GENNARO   Of course you didn't. If you did, we wouldn't be in the mess we're in now.

AMALIA   Why don't you finish your shaving and get dressed?

(GENNARO *glares at her and goes back to his shaving*)

PEPPE   All I want to know is one simple thing – when are they going to give us some petrol so we can get our taxis back on the road again?

GENNARO   Aha. An edict with immediate effect. There are to be nine drivers to every taxi. One behind the wheel and the other eight pushing.

(RICCARDO *enters from the street, skimming through a newspaper. He is the Clerk in the Accounts Department of a small firm, unassuming and dignified and wearing a dark suit and pince nez*)

RICCARDO   Good morning, everyone.

AMALIA   Good morning, Don Riccardo. The coffee won't be a moment.

RICCARDO   Thank you, Donna Amalia. Most kind. Do you know, I don't think I closed my eyes once during the night. Not once. And now I've got the most dreadful, splitting headache. Quite excruciating. My dear wife, poor soul, goes completely to pieces when she hears the sirens. Of course we got back safe and sound from the shelter with the children – our three precious handfuls – but it's not the same, is it? I mean, any thought of sleep was completely out of the question. My poor wife was trembling like a leaf.

PEPPE Yes, they certainly threw the shit at us last night right enough.

RICCARDO According to my paper, they got two big houses at Parco Margherita and some more at Capodimonte and a factory.

PEPPE That's right. Bang next door to the tram depot, it was.

ERRICO Looks like they're starting to mean business then.

(*Enter* MARIA *with an enormous Neapolitan coffee machine which they all greet with enthusiasm*)

AMALIA (*to* AMEDEO) You! Go and keep a look out on the street.

(AMEDEO *goes out.* AMALIA *serves coffee to everyone and takes their money as they gush with pleasure*)

ERRICO Congratulations, Donna Ama. Superb. Better than ever this morning.

(*They all concur and savour their coffee with pleasure*)

PEPPE Yes, that bombing – it well and truly put the wind up me last night.

ADELAIDE Me too. Do you know, I've only got to hear the sirens, and I'm away for slates. I am. I don't stop for nothing. I do not. I'm off. It doesn't matter what I'm doing. I could be in on the potty for all it matters. But I just drop everything, grab hold of this (*holds up her rosary*) and off I scoot to the shelter. I've no shame, I tell you.

GENNARO I'll tell you where it gets me. The old guts. Right here. I get this icy cold feeling running up and down my back, and the old guts start. It's no use hanging

round then. Whoosh – lavatory here I come. Well, I'm no
hero. No need to pretend about that. I'm a realist. That's
what I am – a realist.

PEPPE (*to* RICCARDO) How long do you reckon this
war's going to last, if it's not a rude question?

RICCARDO Who knows?

PEPPE Somebody was telling me the other day in the
cake shop it's going to get worse. According to her the
whole of Naples is going to be bombed flat. Well, I was
just wondering like, you know, if there's any truth in it. I
mean, what do you think – are we going to get wiped out
like she said in the cake shop?

ERRICO Exactly. How much worse is all the bombing
going to get?

FEDERICO Christ, it's not going to get worse, is it?

ADELAIDE So they say, love. Next on the agenda is
poison gas.

GENNARO Ah, so that's what they've got in store for us,
is it? Total and utter annihilation.

PEPPE It's bloody barbaric. What's the civilian popu-
lation got to do with it? Why do they want to bomb our
houses and our tram depots? It's got nothing to do with
us.

RICCARDO (*holding up paper*) According to this the authorities are going to bring in another age group for call-
up.

ADELAIDE Oh, my God.

AMALIA What are you saying, Don Riccardo? They're
not going to call up the rejects as well, are they? That'll
mean Amedeo will have to go.

RICCARDO My dear Donna Amalia, who knows what
they'll do?

GENNARO But, my dear sir, you must have some idea.

You read all the papers, don't you? Look, all we want is some sort of hope, something we can hang on to.

RICCARDO Ah, I see. So to make you feel better I've got to tell you the air raids have stopped, have I? All right. The air raids have stopped. No one's being called up. The traffic's back to normal. The shops are all open and bursting with food. What on earth gives you the idea that I know any more than you do?

GENNARO Because . . . because . . . well, someone like you in a collar and tie, well, it stands to reason.

RICCARDO Would that that were the case, my friend. But a collar and tie is not a crystal ball I fear.

GENNARO Maybe. But look at all the people you rub shoulders with. The high-ups and the people in the know.

RICCARDO (*suddenly guarded after his previous smugness*) High-ups? What high-ups? I don't know any high-ups. I don't talk to them. I talk to no one. No one at all. I know nothing.

PEPPE (*to* ERRICO) Come on, let's skedaddle, eh? He's not going to say nothing, him. (*To* RICCARDO) You do right, mate. Keep your trap shut. It's the best road out these days.

ADELAIDE. That's just what I say. It's best not to talk too much. I don't. Oh no, catch me talking too much. What I say is this – what's your business is absolutely nothing to do with me. Keep your nose out of it, Adelaide. Keep them lips buttoned tight shut. And I do. I most certainly do.

PEPPE Okay then? Tarra, all. (*To* FEDERICO) Coming?

FEDERICO Yep. (*To* AMEDEO) Are you fit, mate?

AMEDEO (*who has just come back in*) Half a mo. Just let me finish this. (*Hastily gulps back his coffee*) Right. Tarra, everyone. See you.

(*He exits with* FEDERICO *and* PEPPE. GENNARO *shuffles off to his cubicle.* ERRICO *stations himself just outside the open door, keeping a look out for suspicious strangers and smoking*)

ADELAIDE   Well, I can't stand here megging like this, Donna Ama. I've got work to do. As you know, I'm not one for talking and gossiping. Oh no. I like to get on with things. Take that niece of mine, for instance. Can I trust her? She's supposed to be making soup and . . .

AMALIA   (*firmly*) Goodbye, Donna Adelaide.

ADELAIDE   Goodbye, Donna Ama. (*Giggles*) 'Papa's a bloody idiot.' (*Exits chuntering to herself*) Such a sweet little child, bless her little cotton socks. Such an angelic voice. (*Giggles again*) 'Papa's a bloody idiot. Papa's a bloody idiot.'

AMALIA   Now then, Don Riccardo, what can I do for you today?

RICCARDO   (*uncomfortably*) Yes . . . well . . .

GENNARO   (*poking his head above the cubicle*) You're all right here, mate. Say what you like. We won't give you away. We think exactly the same about things as what you do. Oh yes. No doubt about it. Fire away. Feel free.

RICCARDO   (*hesitating again*) Donna Ama, I was wondering if . . . well, I was . . . have you perhaps managed to get hold of any butter?

AMALIA   Oh no, Don Riccardo. You'll have to come back later I'm afraid. I was promised some, but you know how things are. If they can get a better price somewhere else, that's the last you see of them. If he comes with some, then, of course, it's yours. You know we don't use it. Well, we don't like it all that much and besides it's far too expensive for the likes of us. I mean to say, who can afford it these days?

RICCARDO *(bitterly)* Yes, indeed, who can afford it? And in any case you don't make anything out of it, do you?

AMALIA *(on her dignity)* Don Riccardo, if you're going to talk like that, then you can forget all about me getting butter for you. As you well know, the only reason I'm doing it is as a special favour, because I know you have children – your three precious handfuls. I can assure you, my dear sir, there is absolutely nothing in it for me. Not a penny. If I'm telling a lie, may the Blessed Virgin herself . . .

(At this moment GENNARO *appears dressed in waistcoat and tie. She sees him and stops dead in her tracks. He crosses to where his jacket is hanging on the back of the chair. He stares at her pointedly. She hesitates and then continues)*

. . . may I never set eyes on my dear husband again.

(He nods sadly to himself, picks up his jacket and plods back to his cubicle, muttering softly under his breath. AMALIA *composes herself instantly and takes some packages from beneath the mattress and commences to hand them to* RICCARDO)

Right then, here's the sugar you asked me for. And here's the cocoa. And this is the flour. I've managed to get hold of some special white for you. Now it all comes to . . . hold on, wait a minute. I've got the piece of paper somewhere he left when he came for the money. *(She rummages amongst the clutter on the sideboard, finds a crumpled bit of paper and pretends to read it)* Yes. Here we are. Two kilos of sugar. One kilo of cocoa. Two packets of white flour. Plus what's owing from last week. That makes exactly three thousand five hundred lire.

RICCARDO Oh dear. As much as that? Well, that puts me in a difficult situation. Things are a little bit tight at the moment, you see. My wife, poor soul, hasn't been at

all well lately. It's been a dreadful drain on our finances
and what with the children and the miserable pittance I
get . . . well, it's enough to give you grey hairs, Donna
Amalia. Our savings have long since been gobbled up
and what with soaring prices and . . .

AMALIA   But I thought you'd told me you owned
property, Don Riccardo.

RICCARDO   Property? Well, yes, I suppose I do. Nothing
much, of course. There's the house we live in. Terribly
small, of course. Nothing grand. As a matter of fact we've
just paid off the mortgage. That dreadful mortgage!
You've no idea of the millstone it was. Years and years of
scrimping and scraping and working all the hours God
sends and . . .

AMALIA   And the other property?

RICCARDO   What?

AMALIA   Your other property, Don Riccardo.

RICCARDO   Well, you'd hardly call it property, Donna
Amalia. Two minute apartments out at Magnacavallo –
that's not what you'd call property. I mean, do you know
how much rent they bring in? Can you guess? Two
hundred lire a month in one case and three hundred in
the other. So what should I do? Sell them? Deprive my
family of the one pathetic bit of income that keeps body
and soul together? Surely you don't expect me to do that?

(*She stares at him coldly. He hesitates and then takes out of his
pocket an object wrapped in tissue paper and tied with ribbons. He
unties it and shows it to her*)

I've just had this valued. It's one of my wife's ear-rings.
It's worth five thousand lire.

AMALIA   (*with feigned indifference*) For the two?

RICCARDO   No. Just the one. You see . . . well, I'm afraid
I had to pawn the other one.

AMALIA   All right. Leave it with me. I'll see what I can do. It's just possible that I might be able to persuade my supplier to accept it instead of cash.

RICCARDO   You're very kind. So that's three thousand five hundred lire I owe you.

AMALIA   Correct.

RICCARDO   So with five thousand for the ear-ring it means I'm fifteen hundred lire in credit.

AMALIA   Correct.

RICCARDO   In that case, I wonder if you'd . . .

AMALIA   If the ear-ring is worth what you say, you shall have your credit, Don Riccardo. I'll put it to one side for you.

RICCARDO   Good, good. Tomorrow then.

AMALIA   Tomorrow. I'm expecting some veal in. Interested?

RICCARDO   Yes, I suppose so.

AMALIA   And how are you off for eggs?

RICCARDO   Eggs? Well, if you had a few to spare, I'd be . . . it's for the children, you see. Not for us. Purely for the children.

AMALIA   I'll see you get some.

RICCARDO   You're very kind, Donna Amalia. I just don't know how we'd manage if it weren't for you and your . . .

AMALIA   (*firmly*) Goodbye, Don Riccardo.

RICCARDO   Goodbye, Donna Amalia. Yes, yes, goodbye.

(*He exits almost timorously.* GENNARO *comes out of his cubicle fully dressed, taking his hat which is hanging on a nail in the wall and dusting it with a hankerchief. He is preoccupied with his own thoughts. He sits down*)

GENNARO   I've been thinking, Amalia.

AMALIA   Oh yes?

GENNARO   I can't stop thinking. I can't stop worrying.

AMALIA   About what?

GENNARO   All this trouble we're building up for ourselves. Good God, I can't sleep at nights worrying myself
sick that the police are going to come bursting in and . . .
and . . . Amalia, it's no use trying to pull the wool over
my eyes. It's not just the odd cup of coffee, is it? There's
far too much coming and going for that. Every hour of
the day, every minute, every second there's people
clamouring in the house for butter and rice and pasta
and beans and God knows what.

AMALIA   Look, how many more times do I have to tell
you? This stuff doesn't belong to me. I'm just doing a
favour to the neighbours by keeping it here for them.

GENNARO   Out of pure goodness of heart, eh?

AMALIA   I've told you – there's no profit in it for me.
Absolutely none.

GENNARO   Then how come we manage to live like we do?
The miracle of the loaves and fishes, is it? I suppose
you're going to tell me next we're living off our rations.
Bollocks. If we had to rely on our rations, we'd be
nothing but skin and bone. So how do we do it? How do
we manage, eh? There's nothing coming in from my side,
There won't be a tram left in service soon. The 3's been
taken off. And so have the 5 and the 16. There's men
being laid off right, left and centre. There's only about
half of us still working.

AMALIA   So what am I supposed to do?

GENNARO   I don't know. I've been thinking, you see. I've
had these thoughts – and now they've gone. It was
something to do with . . . with . . . ah yes, the ration
books. That's it – the ration books. I was thinking, if it's
impossible to keep body and soul together on our rations,
why don't we . . . why don't we . . . It's no use. It's gone.
All I'm trying to do, Ama, is think of some way we can

live like decent, honest people without all this black market business and . . . and . . . (*Shrugs his shoulders helplessly*) Well, if we can't, we can't I suppose. We'll just have to keep our eyes open all the time and live with the fear of being caught and sent to prison and put up against . . . oh God, Ama, please, I beg you, please be careful. (*He gets up to go out*)

AMALIA You're not going out?

GENNARO Yes. Only for a spot of fresh air and a chinwag. Two hours I spent in a damp shelter last night. I'm crippled with cramp here. I've just got to get out for a bit. If you want me, just shout.

(ERRICO *stops him at the door*)

ERRICO Hey, you can't go out. I delivered two hundred kilos of coffee here last night.

GENNARO Two hundred kilos! Jesus Christ, you'll be the death of me, Don Erri. I'm going to end up in clink, I am. Me. In clink. Behind bars. I'm the one they'll hold responsible for all this, you know. Oh, it's all right for you, mate. You're on your own. I know we've all got to help each other at times like this. But this! Bloody hell, man, you're bringing everything here. And it's not just the odd load, is it? It's every day. I tell you, Don Erri, I'm petrified. It's a permanent brown trousers job, is this, mate. I can hear the prison doors clanking behind me. I can hear the cries as they drag the poor sods out to the yard and the click of the rifles and the . . . (*To* AMALIA) Where've you put all this coffee then?

AMALIA You know perfectly well. Under the mattress. Two hundred kilos of coffee.

(GENNARO *goes to the bed and feels under the mattress*)

GENNARO God Almighty – and the rest. (*Opens up mattress*) Struth, look at this lot. Rice. Pasta. Cheese. (*To* ERRICO) That's another thing – this cheese. How long has it got to be stuck under here? The pong at night! It's chronic. Dreadful. It's all I can do to breathe.

ERRICO Just try and put up with it for a bit longer, Don Genna. You see, the thing is I've had a bit of aggro on the cheese front.

GENNARO I'm sorry, Don Erri. I'm really sorry. But what about my health? It's getting distinctly parky now in the evenings and we've got to keep the door open. God, the stench is unbearable. Sometimes when the sirens go, I leap up and I say: 'Thank God – it's the liberation.'

ERRICO It's only for a little while longer, Don Genna.

GENNARO (*rummaging again in the mattress*) Sugar. Flour. And what's this? Lard. Christ, what are we? A food depot? (*He goes to leave once more*)

ERRICO Look, Don Genna, stick around, eh? Don't go too far. You never know when you might be needed, you see, and . . .

GENNARO Don't worry. I know what I've got to do. I won't let you down when the time comes. Oh no, I'll be here playing my part like a good 'un. All I'm saying is – get this bloody stuff out of the house. Please. Please, please. (*To* AMALIA) I'll be down on the corner. If I'm needed, give me a shout. But don't bother about the sirens. I can manage the sirens quite well on my own, thank you very much. (*He exits*)

AMALIA Right then. How much do I owe you?

ERRICO Forget it.

AMALIA What? You're not making me a present of all this, are you?

ERRICO I wish I could. I'd do anything for you. I'd give

you my life. You know that. (*She looks at him with a mixture of boldness and coyness*) Look, there's no need for cash in hand now. It'll do, when you've sold all the stuff. Then you can take my expenses out of it and the rest's all yours.

AMALIA What's going on here? You know perfectly well we always split it down the middle. What's the matter with you? (*He shrugs. She shows him* RICCARDO *'s ear-ring after turning away from his stare*) What do you think to this then?

ERRICO (*holds it up to light*) It looks all right to me.

AMALIA What's it worth?

ERRICO I'd have to see the pair.

AMALIA You can't. The other one's been pawned.

ERRICO Well, get me the pawn ticket. I'll need to see whether the stones match.

AMALIA I'll have it for you the day after tomorrow.

ERRICO Good. I'll give you the valuation then.

AMALIA What do you reckon? Four thousand? Five?

ERRICO Who cares? You won't be out of pocket, my dear. (*Smiles*) So that's where you keep the coffee, eh? Under the mattress.

AMALIA (*lifting a corner of the bed cover*) Come and look. No one'll dream of searching here, will they? God, the job I had getting it all in. What I did was to open the corner and put two little fasteners on it, you see, so I can take out what I want. And then I fasten it up again. Fiendishly clever, eh. All I have to do is put my hand in like this and . . .

(ERRICO *has come up behind her. He traps her hand with his hand.* AMALIA *resists, but not violently*)

. . . and then I take it out again.

(*Gently she frees herself from his grip and puts his hand back where it belongs*)

ERRICO   And then back it comes again.

(*He embraces her and tries to kiss her. She tries to disentangle herself, but not with great conviction*)

AMALIA   No, Don Erri. No, let go of me. Please, let go of me.

ERRICO   (*trying to control himself, but still holding her*) Donna Ama, I'm so sorry. I just don't know what came over me. Please forgive me. I can't let you go until you say I'm forgiven. Say I'm forgiven, Donna Ama.

AMALIA   I suppose so. We all get carried away sometimes, don't we?

ERRICO   Thank you, Donna Ama. Thank you so very much.

(*He kisses her over and over again on both hands.* MARIA *has come in from the scullery and is standing there with her hands on her hips, watching in an attitude of defiance.* ERRICO, *catching sight of her, hastily drops* AMALIA'*s hands and tries to look as though nothing has happened.* AMALIA, *taken by surprise, is disconcerted for a moment, but quickly recovers*)

AMALIA   And what do you think you're doing here?

MARIA   I need garlic for the bean soup.

AMALIA   You know where to find it.

MARIA   There isn't any.

AMALIA   Go and get some then. Donna Giovannina'll have some. (MARIA *goes to street door. As she's about to leave she turns to her mother*)

MARIA   Oh, by the way. I'm off to the pictures again tonight. And I don't know what time I'll be back. (*Exits*)

AMALIA   Well, you timed that brilliantly, didn't you?

God only knows what the little madam's going to make of that.

(*The voices of* AMEDEO *and* ADELAIDE *in the street outside*)

AMEDEO (*offstage*) I'll smash her face in, the old cow.

ADELAIDE Now don't be too hasty. Amedeo love. Don't get all aereated. There might be nothing in it.

(*Enter* AMEDEO, *all agitated, followed by* ADELAIDE)

AMEDEO I tell you there is. We're right in it now. She's got us by the short and curlies and . . .

AMALIA What the hell's going on here? What are you doing back home at this time of day?

AMEDEO Listen, I just bumped into a mate of mine, and he told me he was at Donna Vicenza's about an hour ago just after you had that blazing row with her. Right? Well then, he's having a cup of coffee and . . . look, you were there, Donna Adelaide. You tell the story.

ADELAIDE Certainly, love. Well, she was going spare, was Donna Vicenza. She hit the roof. Literally. You should have heard her. The language! 'Who the so and so does she think she is?' 'Does she blankety blankety think she's got a blankety blank monopoly?' 'Does she think she's the only one allowed to sell effing coffee in this effing neighbourhood?' On and on she went. I've never heard anything like it. Disgusting, it was. 'If I'm not allowed to sell coffee, then she's not going to neither. She'll soon find out she's not the only one with connections. If I can't put that blankety blank so and so in her place, then my name's not Vicenza Capece.' And with that she snatched up her shawl, slammed the door and dashed off down the street.

AMEDEO She'll have gone straight to the cops. She'll have reported us. That's what she'll have done. She's landed us right in it, the prize old bitch.

AMALIA Now hold on, hold on. There's nothing to get excited about. Think about it. What are they going to find when they come?

AMEDEO I know all that. But I had to come and warn you, didn't I?

AMALIA You did right, son. Well done. Now go and warn your father. He'll be down on the corner. Trust him to be somewhere else when he's wanted.

(AMEDEO *runs to the street door and calls* GENNARO)

AMEDEO Papa, papa. (*Waves to him*) You're wanted, papa. It's urgent. (*To* AMALIA) Marco's standing at the corner by Donna Vincenza's. He's going to light his pipe as soon as he sees the cops.

AMALIA Good. Now whatever you do, don't move from there. Right? (*Enter* MARIA *from the street with a bulb of garlic*)

MARIA Two lire! Two lire for one miserable bulb of garlic.

AMALIA Never mind about that. Get in that scullery and let your hair down. And wrap your black shawl round you, too. (AMALIA *goes to a drawer, takes out a black shawl and puts it round her shoulders. Sees* MARIA *still standing there*) Well, don't just stand there flashing your hips. Do as you're told and be quick about it.

(MARIA *shrugs and insolently picks up a black shawl and saunters off towards the scullery*)

MARIA Give me a shout when you need me. (*Exits*)

AMEDEO (*at door*) We're okay. He's not lit his pipe yet. (*Enter* GENNARO)

GENNARO Now what's up?

AMALIA Don't stand there fiddling with your do-dahs. Get yourself ready.

GENNARO Oh, here we go again. (*To* ERRICO) What did I tell you? You won't be happy, will you, till you've got us locked away behind bars? He won't. I'm telling you, he won't.

AMALIA (*to* AMEDEO) You'd better fetch Pascalino and Franco.

AMEDEO I already have. They're on their way now.

ERRICO (*trying to appear unconcerned*) Right then, let's all keep our cool, shall we? No need to panic. I'll stick around and pretend I'm one of the family. We're all in this together, remember?

AMEDEO He's lighting his pipe. Marco's lighting his pipe.

(GENNARO *pokes his head over the top of his cubicle*)

GENNARO Oh, lighting his pipe, is he?

AMEDEO The stinking old crone. The old ratbag. She's been to the cops and shopped us. Hold on, here come Pascalino and Franco.

(*Everyone starts rushing round frantically setting the scene for what is to follow*)

AMALIA (*shouting into scullery*) Maria, stop messing round with those beans and get yourself in here. (*To* GENNARO) And you – shift yourself.

GENNARO What do you think I am – a bloody chameleon or something? Get Pascalino here.

AMEDEO He's coming now. And Franco.

(*Enter* PASCALINO *and* FRANCO. *They are two rather shady characters. Without saying a word they take up position on the left of the bed facing downstage. Before sitting down, however, they open the bundle they've brought with them and tie two large black*

aprons round them and cover their heads with nuns' hoods.
AMALIA *meanwhile, with the help of* MARIA, AMEDEO, *and*
ERRICO, *is arranging four lighted candelabra round the bed*)

AMALIA   Gennaro, how much longer are you going to be
in there?

ADELAIDE   Oh, do hurry up, Don Genna. For the love of
God shift yourself.

(GENNARO *comes slowly out of his cubicle. He is wearing a
long white woollen nightshirt. A large white headscarf, folded
several times is passed under his chin and tied in a bow on top of
his head. He is pulling on a pair of white cotton gloves as he makes
his way towards the bed*)

GENNARO   God almighty, what a pantomime. You're
mad, the whole lot of you. You're pots for bloody rags.

ADELAIDE   Don Genna, please. Show some respect. This
isn't the time for blasphemy.

AMALIA   Get yourself into that bed. Now.

GENNARO   Lunatics. Idiots.

(*He stands by the bed resignedly as* AMALIA *dabs his cheeks
with white powder from a large powder puff to make him look
convincingly corpselike. Then she helps him into bed as* MARIA
*takes some flowers from the sideboard and scatters them on the
sheets. They all take their places as if it were extremely well-
rehearsed and stand there, a desolate and tragic group.* AMEDEO
*closes the wooden shutters and the french doors onto the street. Then
after combing his hair he strikes up a dramatic pose at the foot of
the bed.* ADELAIDE *is by herself with her rosary in her hands.*
ERRICO *sits near the street door.* GENNARO *is half sitting up
in bed, waiting. Long pause*)

GENNARO   (*to* AMEDEO) Are you certain about this?

AMEDEO   Yes. (*Pause*)

GENNARO   All this palaver. Bloody ridiculous.

AMEDEO I told you – he was definitely lighting his pipe.

GENNARO Last week I was stuck here like this for an hour and a half.

ALL Shut up. (*Pause*)

ADELAIDE (*trying to make conversation*) I was only saying to the chiropodist the other week . . . (*A sudden violent knocking on the door*)

AMEDEO They're here.

GENNARO Amazing – he's got it right for once.

AMALIA Will you lie down in that bed. (*Screams*) Lie down.

(GENNARO *lies down in bed looking as much like a corpse as he can.* ADELAIDE *starts telling her beads with her eyes turned towards the ceiling.* PASCALINO *and* FRANCO *mutter incoherently trying to sound like nuns at prayer. The others sob quietly to themselves. The knocking grows louder.* ERRICO *opens the door to admit* SERGEANT CIAPPA *and* TWO PLAIN CLOTHES POLICEMEN)

CIAPPA (*to the others in the street*) You lot wait outside.

(*He is a man of about fifty with greying hair, direct manner and a sharp eye. He knows his way around and is not easily taken in. He has the art, so necessary in Naples, of knowing when to turn a blind eye. He comes into the room, takes in the scene and is not impressed. He makes a point of not baring his head*)

Well, well, well, so what have we got here then? A death in the house, eh? Do you know, this is starting to look like an epidemic. Three corpses yesterday and two more today at Furcella. Ye Gods, suddenly they're dying like flies, aren't they? (*Pause*) All right, come on, I don't want to make trouble for you, but . . . (*Suddenly smashes his fist violently on the table*) Nobody's going to take the piss out of me. Do I make myself perfectly clear? Right then, you, Lazarus – on your hind legs. Now. At once. Unless, of

course, you'd like me to slip the handcuffs on you while
you're lying in bed.

AMALIA   Sergeant, for pity's sake. My husband died in
the night. He breathed his last at three thirty-five.

CIAPPA   Did he really? Three thirty-five, eh? How convenient you just happened to have your stopwatch at the
ready, when he snuffed it, eh?

AMEDEO AND MARIA   (*Wailing*) Oh, papa, papa, papa.
(*The two 'nuns' go on muttering their prayers and* ADELAIDE
goes on telling her beads. CIAPPA *stands there watching them
coldly*)

ERRICO   To go just like that, sergeant. Such a fine
outstanding figure of a man. It's an absolute tragedy.

CIAPPA   A fine figure of a man, eh? Listen to me, you
scumbags, pack it in. Right here and now. (*No response.*
ADELAIDE *prays even more loudly*) All right. Okay. So
we've got a dead man on our hands, have we? Well, let's
see if we can bring him back to life, shall we? (*He moves
decisively towards* GENNARO)

AMALIA   No, sergeant. No, no. (*She flings herself at*
CIAPPA, *clasping him by the knees and weeping profusely. She
makes a great drama out of it partly because it comes natural to her
as a Neapolitan and partly because she is genuinely frightened*)
Oh, sergeant, we're not the type of people to try and
deceive you. My husband, God rest his soul, is dead. We
wouldn't play games about something like that. Someone's been spreading lies about us. Someone's got it in for
us. It must be so. It must be. We're just poor, decent
people trying to eke out an honest living. (*She stands up,
dominating the scene now and making large, theatrical gestures*)
Don't you see the agony this family is going through?
Don't you feel any morsel of pity for these two wretched,
innocent youngsters who've lost a dear father? If you feel
no pity for them, if you feel no compassion for us for the

tragedy that's stricken this humble household of ours, go
on up to him. Go on. Go to him and convince yourself.
Touch the dead man. Go on. Commit sacrilege if you're
not afraid of being excommunicated. (CIAPPA *hesitates
and she urges him on more passionately*) Come on, sergeant.
Come on. Go and touch him.

CIAPPA Why should I touch him? If he's dead, as you say,
what's the point? Good God, I don't even know the man.

MARIA (*sobbing*) He's dead, sergeant. Papa is dead.

ERRICO To go just like that! A man in his prime. A man
loved and respected and revered and . . .

CIAPPA Jesus Christ! This has gone beyond a joke. It
really has. Okay. Fine. So you want me to believe he's
dead. Right then, I believe you. I'll go further than that.
As a gesture of friendship I'll offer you a little comfort in
your sad bereavement. I'll sit here with you and keep you
company till the dear departed is carried out of the
house. Right? Does that satisfy you?

(*He takes a chair and sits down. The others exchange glances of
alarm. The nuns increase their muttering.* ADELAIDE *breaks into
a new prayer, glaring at* CIAPPA *out of the corners of her eyes*)

ADELAIDE 'Diasillo, diasillo, receive him into your
arms, Lord. Knight of the Holy Cross, listen to our
prayers. For our deep sorrow, for your enormous power,
show us signs of your benevolence.'

(*Suddenly in the distance is heard the menacing sound of the air
raid sirens. It is followed by the sound of voices in the street. They
look at each other wondering what to do. The nuns pray louder as
the hubbub outside increases*)

VOICES Where are the kids? . . . Stop shoving, will you?
. . . There's no need for panic. For Christ's sake, don't
panic . . . Hurry up, hurry up . . . Get that shelter open

quick. Get it open . . . You haven't got the dog? How many more times do you need telling to bring the dog? (*The siren stops and there is dead silence as they wait for the planes*)

AMALIA   Sergeant, there's a very good shelter just across the way. We don't have to stay here out of bravado, you know.

CIAPPA   (*calmly lighting a cigarette*) Don't you worry about me, my dear. You go off to the shelter. I'll keep watch over the dead man for you. Well, it would be a sin to leave him here alone, wouldn't it?

(*At this the two nuns leap to their feet and make for the door, talking in high-pitched female voices*)

FRANCO   This is no place for us. There's work to be done outside.

PASCALINO   Yes, sister. Wait for me. I'm coming, too. (*As they exit* CIAPPA *catches sight of their backs*)

CIAPPA   Well, well, well. Nuns in trousers. Now that's a sight I never thought I'd live to see. (*Chuckles*) Nuns in trousers, eh? (*The anti-aircraft guns open up*) All right, corpse. Come on. Stop messing about and let's get down to the shelter. (*No movement from* GENNARO)

PLAIN CLOTHES POLICEMAN   Sergeant, for Christ's sake!

CIAPPA   Shut your whingeing. There's no need to stay here. If you're wetting your pants, clear off.

(*In the distance the first bombs begin to fall.* AMALIA, *white with terror, stands with her back against the wall clasping her two children to her.* ERRICO *and* ADELAIDE *are pressed against the other wall*)

PLAIN CLOTHES POLICEMAN   Sergeant, sergeant! Oh, sod this for a game of soldiers, I'm off. (*He runs out followed by his colleague.*)

CIAPPA (*cool, calm and collected*) They're getting nearer. Yes, they're getting nearer all right. Hello, there go the machine guns. Struth, they're gunning us now.

(*A bomb explodes very near and they all, except* CIAPPA *and* GENNARO, *cower instinctively from it*)

Dear oh dear, that was a bit too close for comfort, eh? You know, I don't know whether these houses will stand up to it. A direct hit and – whoosh – we'll all be blown to smithereens. Wayhay, there goes another. Getting really close now, eh?

(*The bombing is at its most violent. The explosions are more and more frequent, rattling the shutters with their blast.* CIAPPA *is unmoved as he watches* GENNARO *lying stock still in bed. The noise of the raid gradually subsides. There's the odd distant explosion. Then silence*)

So. A real live corpse as ever was. Bombs dropping all around you, and you didn't bat an eyelid. My congratulations, sir. Dedication like that in a corpse is not a thing you see every day of the week. Oh no. Such devotion to duty. I take my hat off to you. (*He crosses to the bed and stands at the foot*) Right, you. Out of it. Do you hear me? I said I want you out of that bed now. This instant. (*No response. For a second he loses his cool and shakes the bed violently*) Are you deaf, you bastard. I said Up.

(GENNARO *lies there more 'dead' than ever.* CIAPPA *walks round the bed and lifts a corner of the mattress cover with his swagger stick to reveal every imaginable item of black market food*) Jesus Christ, what have we got here? This isn't a wake. It's a bleeding harvest festival.

(*The all clear sounds and after a moment the voices start up again outside*)

VOICES   Thank God, it's over . . . Anyone seen father?
. . . Get yourself washed. You're covered in dust . . .
What's happened to my slippers? . . . My God, they got
the big house on the corner . . .

(*Noise of fire engines.* CIAPPA *is now looking at* GENNARO
with open admiration)

CIAPPA   Well, I take my hat off to you. I really do. That
must have taken a whole lot of guts. Bravo, sir. Bravo.
It's all right, I know you're not dead. And I also know
there's enough black market food here to feed a regiment
of stormtroopers for a whole year – for the whole dur-
ation. My dear sir, I am not going to arrest you. I don't
know about its being sacrilege to touch the dead, but it
sure would be sacrilege to touch a man who's got as
much bottle as you have. Don't worry. I'm not going to
arrest you. (*Pause*) Just give me the satisfaction of seeing
you move. That's all I want – just a little flicker of
movement from you. I won't even search the place. I've
seen nothing. Right? (*Still no response from* GENNARO)
Come on, matey, let me see you move. I won't arrest you.
I give you my word. (*No response*) I haven't seen anything.
And I'm not going to look. I give you my word of honour.

GENNARO   (*sitting bolt upright*) Well, if you arrest me after
that, you're a two-faced shit.

CIAPPA   No, no, I've given you my word. But there's just
one thing. I'd like you all to bear in mind that I am not a
complete, screaming bloody idiot.

GENNARO   Me neither, sergeant. Me neither, old cock.

(CIAPPA *smiles, goes to pat* GENNARO *on the back. Then he
stops and turns to the door*)

CIAPPA   Well then, everyone, I bid you good day.

(*They all breathe freely again and they are all over him, jabbering and pawing at him. Good naturedly he smiles at them*)

AMALIA   Sergeant, may I offer you a cup of coffee?

CIAPPA   A cup of coffee? Well, thanks all the same, but I had one on my way here. Half a lira cheaper than yours, but nowhere near as nice, I'm sure. (*They all go to see him off*)

CURTAIN

ACT TWO

(1944. Same room.

The allied landings have taken place. In the meantime AMALIA's *house has undergone a transformation. The walls are cyclamen and the ceiling is white stucco with gold decoration.* GENNARO's *cubicle has gone. In its place the walls are tiled white and there's a marble shelf with an enormous and resplendent coffee machine on it. The furnishings of the room are garish and gaudy. On the bed is a luxurious cover in yellow silk. The shrine in the street outside has been completely refurbished with fire-coloured electric lights instead of candles.*

AMALIA *is a different woman, too. She is dressed to kill and looking years younger. She is standing downstage in front of an expensive mirror touching up her hair. She has on a silk dress with matching shoes and stockings. She is wearing expensive, flashy jewellery, including long pendant ear-rings. Her accent is now more refined to suit her exalted position, but from time to time she slips into her old ways.*

In the street outside the voices are still the same as before as they jabber on about the liberation and the luxuries it has brought)

VOICES   Hey, Yank, Yank, got any gum, chum? . . . Here come the doughboys. Got any fags, mate? We pay good money. Name your price . . . Wow, those stockings!

Sheer nylon. Where do you get them from, how much do you want for them? . . . Hey, Yank, Yank, you want to meet my sister?

(AMALIA *takes a large bottle of eau de cologne and puts some on her hands and neck. Then she sprinkles it liberally round the room.*

ASSUNTA *passes in the street. She is* ADELAIDE's *niece, a young woman of about 24, naive, open and a little bit scatty. She is apt to go into hysterical laughter for no apparent reason in the middle of a sentence. She is in mourning in a simple black dress with black ear-rings. Seeing* AMALIA *she enters the house, carrying a half-opened package)*

ASSUNTA Look at this beautiful piece of meat, Donna Amalia. It's for a stew tomorrow.

AMALIA (*slightly annoyed at her intrusion*) Is it really, dear? How very interesting.

ASSUNTA Would you like it for yourself, Donna Amalia? I can easy get another piece. It's only five hundred lire a kilo.

AMALIA Thank you, Assunta. But we've got people coming round tonight. Guests.

ASSUNTA I know. Isn't it exciting? Don Errico's invited me and Aunt Adelaide personally. That's why we're keeping the meat for tomorrow.

AMALIA I see. So you and Adelaide are coming, are you? Well, we won't be short of guests then, will we?

ASSUNTA No, you won't, will you? And how's little Rituccia today?

AMALIA Not at all well, I'm afraid. I don't like the look of her.

ASSUNTA Is Aunt Adelaide in there with her now?

AMALIA Yes. I asked her to pop in. Well, she's only just round the corner, isn't she? And she's so good with young children, isn't she?

ASSUNTA   Oh yes. She's got a way with them, you see. I think it's her voice and . . .

AMALIA   Why don't you nip back home, Assunta, and put that meat out of harm's way?

ASSUNTA   Ah yes, the meat. Silly me. I'd quite forgotten. Bye bye then.

AMALIA   Goodbye, Assunta. (ASSUNTA *exits to street. As she does so* TERESA *and* MARGHERITA *push past her and enter the room. They are two girls of* MARIA's *age, heavily made-up and flashily dressed with teetering high heels and short skirts.*)

TERESA   Hi there, Donna Amalia.

AMALIA   Good day to you, my dear.

MARGHERITA   Is Maria ready yet?

AMALIA   She was well on the way last time I saw her. (*Eyes their clothes coldly*) I see you're all dolled up in your Sunday best. So where are you gadding off to this time?

TERESA   Oh, we're just going for a little stroll round.

AMALIA   Really? You want to be careful of those little strolls of yours, you know. I keep trying to tell that to Maria, but I might as well be talking to a brick wall. And, by the way, who's this American sergeant I keep hearing about? Why has he never come round here? Why has he never introduced himself?

TERESA   I think he's a bit on the shy side, Donna Amalia. But he's a lovely fella. Oh yes, real nice he is. The trouble is he doesn't speak a word of Italian and I think he's a bit worried he might make a fool of himself in front of you, you see.

AMALIA   (*coldly*) I see.

MARGHERITA   It's not like what you think, Donna Amalia. The thing is he's had to send off for all the papers, you see, because over there you have to get the permission of the President himself in person before you can get married, you see. As soon as he gets the papers he'll be round here like a shot to ask you properly for her hand. Oh yes, he wants to do everything right and proper.

AMALIA Really? Is that so?

TERESA Oh yes. Now you're not to worry yourself, Donna Amalia. I know you say we've got to watch out and be careful, but it's not like that. Honestly. The point is they have a different way of looking at things, the Americans. They don't see anything wrong in putting their arms round you in the street. It's . . . well, it's just their way of being friendly, isn't it?

AMALIA Strange it's only girls they do it with. You never see them walking round with their arms round each other, do you? Still, I suppose it's their way of looking at things, eh?

TERESA Course it is, Donna Amalia, course it is. They have a whole different outlook on life from us. They're more relaxed. You know, they're more easy-going and . . . I don't know . . . free and easy. Anyway, Maria's got it made. They're going to get married and he's taking her back to America. Actually it was me he fell in love with first.

AMALIA Really?

TERESA Oh yes. Then he met Maria and said he liked her better. He was ever so honest about it. He said straight to my face: 'Your friend is much nicer than you.' Just like that. Wasn't it honest of him? Next evening he brought one of his mates with him and we got on like a house on fire. He fell in love with me on the spot. And I liked him much better than Maria's bloke. He was nicer, you see. So I said to him: 'Look, I've got this friend called Margherita. Can you find someone for her?' So he brought another mate along and now we're all fixed up – three blokes and three girls.

MARGHERITA I can't stand mine. He's too fat.

AMALIA Well, there's no problem there, dear. Have a word with Maria's bloke and tell him to find you something nicer. I'm sure he'd be only too happy to oblige. They're like that, the Americans, aren't they?

(*Enter* MARIA *from her room. She, too, is flashily dressed*)

So what time can I expect you back home?

MARIA I haven't a clue. I'll come back when I've done what I'm going out for. Right?

AMALIA (*moving towards* RITUCCIA'*s room*) I suppose you know your sister's poorly, do you?

MARIA Yes. I was aware of that.

AMALIA Good. Just as long as you bear it in mind while you're out taking your little stroll. (*Exits to* RITUCCIA'*s room*)

TERESA Right then. Are we all fit?

MARIA Yes. But I don't know why. It's a week now since I've seen him. We make a date, and he doesn't bother to turn up.

TERESA Well, maybe, he'll turn up today, Maria.

MARIA It's all the same to me. I couldn't care less. Ah, it's my own fault. I got myself into it, so I suppose I'll just have to get myself out of it. Still, I wouldn't half mind seeing him one last time. One last time and I could give him a real sharacking. A sharacking he'd remember for the rest of his life.

TERESA Well, I asked mine last night and he promised me faithful he'd bring yours today.

MARIA Look, I'm telling you. He's gone. He's vamoosed and he's not coming back. And in a couple of days yours'll have gone, too.

TERESA Well, if he has, good luck and good riddance.

MARGHERITA I can't stand mine. He's too fat.

TERESA Honest to God, Margherita, here we are up to our necks in it and all you can do is gripe about his weight.

MARGHERITA I know. And he's bald, too.

(*Enter from* RITUCCIA's *room* AMALIA *and* ADELAIDE *just as the girls are about to leave*)

AMALIA Hoi. You. Maria. Just make sure you're back at a decent time tonight. Understand?

MARIA Yes, mother, yes. As I said – I'll be back when I'm ready. Come on then, you two. Let's scoot. (*They exit into street*)

ADELAIDE Wasn't it lovely seeing her sleeping there so peaceful, bless her little cotton socks? You know, she doesn't look as feverish to me as she did. She seems better in herself, doesn't she?

AMALIA It's always the same with kids. One minute they're up. Next minute they're down. You never know where you are with them.

ADELAIDE Oh, you're right there, love. You're dead right. Now then, if there's anything else you want, please don't hesitate to ask, will you?

AMALIA Well, as a matter of fact, I was wondering if you'd mind sewing a button on this shirt of Amedeo's. (*She brings out a work basket and indicates the shirt and the button*) You'll find a needle and thread in the basket.

ADELAIDE I'll do it right away, love. Only too happy to oblige.

(*She sits at the table to start the work. Enter from street* FRANCO *carrying various packages of food. He is followed by the wine man with a cask of wine on his shoulders and carrying a length of rubber tubing for siphoning the wine into bottles. The wine man goes straight through into the scullery*)

FRANCO *(calling to wine man)* Okay, mate? You know
where to go? *(To* AMALIA*)* Donna Amalia, Don Errico
said to tell you it's the finest wine money can buy. I've
forgot its name, but I do know it's shit hot.

AMALIA That's just what I'd expect from Don Errico.
He's a man of real taste and discernment, you know.
(Bellowing into scullery) Oi, you! The flasks are all ready
and rinsed out. And don't break nothing or you'll get my
boot up your backside. *(Sweetly to* FRANCO*)* You were
saying?

FRANCO Well, I've got a load of gear for you, haven't I?
Six white loaves. Genuine army flour. The best I could
get and baked proper in a local bakery. *(She puts loaves
onto a shelf)* Now then, I've got a consignment of fags for
you from Teresino at Furcello. *(Hands over a carton of
American cigarettes)* Oh aye, and she asked me to give you
this note.

*(*AMALIA *takes the note and puts the cigarettes away in a
drawer. She makes a show of reading the letter, but it is obvious
she can't read)*

AMALIA I just can't see a thing in this light. Donna
Adelaide, see what it says, will you?

ADELAIDE Of course, love. Anything to oblige. Give it
here. *(She takes the note and she, too, has difficulty in reading it)*

FRANCO I tell you what, Donna Adelaide. That boy of
yours has managed to get his hands on a joint of lamb for
tonight. You should see it. Fit for Royalty it is. Bloody
enormous. I've taken it down to the baker's for roasting
and I'll be picking it up this evening round about half
seven. I'll bring it round with roast potatoes and all the
trimmings. I tell you, ladies, it's fit for Royalty, is that
joint of lamb.

AMALIA Good, good, I'm very pleased to hear it. Now,

Donna Adelaide, if you can't read it, don't just sit there staring at it. It won't read itself, you know.

ADELAIDE No, it's not that. It's this right eye of mine that's playing me up. I can't see out of it proper. It's all blurred and this letter's written in pencil, too. It's not in ink. It's in pencil, you see.

FRANCO I think I'll slip into the scullery and give old buggerlugs a hand. (*Exits*)

ADELAIDE Ah, here we are. I think I've got in the right light now. It's all a question of the right light, you see.

AMALIA Well, get cracking then.

ADELAIDE Right. (*Reading*) 'Dear Donna Amalia, these cigarettes were some I got from an American sergeant who brings things round. He wanted ten lire a packet more than the last time. So I said to him: "Whose side are you on? I thought you were supposed to be on ours." But I couldn't budge him. He said: "If you want them, that's the price you've got to pay. Take it or leave it." '

AMALIA God, what a song and dance she always makes about things. Long-winded old whorebag. Go on, Adelaide. Carry on.

ADELAIDE Right. Where was I? Ah yes, here we are. (*Reading*) 'So what could I do? You have to go along with it, or you end up undercutting one another, don't you? The punters'll have to go without for a day or two and then, God willing, we can all come out together with the new prices. Best wishes. PS: Let me know what you're charging for army blankets and the woollen mufflers, because with the cold weather coming along, the price will have to go up. And you'd better stock up with tomato puree for the winter.'

AMALIA I've already done it.

(*Enter* ASSUNTA *from the street*)

ASSUNTA   Aunt Adelaide, I've got all the potatoes
prepared, but I'd like you to come and check if you don't
mind.

ADELAIDE   (*getting up*) Right. I'll just put this sewing to
one side for a minute, Donna Amalia. If you want
anything else doing, just give me a call, won't you?

AMALIA   Well, if Rituccia wakes up . . .

ASSUNTA   Oh, I can cope with that. I don't mind. I'm
quite happy to sit with her.

ADELAIDE   There's a good girl. Isn't she a lovely girl,
Donna Amalia? Bless her, I could eat her I could. I could
eat her all up. See you later then. Bye. (*Exits*)

ASSUNTA   (*hesitantly*) Donna Amalia.

AMALIA   Yes?

ASSUNTA   There's something I wanted to ask you. What
it is, you see, is that . . . Oh I say, what a lovely smell.
You're wearing scent, aren't you? (*Goes to the dresser and its
multitude of bottles*) Oh, I do love things like this. I like to
call them toiletries, you know. (*Picks up bottle of eau de
cologne*) Is this what you're wearing? What a gorgeous
bottle. Ever so glamorous, isn't it? I suppose Don Errico
bought it for you, did he?

AMALIA   No, he did not. I bought it myself. With my own
money. What's Don Errico got to do with it?

ASSUNTA   Well, I mean to say . . . I mean . . . well,
everyone's talking, aren't they? They're saying things
about you and . . . and . . . Oh dear. (*She starts to giggle*)

AMALIA   What are people saying? Come on. Spit it out.
What are people saying?

ASSUNTA   Nothing. Honestly. It's just me. I'm always
putting my foot in it. Honestly. Aunt Adelaide's always
going on at me about the way I blurt things out I didn't
ought to. She says I talk too much. Don't take any notice
of me. Ignore me. It's just the way I am. I'm a bit scatty,

you see and . . . (*Her giggling turns into near hysterical laughter*) Oh dear. It's always the same. I just start laughing for no reason at all.

AMALIA   Why?

ASSUNTA   Oh, don't say things like that. It only makes matters worse. Oh dear, oh dear, I just don't know what comes over me. I don't. Honestly.

AMALIA   Assunta, I have to tell you there are times when you drive me clean up the wall.

ASSUNTA   I know. I can't help it. I do it to everyone. I think I must have a weakness somewhere. (*Struggles desperately to control her laughter. Finally succeeds*) There. It's over now. Fingers crossed, eh? Right. Well, what I wanted to ask you was . . . well, I was going to ask Aunt Adelaide, but she knows less than I do about it, and what you being a woman of the world and . . .

AMALIA   For heaven's sake, spit it out, will you?

ASSUNTA   Yes. Right. Well, what I wanted to know is this – am I a virgin?

AMALIA   How in God's name am I supposed to know?

ASSUNTA   Well, the thing is, you see, the thing is I got married by proxy.

AMALIA   What?

ASSUNTA   To Ernesto Santafede on the twenty-fourth of March 1941. He was on military service, you see, and . . . isn't that a lovely dress? Is it new?

AMALIA   Yes. The dressmaker came round with it special yesterday. Now get on with it, will you?

ASSUNTA   Yes, certainly. Well, the thing is, you see, he had to go off to North Africa while we were engaged, and that was the last I saw of him till after we were married. But we never got together properly as husband and wife, you see, because when he came back home on fourteen days leave, we were supposed to have this room all to

ourselves. Oh, it was a lovely room. Aunt Adelaide had
done it up special with clean sheets so we could . . . we
could . . . well, you know – so we could be alone. It was
so romantic. I'd got myself all dolled up really nice. I
used up a whole bottle of scent and then . . . (*Mimics
sound of air raid sirens*) . . . well, we had no time to do
anything except make a bolt for the shelter. We were
down there the whole fortnight he was on leave. And
then he had to go back. And I haven't seen or heard of
him since. Actually I tell a lie. He did get a message
through once. He didn't send it personal. It came via this
cousin by marriage of a friend of mine who was in Rome
at the time. And he bumped into this old lady who
happened to be coming through Naples on her way to
Calabria and . . .

AMALIA   Yes, yes, yes. But what was the message?

ASSUNTA   Well, there was nothing to it really. She said
he'd been taken prisoner. And then a friend of his who'd
come back from the front said he'd been killed. And then
someone else said they'd seen him alive. And then
someone else said . . . So what I'm asking is this – am I
technically a virgin or not?

AMALIA   Of course you are, if you haven't been with your
husband properly. But until you know one way or the
other what's happened to him, you're still a married
woman.

ASSUNTA   Oh, I see.

AMALIA   You can't get married again, if that's what
you're thinking.

ASSUNTA   Oh no. I don't want to get married again. I
couldn't anyway. Out of respect. (*Shows* AMALIA *her
husband's photograph in a locket she's wearing round her neck*)
See? That's him. The one with the bemused expression.
That's why I always wear mourning. Except when

someone comes along and tells me he's alive. Then I take it off. Then someone else says, no, he isn't, and so back it goes on again. It's on off, on off all the time. It's making me dizzy. It's ridiculous. I just want to be one thing or the other. Not that anyone notices. Who cares about me? Who gives a fig?

(*Enter* ERRICO *from the street. He wears a flashy light grey suit with a flower in his buttonhole, an expensive hat, a brightly coloured tie and yellow shoes. He has an enormous diamond ring on his finger and comes in slowly as though he owns the place. He's very pleased with himself and conscious that he has all the women of Naples eating out of his hand*)

ERRICO   Donna Amalia! Here I am. All yours.

AMALIA   My oh my, Don Errico. Just look at you. Happy birthday, my dear.

ERRICO   Thank you. Thirty-six today. Getting on a bit, eh?

ASSUNTA   Thirty-six? That's not old. You're still in your prime. You've got years to go before your teeth start to drop out.

AMALIA   (*hurriedly*) I was expecting you sooner, Errico.

ERRICO   Well, I did try. I wanted to thank you for that enormous bunch of roses you sent round this morning. And, of course, for all the trouble you've gone to over my birthday. I mean, having it in your own house and everything, it's . . .

AMALIA   It's no trouble at all, Errico. Good Lord, you can't spend your birthday on your own. You have to spend it here with us like one of the family.

ERRICO   I'm very touched, Amalia. But I don't want you putting yourself out on my account. There's no need to. Amedeo and I are seeing to everything. All you've got to do is sit there and look stunning. (*He sits at the table*) Yes, as I was saying, I did try to get round earlier, but I got held up. I had these trucks leaving for Calabria, and you know how it is – if I'm not there while they're loading, things have a mysterious way of going missing. Anyway, I got all that sorted out, and then, bugger me, I had to waste half a day chasing round after a permit. And you know what that's like. Filling in forms, dealing with clerks. (*Mimes the dishing out of back-handers*) Dear God, what a palaver. Anyway, while I was waiting for the documentation I nipped round to the jeweller. I want to talk to you about that later by the way when . . . (*Nods towards* ASSUNTA) So when it was all over, I went home to change into something a bit more presentable, and here I am. Amedeo back yet?

AMALIA   No. He went out first thing this morning, and I haven't seen him since.

ERRICO   Fine, fine. (*To* ASSUNTA) Haven't you got a home of your own to go? (ASSUNTA *is not sure how to respond*)

AMALIA   She's here in case Rituccia wakes up.

ERRICO   Ah yes. And how is Rituccia today?

ASSUNTA   She's a bit better, thank you. Listen, I'll go if I'm not wanted. I know I've got to make myself scarce when you're around. Well, with you two being . . . well, you know . . . I mean . . . Oh dear. Here it comes again. (*Breaks out into laughter again*)

AMALIA   Jesus Christ, you're not starting that again?

ASSUNTA   I can't help it. What am I supposed to do? It's a weakness. It just comes over me. I just laugh for no reason at all. People don't believe me, but it's true. I'm sorry, but . . . but . . . excuse me, I've got to go. (*Exits to street still giggling*)

ERRICO   Has she got a bloody screw loose or something? (*FRANCO comes in from scullery with wine man who carries the empty flask on his shoulder*)

FRANCO   Right then. That's it. You're all bottled up out there.

ERRICO   (*handing him a bank note for the wine man*) Here, Give him this.

FRANCO   (*hands note to wine man*) Say ta very much to the gentleman. (*The wine man nods his thanks furiously and exits to street*) He's dumb, poor sod. Anything else you want?

ERRICO   No. Hang about outside. I'll give you a call, if I need you.

FRANCO   Whatever you say, boss. (*Exits to street*)

ERRICO   Amalia, Amalia, at last. At long last we're . . . (*Enter from street PEPPE and FEDERICO in animated conversation*)

PEPPE   Nothing doing, mate.

FEDERICO   What's the matter with you? I'll write you a cheque. I'll do it now.

PEPPE   I don't want a cheque. Not unless it's for two hundred and thirty thousand lire. I'm not letting them go for less than that.

FEDERICO   You're talking a load of bollocks, man. (*To AMALIA*) Two coffees, if you please, Donna Amalia. (*AMALIA goes to get them*) Hey, Errico! How's it going, old cock?

ERRICO   It was going extremely well till you came in.

PEPPE   Course it was. He's a bloody nuisance, him. Listen. About this deal. Forget it. If you don't want to pay the fair price, stuff it.

FEDERICO   But it's only five tyres.

PEPPE   Nine. Nine tyres. And all brand new. They're all straight from the factory. Not a mark on them. They've never been used. Old Errico here knows what they're worth, if you don't.

FEDERICO   Now look here, with all due respect to present company, I do not need a second party to tell me what those tyres are worth. I know their value.

ERRICO   Dear oh dear. Just look at you two. Don't you think it mightn't be a bad idea if you tried to get your act together?

PEPPE   That's what I'm saying, Errico. That's just what I'm saying. By the way, what do you think to that Fiat?

ERRICO   Well, I had a run in it. It's in the garage now. I wouldn't go above seven hundred thousand for it.

PEPPE   But that's what I was asking.

ERRICO   In that case this is your lucky day, eh? (*Takes out a wad of banknotes and hands two to Peppe*) I think you'll find that's correct.

PEPPE   Great. There you are, you see, mate. Thank God for someone who doesn't fart about. It's a right pain in the backside trying to do business with you.

FEDERICO   All right, all right. (*Takes out cheque book and writes out a cheque*) Two hundred and thirty thousand lire. On the nail. Right? My God, what we could do with Don Gennaro now and one of his famous legal whatshis-names. Oh boy, oh boy, could we do with him now. (*Enter* AMEDEO *from street. He, too, is dressed sharply*)

AMEDEO   Hello there, chaps. (*He goes to a chest of drawers, looking anxiously for something in it. With great relief he finds it. It is a small package wrapped in newspaper*) Thank God for that. I thought I'd lost it.

(*Enter* RICCARDO *from street. He is rather subdued. He is thin and pale and shabbily dressed*)

RICCARDO   Good day to you all. Not interrupting any-thing, am I?

(AMALIA *is furious to see him and exchanges glances with*
ERRICO)

AMALIA Good day, Don Riccardo. Were you wanting
something? (RICCARDO *indicates that he would like to talk
to her alone*) Very well. If you can wait a minute.

RICCARDO Oh, of course. Certainly. I don't mind waiting. I'm at your convenience, Donna Amalia.

PEPPE (*to* AMEDEO) Can we have a chat this evening?

AMEDEO Well, we've got people coming round. I suppose
you could always come, too.

PEPPE I *am* coming, prat. I've already been invited.

AMEDEO Great. We can talk then.

PEPPE Yes. But not in here. (*Furtively*) There's a little job
coming up tonight. Five new tyres.

AMEDEO Let's talk about it outside.

PEPPE Right. Donna Amalia, I'll pay for the coffee.
(*Hands her money*) You don't happen to have any cigarettes, do you?

AMALIA Sorry, I'm just out. I'm waiting for my supplier.

PEPPE Ah, I see. They've all gone under the counter,
have they?

FEDERICO Surprise surprise.

PEPPE Right then. Are we off?

FEDERICO Sure. Are you coming or staying. Amedeo?

ERRICO Amedeo's staying. I want a word with him.

PEPPE Right. See you all tonight then. (*To* FEDERICO)
Okay then, we'll sling our hooks. (*They exit to street
chattering*)

AMALIA Now then, Don Riccardo, what can I do for
you?

RICCARDO It's about the arrangement we made.

AMEDEO (*to* ERRICO) I'll be outside when you want me.
(*He makes to go then remembers his package*) Struth, I almost

forgot my dosh. There's three hundred thousand lire in there. (*Realises the mistake he's made in front of Riccardo*) Yes. Well. It's not mine, of course.

AMALIA   (*furious with him over his gaffe*) I should think not indeed. Three hundred thousand lire! When have we ever owned money like that?

AMEDEO   Exactly. (*To* RICCARDO) It doesn't belong to me. No, it belongs to someone else. He asked me to look after it for him. I'm doing him a favour. Yes. Well. I'll be off. (*He takes the package and hurries off into the street*)

AMALIA   So, Don Riccardo, we'll try again, shall we?

RICCARDO   Yes. (*Hesitates then blurts out*) It's not that I've any right. God knows, I haven't. I've no right at all, but . . . but I was wondering if I could make an appeal to your better nature, Donna Amalia.

(AMALIA *sits down at the table, half turning her back on* RICCARDO *as if not interested.* ERRICO *adopts a similar position smoking contentedly*)

How can I put it? Well, when I first found myself short of funds some time ago, you were kind enough to suggest that I dispose of one of the two small apartments I owned. You said you knew someone who might be interested in buying. Well, there was nothing else I could do. I was desperate. So I did as you suggested. I sold the apartment. We struggled on for a while and then – calamity. Disaster. I lost my job and I had to sell the second apartment. Donna Amalia, I know it was you who bought the properties. Good luck to you. I hope they give you years and years of enjoyment. I really do.

ERRICO   Get on with it, Don Riccardo.

RICCARDO   Yes. Well, things got even worse and you were kind enough to make me an advance of forty thousand lire on the house where I live presently with my

family. I was extremely grateful. Believe me, I was quite
happy to sign an agreement undertaking to repay the
loan within six months. Well, as you know, that period
elapsed three weeks ago and ... and ... (*Suddenly
passionately*) Donna Amalia, your lawyers have sent me a
letter demanding I pay a monthly rental of four thousand
lire or they'll force me to vacate the premises. Surely to
God, you're not telling me that you're going to seize my
home and throw me and my family out on the streets for
a measly forty thousand lire? Surely you haven't got the
heart to do that?

ERRICO Yes, but it's not just forty thousand lire, is it, old
man? The agreement stated specifically that if the forty
thousand lire you've already had isn't paid back within
the required time, then Donna Amalia here has the
option of buying the property outright for a further
payment of fifty thousand lire. That's my understanding
of it. So it's very simple, old man – take the fifty thousand
lire and find somewhere else.

RICCARDO Find somewhere else? With a wife and three
small children? You can't be serious.

ERRICO Well, what's the alternative, old man?

RICCARDO Look. Here's ten thousand seven hundred
lire. (*Takes money out of his briefcase*) I've sold a couple of
jackets and a pair of winter trousers. I didn't get much,
but you know how much things fetch these days. It's all
you can do to ... Look, I can offer this to Donna Amalia
on account of what I owe her. I've still got eighty
thousand lire due to me in back pay. It should be only a
matter of days before it comes through.

AMALIA That's all very well. But this money was due
three weeks ago.

RICCARDO Donna Amalia, you must believe me when I
say I simply could not raise the money at the time. It was

totally impossible. Surely you understand my position? I'm asking you a favour. Just one small favour, Donna Amalia.

(*No reply. He seems to crumple. He speaks as though talking to himself*)

Moving house? It's just a pipe dream. Once upon a time it was no problem. It was simplicity itself. If the house you were in was too cramped or wasn't up to standard, you changed it for something better. You could go anywhere. Because your roots and your heart and your soul were in Naples, one district was just as good as the other. Yes, once upon a time you could go out in the evening for a quiet stroll and you'd meet other people and they'd be calm and tranquil and you'd say hello and you'd smile and you'd chat. You had the feeling – we're all in this together, we've all got each other's interests at heart, we all care about each other and grieve with each other and . . . and . . . Once upon a time you could stroll round the shops looking in the windows. You didn't have to buy anything. You weren't envious or resentful about things you couldn't afford. If you saw something you fancied, you'd say: 'Oh, that's nice. We'll save up and buy it later.' But now? Moving house? How can you move house when that's the only place on earth where you feel any security? Now the moment you set one foot outside your own front door you feel as though you're in a foreign country. Once upon a time. Oh yes, once upon a time.

ERRICO Well, it's nothing to do with me, old man. It's for Donna Amalia to make the decision.

RICCARDO Donna Amalia, I'm pleading with you. Here's ten thousand seven hundred lire. Take it on account. Please. It's not for my sake. It's for the sake of my children. My children are starving. Right now at this moment there is nothing for them to eat.

AMALIA Oh yes, this is all very well. All this fine talk. All this eloquence. All this drama and tragedy. Well, listen to me, sunshine, you weren't behind the door when it came to grabbing the money I offered you. You knew when you were onto a good thing. Okay, so it was me bought your two apartments. What are you suggesting – that you weren't paid for them? (*Before he can answer she ploughs on with increasing anger*) You make me sick. You make me want to throw up. When we were starving, did we come grovelling to you? Did we come whingeing and whining? I suppose my children never went hungry, did they? Oh no, they never had to go without, did they? And you? While we were pinching and scraping, having to eat any old shit we could lay our hands on, you were in your secure and comfy well-paid job, weren't you, and you'd all the time in the world to gossip and go window shopping. You piss me off. All you had to do was find the money you owed me, and the house would still be yours. Well, you haven't, have you? So go round to my lawyers, collect your fifty thousand lire and get out of my hair. On the other hand if you want to stay on in the house to remind you of the times you were doing fine and dandy and we were wondering where the next meal was coming from, then pay the rent. That's all you've got to do, sunshine – pay the rent. If you can't, that's you problem. It's not mine. Right? So just go, will you? Bugger off. (*She pushes him towards the street door*) Clear off out of it. Out, out.

RICCARDO All right, I'll go. I don't want to be a nuisance. I don't want to upset you. I'll start looking for somewhere at once. I'll call on your lawyers tomorrow and . . . and . . . Goodbye, Donna Amalia. (*Exits*)

AMALIA Goodbye. And bloody good riddance, too. Thick. Thick as shit, he is. Ah, forget him. Now then, Errico, you were saying you went to the jewellers.

ERRICO That's right. I took him two diamonds I bought six months ago. And on top I paid him four hundred thousand lire for these little beauties. (*Shows her two stones wrapped in tissue paper*) Look at them. At a rough guess, worth at least three and a half million.

AMALIA They're beautiful.

ERRICO Not a flaw in them. (AMALIA *has a quick look outside and then lifts a floor tile by the bed. She takes out a small bag in which she keeps her valuables*)

AMALIA You can't be too careful, eh? (*She puts the diamonds in the bag and replaces it, taking care to see that the tile lies flat on the floor*) So they're really for me, are they? They're all mine.

ERRICO Of course. It's your share of the profits. That's the way it has to be, if you want to regularise our partnership. And I'm not just talking about business.

AMALIA Errico, you know perfectly well what my feelings are to you. When you look at me that way, don't you understand that my heart melts and my knees tremble and I feel a long slow aching in my heart? Do you really think I don't want you just as much as you want me? But what can we do? What can we do? (*Pause*) Look, business is going well. I do the buying and the selling and you see to the delivery side. Fine. Great. We're doing marvellously out of it. So why spoil it by doing something we know is wrong? I've got grown-up children, Errico. What would they say? And then there's Gennaro. What about him?

ERRICO For Christ's sake, it's more than a year since you heard from Gennaro. I'm not trying to be a wet blanket, Ama, but don't tell me that if he were alive, he wouldn't

have found some way of getting in touch with you and
letting you know where he was. Course he would. Be
practical. Face up to facts. He went out the morning of
the air raid and nothing's been heard of him since. All
right, he could have been captured by the Germans. But
what would they want with him? He'd be just as big a
bloody nuisance to them as he was to us. No, Ama, he's
stopped a bullet on the road. He's been killed by a bomb
or ripped to shreds by shrapnel. Anything could have
happened to him. He's a goner. Kaput. Goodbye, Gennaro, nice to have known you.

AMALIA   What about this then? (*She gets a letter from the
drawer of the dresser*) It's addressed to Gennaro. It came
three days ago. I opened it in case there was any news
about him. Maria says it's from someone who's been with
him all the time till quite recently. He sends him his
regards and all his news. Gennaro must have given him
our address. And not long ago either. He's alive, Errico.
He must be. The fact that he hasn't been in touch is . . .
is . . . well, he's not been able to, has he? He's alive. I
know it. And one fine day he's going to turn up here. You
mark my words. He's going to walk through that door
with his shuffle and his stoop and his . . . I know it. I just
know it.

ERRICO   And you'd like that, wouldn't you?

AMALIA   I don't know. How can I know? I tell you one
thing, though – there'll be none of that old nonsense of:
'Oh, Ama, what are you up to now? I don't mind you
doing so and so, but I do mind you doing such and such.'
Christ, he'll be under my feet morning, noon and night.

ERRICO   Well, there's your answer then.

AMALIA   (*carried away by her mimicry*) 'It's too risky, Ama.'
'Be careful what you're doing, Ama.' 'Watch out for this.
Watch out for that.'

ERRICO   Is that the only reason you're worried about him?

AMALIA   There's any number of reasons.

ERRICO   But they don't include me? (AMALIA *is unable to keep up the pretence. She slowly and sensuously puts her arms around him*)

AMALIA   Oh yes, Errico. You're well and truly included, my dear.

(ERRICO *clasps her tightly and kisses her long and hard and passionately. Enter* FRANCO *from the street, feeling in his trouser pockets and making for the scullery. When he sees them he stops dead in his tracks. Not knowing what to do, he tiptoes back, stands by the open door and turns his back to them. A customer bursts in from the street*)

CUSTOMERAF54Hi there. Is there a coffee going?

(FRANCO *springs across and hastily bundles him out, slamming the door*)

FRANCO   (*shouting after him*) We're closed. Try the place on the corner. (*Meanwhile* ERRICO *and* AMALIA *have leapt apart.* AMALIA *exits to her room*)

ERRICO   What the hell are you doing here?

FRANCO   I left my matches in the scullery.

ERRICO   Well, go and get them.

FRANCO   It's not all that important really. I can always . . . (*Sees* ERRICO's *menacing look*) . . . All right. I'll go and get them. (*Exits to scullery as* AMEDEO *enters from street*)

AMEDEO   You still want that chat?

ERRICO   Yes I do. And it's important.

AMEDEO   Oh?

ERRICO Look, my lad, I've been round a bit longer than you. I was brought up on the streets. You weren't.

AMEDEO So?

ERRICO So, reading books is fine. But books don't tell you everything. Oh no. In these parts you learn by keeping your eyes open and keeping your wits about you and listening to people who know a damn sight more about life than you do. So you listen to me. Listen good and hard. You, my lad, are heading for trouble.

AMEDEO Heading for trouble? What do you mean?

ERRICO You're going round with Peppe. Peppe 'The Jack'.

AMEDEO So?

ERRICO Dear God, you're just a babe in arms, you. A total bloody innocent. You know what's going to happen to you? You're going to end up in clink.

AMEDEO Clink?

ERRICO Where do you think Peppe gets his nickname from?

AMEDEO (obviously lying) His nickname? I never thought of it.

ERRICO Then I'll tell you. He's called Peppe 'The Jack' because whenever he spots a likely-looking car, the pair of you wait till after dark and he gets under it and lifts it up with his shoulders while you scamper underneath and whip the tyres off.

AMEDEO Who me? (Enter AMALIA from her room having tidied herself up)

ERRICO It's high time you were taught a few of the facts of life, my old son. (Takes him by the arm and leads him to street door) We're just off out for a minute, Donna Amalia.

AMEDEO You've got it all wrong. You don't know what you're talking about.

ERRICO Come on, big cheese. Out. (They exit as MARIA

*enters without talking to them. It's obvious that something is
wrong.* FRANCO *enters from the scullery, crosses the room and
exits into the street*)

AMALIA   You're back early. (MARIA *grunts*) So what did
he have to say then, this fiancé of yours?

MARIA   There is no fiancé. He's gone. For good.

AMALIA   (*with heavy irony*) Oh dear, oh dear, what a blow.
You'll have to find yourself another one now, won't you?

MARIA   It's got nothing to do with you. It's my life, not
yours. I'll do as I like. You mind your own business.

AMALIA   Ah, my poor angel. Mama's little cherub. She'd
quite set her mind on it, hadn't she? America, here I
come. Well, what's coming now, my sweetheart?

MARIA   Trouble.

AMALIA   Trouble? What trouble?

MARIA   You should have taken more interest in me,
shouldn't you?

AMALIA   What the hell are you talking about? What have
you been up to?

MARIA   You should have taken more notice of me when I
was going out with my mates. But no. You were just glad
to see the back of me, weren't you? It was all so very
convenient for you, wasn't it? You should have taken
notice of me. But no, it was business business all the
time. Making money. Piling up the dough. That's all you
thought about. Well, you should have thought about me.

AMALIA   You've got the cheek to stand there and tell me I
didn't care about you? Me who worked myself into the
ground to give you a decent home and feed you and
clothe you. Me, who thought about you every single
second of the day.

MARIA   I don't know how you found the time. I really
don't. Not with having to think about Errico every single
second of the day as well.

AMALIA   What's Errico got to do with it? Look, you can get this into your head right here and now. Errico is a business partner. Nothing more. Nothing less. He is simply a business partner. Understand? (MARIA *shrugs*) And now, madame, let's talk about you, shall we? Let's talk about your trouble. When did it start? Where did it start?

MARIA   Here.

AMALIA   Here?

MARIA   In the evenings. When you were out with Errico. Gadding round in flashy cars. Having meals at his house. Discussing 'business'.

AMALIA   I don't believe this. I do not believe it. You did it here? In this house? You little trollop. You filthy little whore. You've got the impudence to stand there and come out with it just like that. And then you talk about me. You're not fit to live under the same roof as me, you dirty little tart. I've a good mind to beat the living daylights out of you.

MARIA   Go on then. And bring Errico over while you're about it. Let him have a go, too. After all, you've given him the right, haven't you?

AMALIA   You slut. You filthy little cowbag.

MARIA   I'm no more of a slut than you.

AMALIA   I'll kill you. Do you hear me? I'll bloody well kill you. (*She makes a move towards* MARIA *who dashes off into scullery.* AMALIA *chases after her and we hear them screeching and bawling. At the same time there are voices in the street*)

VOICES   It is him, I tell you . . . He's back. Good God, he's back . . . Don Gennaro, where have you been all this time? . . . I don't believe it. We all thought you must be dead . . . It's you, Don Gennaro. It's you.

GENNARO   (*offstage*) Yes, it's me. And I'm still alive. (ADELAIDE *comes bursting in from the street*)

ADELAIDE Donna Ama! Amedeo! Maria! Where is everyone? Oi, where are you all? Donna Ama, Donna Ama. (AMALIA *enters from the scullery*)

AMALIA What's all this racket? What's going on?

ADELAIDE It's your husband. He's back. Don Gennaro's back.

(GENNARO *comes in from the street, a little dazed by it all. He is wearing worn and tattered clothes. He has an Italian army forage cap, American army trousers and a camouflage German windcheater. He is much thinner than in Act One and utterly exhausted. He is carrying a bundle over his shoulder with a billy can attached to it*)

GENNARO (*to the people in the street*) Thank you. Thank you so much. You're very kind. I'll tell you all about it later. Yes, later on I'll tell you everything that's happened.

(*He is pulled up short by the changes in the room and fails to recognise* AMALIA *in her new finery. He makes to withdraw, thinking he has come to the wrong house*)

Oh, I'm sorry. Do forgive me. I'm so sorry.

ADELAIDE (*tugging him back*) It's all right, Don Gennaro. Come on in. This is your house, you silly old bugger. It's your home. Look. There's your wife over there. (GENNARO *and* AMALIA *stare at each other speechless*)

AMALIA (*quietly, overcome and unable to believe her eyes*) Genna.

GENNARO Ama, Ama. I didn't recognise you. I didn't . . . Oh, Ama, Ama. It's been an eternity. (*They embrace in tearful silence*)

AMALIA Come and sit down. Rest yourself. Tell us all about it. Tell us where you've been.

GENNARO Not just like that, Ama. I wouldn't know where to begin. I'd be here till kingdom come, if I were to tell you everything that's happened. It's only just over a year, but it seems like a lifetime. I feel as if I've been away for ever. If I had to write it down, I'd be here till doomsday. But it's all here, Ama. In my mind's eye. I can see it all. (*Taps his head*) It's all stored away up here. But where do I start? How do I start? All this. It belongs to a different world. You. The house. The street. The people I knew. I need time. Tell me all about you and the children. How they are – Amedeo, Maria, Rituccia?

AMALIA   Rituccia is rather poorly.

GENNARO   Poorly? What's wrong with her?

AMALIA   Oh, it's nothing. It's only a bit of a fever. One of these things kids pick up from time to time.

GENNARO   My little girl. (*Points to her room*) In there, is she?

AMALIA   Yes. She's sleeping. (*He nods and shuffles off into* RITUCCIA'*s room*)

ADELAIDE   Poor man. Poor old sod. He's as thin as a rake. All skin and bone, he is. It brings tears to your eyes. It does. Poor soul. Well, I must be off, Donna Amalia. I've got to attend to my potatoes, haven't I? See you later then, love. (*She exits to the street, pausing to speak to the Madonna*) Madonna, we commit him into your hands. Amen.

AMALIA   (*calls to* MARIA *in the scullery*) You! Come out of there. Your father's back. (*Enter* MARIA, *drying her eyes and tidying her hair*)

MARIA   Papa?

AMALIA   Yes. Now pull yourself together. And don't you dare say a word to him about what's happened. It'll be the death of him in his state now. (AMEDEO *comes rushing in from the street*)

AMEDEO   What's going on? They say father's back. (GENNARO *comes out of* RITUCCIA'*s room*)

GENNARO She doesn't look at all well to me, Ama. I don't like the way she's breathing. I don't . . . (*He sees* AMEDEO) Amedeo!

AMEDEO Papa! (*They hug each other*)

GENNARO Oh, Amedeo, this is a dream come true.

AMEDEO It's wonderful to see you, papa. (GENNARO *sees* MARIA, *standing by herself in a corner*)

GENNARO Maria. It's me, your papa. I've come home. (MARIA *rushes to him and he hugs both his children*) If only you knew. Oh, if only you knew. I'll tell you all about it later. (*He lets them go and begins to prowl round the room, taking in all the alterations*) My little room! What's happened to my little room?

AMALIA Well, you weren't here and . . .

GENNARO Very true. I wasn't here. But, oh, my little room. What a pity you've gone. (*He continues his prowl*) My word, you've certainly made it look very nice while I've been away. It's lovely.

AMEDEO Papa, papa, we're dying to know. Where have you been all this time?

GENNARO Where have I been? I wish I knew. I don't know where to start the story. I'm confused, you see. Shall we sit down.

(*They sit down and wait for him to begin. He struggles to get his thoughts in order*)

You remember when they evacuated the houses along the coast road? Everyone was given an hour and a half to get out. Do you remember? Streams and streams of people with bundles and suitcases and children.

AMALIA I remember, Genna.

GENNARO Well, I was caught up in it. I was coming back from Frattamaggiore. I'd got about ten kilos of apples with me and I was loaded up with bread as well.

And you know how far it is. I was ready to drop.
Anyway, suddenly out of nowhere there was this rumour
that they were starting to shell us with naval guns. 'The
shelter quick.' 'Quick, let's get to the shelters. The
Americans are shelling us.' The first thing I thought
about was you. All I wanted to do was get back home to
you and the kids. Christ, what was happening? Shelter?
What shelter? Bombs can drop anywhere. You can be
bombed from the sea, from the air, from the ground.
Landmines, you see. Landmines. All I wanted to do was
to get home. And so there I was staggering along under
the weight of fourteen kilos of apples and bread. Shooting. It was going on all over the place. It was all hell let
loose. They were firing from the rooftops, from windows,
from cellars. People running for dear life. Machine guns.
Germans. Dead bodies. And in the middle of it I . . .
Well, I came a purler. Arse over tit I went. Christ, there
was bread and apples everywhere. I hit the ground with
my head and did all this. (*He shows them where his head was
split wide open*) I remember seeing blood all over my hands
and hearing the shooting. And then I lost consciousness.
God knows who ended up with the apples. When I came
too, I felt as if I were suffocating. I could hear voices and
people shouting and screaming. I wanted to move, but I
couldn't. I knew my legs were still there, but I couldn't
feel them. Perhaps I was under the rubble somewhere
when the shelter was hit. What shelter? Then suddenly I
heard what sounded like the rumble of a train. In the
distance, it was. It kept getting louder and louder and the
ground started quivering so I shut my eyes and listened.
Could it really be a train? I could hear the rattle of the
wheels. It was a train. I wasn't in a shelter. I was in a
train. There was this dim light that seemed to keep
flashing on and off. How long it went on for I don't know.

Then everything went quiet. I felt freer. There was room
to move. It was getting lighter and I could breathe again.
People were moving, getting off the train. So I got off
with them. Where was I? God knows. They treated my
injury in a first-aid unit somewhere and then after a
couple of days this German sergeant came up and asked
me what my trade was. I thought suddenly: Dear Christ,
if I tell him I'm a tram driver, he's going to say: 'We
don't have trams here, pal. So you're no use to us, are
you?' (*Pretends to aim a sten gun*) Rattatattatattat. Goodbye, Gennaro. Goodbye, old son. So I squared my
shoulders, puffed out my chest and I said: 'I'm a
labourer, mate. I hump stones. I'm a humper of stones.'
And so I humped stones. My God, it was no joke, Ama.
No food. Nothing to drink. Air-raids every five minutes. I
think this German sergeant took a shine to me because he
was always coming across for a chat. I couldn't understand a word he said, so I just said Yes and No when it
seemed appropriate. That went on for three months. And
then one day some of us – all from Naples – well, we
managed to escape. Someone said: 'Christ, they're firing
at us.' And I said: 'Let them. We'd be better off dead.' It
was no life, Ama. It was no life. We moved at night
mostly from one village to the next. We picked up lifts
wherever we could – farm carts, trains, anything. And
then we were on foot. Walking, walking, walking. The
destruction, Ama. The desolation. You've never seen
anything like it. Whole villages wiped out. Children with
nowhere to go. Shootings. Bodies everywhere. Theirs.
Ours. I've never seen so many dead bodies. People all
look the same when they're dead, Ama. I'm not the same
person any more. It's done something to me. Do you
remember last time? I served all through the war last
time, and when I got back, I was full of it. I couldn't stop

talking about it. I was like a madman, blazing with anger, picking fights with everyone. But not this time. This isn't war. This is something entirely different. It's something we'll never ever properly understand. I'm fifty-two, and it's only now I feel I've really grown up. (*Pause as he struggles with his thoughts again*) War takes away all desire to hurt people. All you want to do is to be kind. Oh, Ama, don't let's do harm to anybody. Don't let's hurt them. (*He breaks down in tears*)

AMALIA   It's all right, Genna. It's all right, my love.

AMEDEO   Papa, papa.

GENNARO   What was I saying? Where did I get to? Ah yes – village to village. And I got friendly with someone and he and I found a deserted stable and we used to sleep in it. In the mornings I'd go and look for work and come back in the evening. And then I realised he never went out at all. Never ever. He'd got hold of some bits of wood and made a sort of rabbit hutch for himself in a corner. At night he used to talk in his sleep. 'Help. Help. Leave ma alone.' He used to wake me up with it. You know what it was, Ama? He was a Jew.

AMALIA   Poor man.

GENNARO   We'd known each other for a couple of months before he told me. I'd get back in the evening with bread and cheese or fruit or whatever I could get hold of, and we'd make a meal of it together. After a time we became real buddies. We shared everything. But he'd got it into his head that I was going to denounce him to the Germans. He used to look at me as though he were raving mad. He'd be as white as a sheet with his eyes all bloodshot and terrified out of his wits. Petrified. One morning he grabbed hold of me. 'You denounce me,' he screamed. 'I don't denounce you. Why do you denounce me?' It was terrible to see, Ama. This man with grown-up children. He showed me their photograph. A fine-looking man with iron-grey hair, and he was crying his heart out. What have we allowed to happen, Ama? What have we come to? It's going to have to be paid for one day. I can see him now, pleading with me. I tried to make him understand. 'I wouldn't denounce you. Christ, what do you think I am?' But no. Nothing would convince him. He just had this one thought in his head all the time. And so it went on – one village to another. We even crossed the enemy lines without meaning to. The first we noticed was when we saw the soldiers were wearing different uniforms. I can't tell you the relief. We just flung our arms round each other in sheer joy. We'd become like two brothers. I gave him my address. 'Just in case,' I said. 'Just in case.'

AMALIA   That explains this then. (*Holds up letter*) It came the other day. It must be from him. (*Hands letter to* GENNARO)

GENNARO   Yes, yes, this is from him all right. So he got back safely. Good. That's good. (*Reads*) 'Dear Gennaro, I imagine you will by now be back home with your wife and your family and send you my greetings and warmest good wishes.' He was as good as his word, you see. 'Your wife and children, whatever they may have been through, will, I am sure have been fully worthy of their sufferings and your own.'

(*They all react with uneasy guilt*)

'The joy of you having returned will make up for all their anxieties. I am well.'

AMEDEO   (*half relieved that it's all over*) Well then, papa, it sounds as though you've really been through it, eh?

GENNARO   Oh, you've not heard the half of it, my son. I haven't even scratched the surface.

AMEDEO Yes, but you're back home with us now, papa. You don't have to think about it any more.

GENNARO Not think about it? You must be joking. As if I could ever forget one single second of it.

AMEDEO But it's all over now, papa. Relax.

GENNARO No, no, you're wrong. It's not all over. You haven't seen what I've seen. The war is not over by a long chalk.

AMEDEO Papa, don't upset yourself. There's absolutely nothing to worry about now.

GENNARO Maybe, maybe. Anyway, I'm alive. I'm still alive. God, the number of times I missed being killed by the skin of my teeth. And if they'd got me, I'd never have seen all this, would I? (*He looks round the room with wonder*) All the new decorations. All the new furniture. And Maria in her new dress. And Amedeo here, so smart, so dashing. And you, Ama, looking like a great lady in that lovely dress and all that jewellery. (*He looks closer*) Are those diamonds? Christ, those are diamonds.

AMALIA Well, yes . . . they're sort of diamonds. (*Long pause as he takes it all in and looks at the others.* MARIA *avoids looking at him*)

GENNARO Is there something you should be telling me, Ama?

AMALIA What is there to tell you, Genna? We're a little better off than we were, that's all. Amedeo's working and doing quite well. And I've got a nice little business going now as well.

GENNARO I see. So do I have to go away and be given up for dead all over again?

AMALIA Gennaro! What on earth are you saying?

GENNARO I'm not going to play the corpse again. I don't like being a corpse. It brings bad luck.

AMALIA Gennaro, don't be so silly. It's lovely to have

you back. We're all thrilled to bits. Things have changed
a little, that's all. We've got the British here, and the
Americans.

GENNARO   But of course. They've all come to help us.
They said they would, and they have. They've kept their
word. Bravo. So, Amalia, you say you've got a business
going. Tell me about it.

AMEDEO   She's in partnership with Errico.

AMALIA   That's right. We decided to go into partnership.
He's coming and going all the time with his trucks, so it
seemed a good idea for him to look after the delivery side
of things.

GENNARO   Trucks? He's got trucks?

AMALIA   From the Americans.

GENNARO   Ah, so you've formed a company with trucks
supplied by the Americans?

AMALIA   Oh yes. We only have to mention we'd like a
couple of lorries, and they give them to us just like that.

GENNARO   Good, good. They really kept their promise.
Good. (*To* AMEDEO) And what have you been doing,
Amedeo, since I've been away?

AMEDEO   Oh this and that. I sort of deal in second-hand
cars sort of thing. If I see a car I like the look of, I try and
find someone who's interested in doing a deal cash down
and then . . . (*Diverting attention to* MARIA) Maria's got a
wonderful surprise for you, papa. She's going to America,
aren't you Maria? She's got herself engaged to a Yankee
soldier.

(MARIA *tries to avoid looking at* GENNARO, *and* AMALIA
would like to die)

GENNARO   You? You're going to leave me? Papa's little
girl, and you're going away?

(*He hugs her tenderly and she bursts into tears, hiding her face in her hands*)

Don't cry, my little pet. I won't let them take you away. Papa will find you a nice young man from Naples. Someone from your own country, my little angel.

(*As he comforts her* ERRICO *enters softly from the street*)

ERRICO   Ama! Ama! (*Suddenly he sees* GENNARO. *He can hardly believe his eyes*) Dear God – Don Gennaro!

GENNARO   (*genuinely pleased to see him*) Errico! Errico as I live and breathe! (*He flings his arms around him*) I only got back half an hour ago. My God, the stories I've got to tell you.

ERRICO   But where on earth have you been?

GENNARO   Errico, my friend, how can I begin to tell you? Where to start? It's like a dream. It's like . . . I hear you're running a partnership with my wife. And it's going well, too. Congratulations.

ERRICO   (*glancing at* AMALIA) Oh that. Yes. Well . . . I tell you what, old man. Donna Amalia was only saying not half an hour back she was convinced you'd turn up sooner or later. And here you are. Amazing. And you couldn't have chosen a better moment.

GENNARO   Is that so?

ERRICO   Certainly. It's my birthday and, knowing that I was on my own, Donna Amalia insisted that I spend it here with her in the bosom of the family.

GENNARO   Well, what could be better? What a wonderful thing to do, Amalia. He's on his own, poor chap, and you've all rallied round to help. Well, it's at times like these that we should all stick together and be amongst friends. Ah, Don Errico, it's a dreadful time to be alive, believe me. Where I've been – my God, I can still hear

the guns now. And the shellings and the bombs and the
rockets. On and on and on. Never stopping for a second.
I only have to hear someone knocking on the door and
I jump clean out of my skin. I remember one time
when . . .

ERRICO (*hastily*) I know, I know. But don't think about it,
Don Gennaro. Put it right out of your mind. We've got
friends coming round tonight and we're really going to
live it up.

GENNARO Live it up? You can't be serious. Good God,
you all think the war's over, don't you? Well, it isn't. It
isn't. Not by a very very long way it isn't.

ERRICO (*pointing to decorations*) Yes, yes, old man. But
what do you think to all this little lot then?

GENNARO (*confused again and tired*) Very nice. Lovely.
Beautiful.

(MARIA *exits to her room*. FRANCO *enters from the street with
a huge roast in a pan covered with a white cloth*)

FRANCO (*blows a mock fanfare*) Here we are then, lads.
The roast lamb. In person. (*Suddenly sees* GENNARO)
Jees, Don Gennaro! How are you, my old mate?

GENNARO Franco, my dear old chap. So you've come
through it all as well, eh?

FRANCO Oh aye, I'm still alive and kicking. Miracles still
happen.

ERRICO Don Gennaro, this is the little birthday supper I
was telling you about. Roast lamb, roast potatoes and all
the trimmings.

GENNARO Roast lamb! Ye Gods, that looks good. And it
smells delicious. You know, there were times when if
something like that had come our way, we'd have killed
for it. Ripped each other apart with our bare hands. God,
what times those were. What times. Imagine us there in

the open country, crouched down in a ditch with shells and bombs raining down all around us. All hell let loose, Errico. Stuck there day and night with nothing to eat, nothing to drink. Seven of us huddled together with these two dead bodies. They'd been torn to bits by shrapnel, you see. And then suddenly out of the blue, without any warning . . . (FRANCO *who has been standing at the door looking out into the street shouts*)

FRANCO Here we are. Here it comes. The rest of the feast. (*Enter a man staggering under the weight of two more roasting tins*) This way, mate. Over here. Follow me. (*He leads the man into the scullery*)

GENNARO A four course meal! Ye Gods and little fishes. Yes, as I was saying – well, there we were crouched in this ditch with shells and bullets flying round all over the place, and suddenly, without any warning . . .

AMALIA Not now, Genna. Not now. Tell us all about it later. We're just about to lay the table.

GENNARO It's not a very long story.

AMALIA When we've eaten, Genna. We've got people coming round.

ERRICO All our friends.

GENNARO In that case I'd better go and get myself cleaned up. See what a bit of soap and water will do, eh? I'm a bit grubby, you see. Yes, I'm rather grubby if the truth be known.

ERRICO That's it, old man. Get yourself spruced up. You'll feel like a new man.

GENNARO (*moving off*) Yes, yes. And then I'll tell you something that'll really make your hair stand on end, Errico. The things I've seen! I tell you, the last war was a picnic compared to this one. An absolute doddle. (*Exits to bedroom.* AMALIA *tries not to look at* ERRICO, *who rather grumpily sits at chair by the front door. Enter* ASSUNTA *from street)*

ASSUNTA   I was wondering if you needed a hand, Donna Amalia.

AMALIA   Ah, Assunta. Just the person I need. I don't know if I'm on my arse or my elbow. Look. The table isn't even set yet.

ASSUNTA   No problem. Let's get cracking, shall we? (AMALIA *takes a tablecloth from a drawer and hands it to* ASSUNTA, *who starts to lay the table helped by* AMEDEO) You should see Aunt Adelaide. She's been ages getting herself all dolled up. She's got a new dress and it looks absolutely smashing on her. Honest to God, you wouldn't believe how much money she's making. She's coining it in. Mind you, she works hard for it. Oh yes, she . . . it's a smashing dress. I say it myself, but it's absolutely gorgeous. I'm not going to change, though. I'm going to carry on wearing my mourning. I'm coming like this.

(AMEDEO *potters off to the scullery to fetch something*)

Hey, is it true Don Gennaro's come back? Where's he hiding himself? Aunt Adelaide's full of it. She says he's ever so thin. She says he looks like something the dog's brought home. We were just talking about it. We were wondering about you two. You know, how you were taking it and whether Errico . . . well, it'll have to stop now, won't it?

ERRICO   What'll have to stop?

ASSUNTA   Oh nothing. Nothing at all really. I was only saying.

ERRICO   I'll tell you something, sister.

ASSUNTA   What?

ERRICO   You get right up my bloody nose.

ASSUNTA   Yes, I suppose I do. I'm like that, you see.

(AMEDEO *returns to help* ASSUNTA. AMALIA, *furious at*
ASSUNTA's *gaffe, exits to her room to get ready. Enter from
street* FEDERICO *and* PEPPE *and other people invited for the
meal. They all make for* ERRICO *with animated birthday
greetings. The men are all wearing snappy dark suits and the
women all have sumptuous furs and flashy jewellery. A few
moments later* ADELAIDE *arrives noisily in her Sunday best.
Some of the guests have brought bunches of flowers and others
baskets of fruit. All have brought gifts.* FRANCO *has taken it
upon himself to arrange everything decoratively round the room.*
ERRICO, *as star of the show, basks in it all, smiling his thanks
to one and all with a slightly patronising and superior air*)

PEPPE   Well, Errico, the birthday boy himself. You're the
man we've all got to drink to, eh?

ERRICO   No, no. This isn't for me. We've a change of
plans now. All this is for Don Gennaro's homecoming.

FEDERICO   Yes, I heard the poor old sod was back. Great
news, eh?

(*Enter* GENNARO)

PEPPE   Here he is. The man of the moment. Welcome
home, Don Gennaro.

GENNARO   Peppe! Wonderful to see you. (*He welcomes*
PEPPE *and then the whole company with handshakes and
hugging*)

PEPPE   For pete's sake, Don Gennaro, where have you
been all this time, you old bugger?

GENNARO   Ah, don't let's talk about it now. I'm back –
that's all that matters. It seems like a miracle, I know.
But here I am.

(Suddenly notices how everyone is dressed and looks down at his own tattered clothes. He feels totally out of place)

Oh, my Lord, what a glamorous lot you are. And just look at me. I'm letting you down, aren't I? I'm so sorry. Still, these are my battle honours you're looking at here. Oh yes. If this old tunic could speak, what a tale he'd have to tell. Just picture it, my friends – out in the middle of nowhere, crouching in this ditch with shells and God knows what raining down on us from every side.

(He sees that they are all nodding their heads out of politeness. But, nonetheless, he is determined to plough on)

Three days without food or water. Seven of us huddled in a ditch with two dead bodies torn to bits by shrapnel. And then all of a sudden, without any warning . . .

FEDERICO   Steady on, Don Gennaro. Everything's all right now, mate. You're back home. You're with friends. Forget it. Wipe it all out of you mind.

ADELAIDE   He's right, Don Gennaro. You've got to eat. And you've got to drink. We want to see the flesh put back on those old bones of yours.

FEDERICO   Too true, missus. The whole thing in a nut-shell. Hey, Don Gennaro, eat, drink – and that's an edict with immediate effect. (FRANCO *exits to the scullery.* PEPPE *takes* AMEDEO *by the arm and draws him downstage away from the others*)

PEPPE   Well then? Are you fit?

AMEDEO   No. It's off.

PEPPE   What do you mean – it's off?

AMEDEO   Because I don't want to end up in clink. Errico's been going on at me. And besides the old fellow's back now.

PEPPE   But it's a doddle, you stupid berk. Where's the risk? There's nothing to it. He leaves the car outside the road at the top of the slope. Simple. I've squared the night-watchman. In the morning they'll find him tied and gagged. Simple. What the hell can go wrong? (*They move away and continue talking in undertones*)

GENNARO   Well then, everyone. Let the party commence. On with the festivities. (*Enter* AMALIA *from her room followed by* MARIA. *She's wearing a magnificent stole of silver fur.* MARIA *goes off into a corner by herself*)

AMALIA   Welcome, everyone. (*They all cry out with admiration*)

PEPPE   Gordon Bennett, missus, you look fantastic. (*They all cry out in admiration*)

AMALIA   Thank you, thank you. Thank you so much. You're very kind. Assunta, go and tell Franco to start dishing up.

ASSUNTA   Right away. Oh, that stole. It's gorgeous. It's going to bring on one of my turns. (*Runs off to scullery trying to stifle her giggling*)

AMALIA   Well then, everyone. Please be seated. (*They sit themselves at the table.* GENNARO *looks around with bewilderment, eyeing his wife's appearance with more and more unease*)

ADELAIDE   Come on, Don Gennaro. Sit down. Park your arse, lad.

GENNARO   This is like something out of a film. Here I am back with you all, yet I can't believe my eyes. I keep thinking I'm dreaming. (*Slowly he sits down*)

ERRICO   Well, that's the way it goes, old man.

GENNARO   Yes, yes, I suppose it does. My goodness, what we went through. It wasn't the fact you had nothing to eat or nothing to drink. It was the fact that it preyed on your mind. Do you understand that? And then on top of it all there was death staring you in the face every minute of the day. As I was saying, we were right in the middle of nowhere, crouched up in this ditch away from the shells and the bombs and suddenly, without any warning, this truck looms up out of nowhere and . . .

ERRICO Ah, talking about trucks . . . Sorry, Don Gennaro, but if I don't mention it now, I'll forget it. Federico, there's a truck going for sale all taxed and licenced. Right? I'm going to look at it tomorrow, if you're interested.

FEDERICO Course I am. I'll come with you. And I'll bring Peppe as well.

ERRICO I shall want my ten per cent, you know.

PEPPE But of course. You're on, mate. We'll make a day out of it.

GENNARO Anyway, there we were in this ditch all seven of us huddled together with bombs dropping all around and . . .

PEPPE And the shells. Don't forget the shells, mate. (*Before* GENNARO *can reply* FRANCO *enters triumphantly with the roast lamb*)

FRANCO Here it is, lads. Here we go. Tuck in, eh? (*He puts it on the table in front of* AMALIA)

PEPPE By heck, I can't wait to get stuck into that, I tell you.

ASSUNTA And you must get stuck into it, too, Don Gennaro. We've got to fatten you up, haven't we?

GENNARO Have we?

ASSUNTA Course we have. Don't look so worried. Don't look so glum. It's all over now. It's all over and done with.

GENNARO All over and done with? What are you on about? What's over and done with?

ERRICO All right, all right, have it you own way, old man. But can we just for one moment concentrate on the festivities and forget all about your woes for an hour or two, eh?

(AMALIA *is serving and they all start to tuck in, jabbering and grinning.* GENNARO *watches silently for a moment or two and then stands up*)

GENNARO Ama, I'm just popping in there for a minute to see how Rituccia is. (*He goes towards her bedroom*)

ERRICO Don Gennaro, where are you going? You're not leaving us now? (*They all shout out in support of* ERRICO)

GENNARO No, I'm just going to sit with my daughter. She's a bit feverish, you see.

AMALIA I'll come with you.

GENNARO No, no, Ama. You stay with our guests. I don't seem to have any appetite. And I'm feeling tired. A bit weary. You stay at table. It's better for you to stay. (*As* GENNARO *makes to leave* MARIA *gets up and joins him*)

MARIA I'll come with you, papa.

ADELAIDE (*getting up*) Now, Don Gennaro, this isn't right, you know. It's not right and proper, love. I know you're upset. Well, you would be – what with all you went through in that ditch. But you're all right now. It's all nice and peaceful now. All you've gone through – it's in the past now, love.

GENNARO (*fairly tartly*) No. Far from it. You're making a big mistake. The war is very far from over. It's not even finished. Nothing is finished. Not by a long way.

(ADELAIDE *returns to table, a little miffed. As* GENNARO *shuffles off with* MARIA *he senses from her manner that something is wrong with her*)

GENNARO (*putting his arm round her*) Is anything the matter?

MARIA (*shaking her head*) No, papa. (*They exit. Silence for a moment. Then* FRANCO *comes in from scullery with two flasks of wine)*

FRANCO   *(blowing another mock fanfare)* Here we are again, lads. The wine! Eat, drink and be merry.

(They all exclaim with delight. They settle down to the meal. All is animation, joy and above all, noise)

CURTAIN

ACT THREE

(*Same room, next day. Late evening.*

The coloured lights in front of the shrine to the Madonna in the street have been switched off. CIAPPA *is sitting at the table.* GENNARO *is walking up and down, glancing occasionally into the street*)

CIAPPA (*after a pause*) I've often thought about you since that time I dropped in on you. Remember? The air raid. The bed. The corpse. Quite a night. I used to pop in if I was in the neighbourhood to see if they'd heard any news of you. I'm glad you're back. Pity I've had to come on a different errand this time. (*Pause*) Listen. I've got sons myself – three of them. But when you've been around as long as I have you get a nose for trouble. Know what I mean? You've got this sixth sense. You know when you can turn a blind eye, or when it's something more serious.

GENNARO I understand what you're saying, sergeant. And I thank you. At any other time what you've just told me would have sent me bananas. I wouldn't have been able to control myself. But now? What can I do? Throw the boy out of the house? Throw my daughter out of the house? Throw out my wife who didn't know how to be a mother?

CIAPPA   I'm afraid there's more to it than that, Don
Gennaro. As far as your son's concerned, I haven't told
you the whole story. I very much fear that I've no choice
but to arrest him.

GENNARO   (*shrugs*) If he's done something to deserve it
. . . well, it's up to you.

CIAPPA   I've had my eye on him for some time. And the
other one, Peppe. It's getting beyond a joke. No one can
leave their car parked for five minutes with those two
around. You look away for a second, and that's the last
you see of it. According to my information they've got a
job on tonight. So, if we catch them red-handed, I've only
one option – haul them both in.

GENNARO   If you have to, you have to.

CIAPPA · You mean you're not bothered?

GENNARO   No. If they're caught red-handed, that's their
look-out, isn't it?

(*Enter* ASSUNTA *from* RITUCCIA'*s room, full of anxiety*)

ASSUNTA   Isn't Donna Amalia back yet?

GENNARO   No.

ASSUNTA   Or Amedeo?

GENNARO   No.

ASSUNTA   Well, how long are they going to be? The
doctor's waiting for them in there. (*The* DOCTOR *comes
out of* RITUCCIA'*s room, followed by* ADELAIDE. *He's
young and newly qualified. He's businesslike and obviously knows
what he's about*)

DOCTOR   Is anyone back yet?

GENNARO   No one, doctor.

DOCTOR   Good God! I told them it was urgent. Where
the hell are they? We can't wait all night. That child is
seriously ill.

ADELAIDE Santa Anna! (ADELAIDE *and* ASSUNTA
start muttering the Ave Maria quietly)

DOCTOR She's in a very bad way. And you know why?
Because you idiots always leave it to the last possible
minute before you call me in.

ADELAIDE Vergine Immacolata! (*She bursts into the Ave
Maria again*)

DOCTOR It's always the same with you lot. It's a wonder
how you manage to stay alive.

ASSUNTA You know perfectly well why we do it. It's
because we think doctors bring bad luck.

DOCTOR And as a result you die. Good grief, what do
you expect when you don't call the doctor in till the last
minute? Bad luck! What impertinence! Anyway, bad
luck or not, the top and bottom of it is that the little girl
has not got long to live.

ADELAIDE Sant' Arcangelo Gabriele. Santa Rita, Santa
Rita, the poor child is named after you. Bring down your
goodness on her, we pray, and enfold her in your
bounteous love and pity. (ADELAIDE *and* ASSUNTA
break into the Ave Maria again)

DOCTOR It's no use calling on the saints. I'm sure it does
you great credit. Faith's a fine thing to have. But I tell
you this for nothing – unless someone gets here with the
prescription I made pretty damn quick, that child in
there is going to die.

ADELAIDE Doctor, what a wicked thing to say. It sounds
as though you're wishing it on the poor little mite.

DOCTOR Does it indeed?

ASSUNTA Yes, it does. You could at least give us some
hope. Surely to God the last word hasn't been said?

DOCTOR Oh yes it has, my dear. By me. By all means
let's keep hoping. There's no harm in that. The last thing

we want is to lose hope. And there's not the slightest need to. If that medicine comes in time, there's a ninety per cent chance she'll pull through. Without it? (*Shrugs*)

ADELAIDE Sant' Antonio e' Pusilleco! (ADELAIDE *and* ASSUNTA *return to* RITUCCIA's *room both praying hard*)

DOCTOR (*looking at watch*) It's getting late.

CIAPPA Surely to God it shouldn't be that difficult to find, doctor.

DOCTOR Everything's difficult to find these days, sergeant. Especially at this time of night. It's bad enough during the day. Medicine's like gold dust. The only place you can get it is on the black market. And even that can be dodgy unless you've got contacts. Well, I suppose I'd better give them a minute or two longer.

GENNARO I'm sorry about all this, doctor.

DOCTOR There's no need to be. It's me sounding off. It's just that it makes me furious that . . . (*Shrugs*) Oh, what the hell! (*He goes back into* RITUCCIA's *room*)

GENNARO 'The only place you can get it is on the black market.' (*Laughs bitterly*) When the doctor said the child would die if she didn't get the medicine, you should have seen her mother. Dashing round Naples like a mad woman. Hammering on doors. Banging on windows. And has she got it? Who knows? 'The only place you can get it is on the black market.' Jesus Christ, she went as white as a sheet.

(AMEDEO *comes running in from the street out of breath. He pulls up short when he sees* CIAPPA. *But then he recovers himself quickly*)

AMEDEO No good. Nothing. There's only one or two chemists open and they haven't got it. I've been right out to Furcello and Palmetto. I've tried everywhere. I knocked on every single door. Nothing. They all say:

'Tomorrow – if you're lucky.' (FRANCO *enters from the street, panting and collapses into a chair*)

FRANCO Bloody hell, my feet! (DOCTOR *comes in from* RITUCCIA's *room*)

DOCTOR Well?

FRANCO All I could get was this. I don't know if it's any use.

DOCTOR Well, if it's what I asked for, of course it will. (*Takes bottle and looks at label*) This is for scabies.

FRANCO Is that no good?

DOCTOR God, we've got a blithering idiot here.

FRANCO Hold on. (*Rummages in his pocket and produces a bottle*) What about this?

DOCTOR (*takes bottle and looks at it*) Wonderful. Just wonderful – if you're a nursing mother.

FRANCO Wait a minute. I've got something else. (*Rummages again*) Here we are. Pills. I don't know what they are, but they're bound to be medicine of some sort, aren't they?

DOCTOR They haven't got a label. What's the use of pills without a label? I wrote down specifically what I wanted, and you come back with pills without a label. Tremendous. Thank you very much.

FRANCO But, doctor, things aren't like they were before the war. These days we've got to make do with what we can get. I mean, when all's said and done this *is* medicine, isn't it? We've just got to make do with what we can get.

DOCTOR If you say that once more, I swear I'll . . . What the hell do you think I'm doing here? Trying to patch up the roof or something? (*Angrily writes out another prescription*) We'll have one more try. Take this to the address on here. It's an old colleague of mine. With a bit of luck he might have it in. And hurry. Don't hang around.

FRANCO   Right. It's not too far, is it?

DOCTOR   You can be there and back in ten minutes. And don't come back with something else, or I'll ram it down your bloody throat. Do I make myself clear?

FRANCO   Sure. Right. The address. Written down here, you say?

DOCTOR   (*almost screaming*) Get out! (*Composes himself as* FRANCO *hurries out*) Sorry about that. It's just that I get absolutely insane about these things. I get . . . Sorry. Excuse me. (*He exits into* RITUCCIA's *room*)

(AMEDEO *has been on edge ever since he came in, looking at* CIAPPA, *his father, the clock and into the street*)

AMEDEO   Mother's sure to have found something. I bet she'll be back in a bit. (*Pause. Then to* GENNARO) You'll be here for a while, won't you? Only, you see, I'm supposed to be meeting someone, you see.

(CIAPPA *and* GENNARO *exchange glances*)

GENNARO   Okay. You'd better go then.

AMEDEO   (*shiftily*) Well, it's something I can't very well put off, you see. It won't take long. I'll be straight back.

GENNARO   (*to* CIAPPA) You know, sergeant, it's been going through my mind that with one thing and another you must have your hands pretty full these days. Racketeers, wide boys, spivs, petty thieves. (*To* AMEDEO) How much of a hurry are you in, Amedeo?

AMEDEO   Well, not that much, I suppose.

GENNARO   Good. Sit down a minute. Yes, sergeant, it's a breeding ground for petty crime, is war.

CIAPPA   Very true, Don Gennaro.

GENNARO   All this smuggling and profiteering – false number plates, forged documents, car thieves. I can't help remembering something you said to me when you came round during the air-raid and I was playing the part of the corpse. You said: 'It may be sacrilege to touch the dead, but it would be even greater sacrilege to lay my hands on someone like you.'

CIAPPA   I did indeed.

GENNARO   There are certain things it's better to turn a blind eye to, aren't there?

CIAPPA   Oh yes.

GENNARO   People have to live. They have to get by the best way they can. You know perfectly well what they're up to, but you say to yourself: 'It's all a question of survival.' In spite of yourself you have a sneaking respect for someone with enough initiative, enough nous to get away with things. Like driving around in trucks with false papers. You say to yourself: 'Now there's someone with guts. He's on the ball, that one. He's helping to keep things going.' Oh, there've been dangers to it. They've chanced their arm, stuck their necks out, risked being gunned down on the road. But they've got things done. Who can blame them? And look at all this prostitution. So what, sergeant? War brings misery. Misery brings hunger. And what does hunger bring? Look around you. Look at the whores in the streets. Some do it out of sheer misery. Some do it out of hunger. Some because they know no better. Some because they were too trusting. But then it passes. It's all forgotten. It's over and done with. War's always like that. Finally we all have to pay for it. War is paid for with everything we possess. But when it comes to theft – no, no, no, no. No one can blame the war for becoming a thief. Oh yes, you can blame it for plenty of other things. But a thief is born. You can't say of a thief that he's a Neapolitan or a Roman. Or Milanese, English, French, German, American. A thief is simply a thief. He's on his own. He doesn't have parents.

He doesn't have a family. He doesn't have a nationality. And there's no place for him here.

AMEDEO Why are you making me stay and listen to all this balls?

GENNARO We've got an appalling reputation here in Naples. We don't deserve it, but, my God, have we got it. People have only to hear the word, Naples, and they're on their guard. Every time some big robbery hits the headlines – it doesn't matter where it is – people say: 'Ah, it's Naples that's behind all that. What do you expect? It's always been like that.' Gossip, gossip. Chatter, chatter. 'In the docks – did you hear? A freighter's gone missing with its entire cargo. Naples, of course. It's bound to be the Naples connection.' A truck disappears. Chatter, chatter. 'Oh yes, I heard all about it. One truck – more like five hundred. Oh yes. All vanished into thin air. Never been seen again. Well, that's Naples all over for you.' It isn't true, of course. None of it's true. But it's the reputation we have, and it sticks. (*To* AMEDEO) And that's where you come in. You're the ones, you young-sters, who've got to try and dig your city out of the mire. You've got to set a good example, so that when you hear people slagging off Naples, you can stand up to them and say with a clear conscience: 'Yes, there are thieves there. But there are honest people, too. Hundreds and thousands of honest people. Just like there are in any other part of the world.' But to say that, my son, you have to have a clear conscience.

AMEDEO All right, there's no need to go on about it. I can't stand around here listening to all this rubbish. I've got a mate to meet.

GENNARO Off you go then. Got your scarf?

AMEDEO (*feeling in his pocket*) Yes, I think so.

GENNARO And you'd better take a coat, too.

AMEDEO What do I need a coat for?

GENNARO In case you're back late. It's getting chilly out there.

AMEDEO I'm not going to be late. I've already told you. (*Shrugs*) All right then, if it makes you happy. (*Takes his coat and goes to street door with it over his arm*) Cheers. I won't be long. (*Exits*)

CIAPPA I guess I must be off, too.

GENNARO All the best, sergeant. And thank you.

CIAPPA You're welcome. Good night, Don Gennaro. I hope the little girl pulls through.

(*CIAPPA goes out as MARIA enters from RITUCCIA's room. She crosses to the dresser, takes a cup and goes back with it. She does not look at GENNARO, who follows her with his eyes full of tenderness and pain. At the same time PEPPE enters cautiously from the street, smoking a dog end. He seems suspicious and tentative. He spots GENNARO*)

PEPPE Ah, Don Gennaro. Evening. Any sign of Amedeo?

GENNARO You've just missed him.

PEPPE Ah. We were supposed to be meeting, you see. (*Glances at his watch*) He's a bit early. How's the little girl?

GENNARO So so.

PEPPE I'm not too good myself to tell you the truth. This shoulder's giving me gyp. I can hardly move it.

GENNARO Cars.

PEPPE What do you mean – cars?

GENNARO I thought you said your shoulder was bad.

PEPPE Bad? It's giving me hell.

GENNARO It'll be the cars then.

PEPPE I don't get it. What have cars got to do with it?

GENNARO You're driving with the window open. Your shoulder's in a draught all the time.

PEPPE Ah yes. The draught. No, actually, it's not that, Don Gennaro. It's to do with . . . Look, the money's coming in all right, but it takes it out of you. I'm shattered. I'm going to have to tell Amedeo I need a break.

GENNARO You do that, Peppe. What sort of break are you talking about? Two years?

PEPPE Two years? I should cocoa. Very nice, if you can get it, mind you, but . . . No, what I'd like, Don Gennaro, what I dream about is finding a place right off the beaten track. Miles and miles from anywhere. You know, some place where I don't have to see anyone or speak to anyone. Know what I mean? Something like the Trappists really.

GENNARO Something on the monastic side.

PEPPE That's it. You've got it. Nothing plush. Something very very simple. Just a single room would do.

GENNARO A cell, perhaps.

PEPPE Absolutely spot on. A cell all to yourself! And there's someone constantly on hand outside to look after you and pamper you and cosset you and . . .

GENNARO . . . and bring you food dead on the dot every mealtime.

PEPPE Right.

GENNARO And you won't have to bother your head about what you're going to eat. That's always decided for you, isn't it? That bloke outside. Takes all those cares off your shoulders, eh? A really reliable sort.

PEPPE Sure. Even if you have to pay him.

GENNARO Oh, there's no need for that. It's so much nicer, anyway, to be waited on by someone who doesn't need paying. Do you know, I like the idea of this set-up of yours, Peppe. A nice little room with a nice little window with nice little bars on it, eh?

PEPPE   Oh no, I don't fancy that. I don't fancy bars on the windows.

GENNARO   But you'd need them.

PEPPE   What for?

GENNARO   Well, I thought you were hankering for somewhere nice and isolated. And these days, Peppe, old chap, what with all the crime about, it's difficult to know who's a friend and who isn't. So you'll need to feel safe and secure in there. And these monastery places all have bars on the windows, you know.

PEPPE   Yes. I suppose they do.

GENNARO   I admire you, Peppe. You've certainly worked out the best place to go to be well looked after and insulated from the cares of the world outside.

PEPPE   Too bloody true, mate. I've got it all worked out. There are no flies on me.

GENNARO   So there you are then.

(PEPPE *gets up to leave rubbing his shoulder painfully*)

PEPPE   This shoulder! It's so stiff I can hardly move it.

GENNARO   Not to worry. Just do one last job and then take a nice long rest, eh?

PEPPE   That's it. (*He starts to go*) All the best then.

GENNARO   I'll come and pay you a visit in your little cell.

PEPPE   Yes?

GENNARO   Sure. I'll bring you some cigarettes.

PEPPE   Terrific. I'll be expecting you then.

GENNARO   Of course. I'll be coming to see my son, so I might as well come and see you at the same time.

PEPPE   What?

GENNARO   So long, Peppe. All the best, my friend.
(PEPPE *exits to street, slightly bewildered. A moment later* ERRICO *enters*)

ERRICO Good evening, Don Gennaro. And how's Rituccia this evening?

(*No response from* GENNARO)

I've just run into Franco. He says she's just the same.
Still got a temperature.

(*Still no reply from* GENNARO)

I've been asking all over for the medicine with the
prescription here. Nothing. All they say is: 'Tomorrow –
if you're lucky.'

(*In face of* GENNARO'*s silence he sits down so as not to meet his
gaze. After a while he forces himself to speak*)

It's a dreadful business, this. Dreadful. Especially as
you've just got back and . . . (*Pause*) Listen, it's not that
she's been neglected. Far from it. But you know how it is
with young kids. You say to yourself, ah, it's nothing
much, nothing to worry about. They're always getting
something the matter with them, kids. And kids being
what they are, bugger me, they spring a surprise on you
and next thing they're back on their feet again tear-arsing
all over the place as though nothing's ever been wrong
with them. (*Pause*) Donna Amalia doesn't deserve all this,
you know. She's the sort of person who runs herself into
the ground looking after her family. All the time you were
away the worry she felt about you was etched deep into
her face. You could see it in her eyes – the sadness, the
despair, the concern. I tell you this, old man, if anyone
ever says a bad word to you about Donna Amalia, he's an
out and out shit. A regular arsehole. You see, I can say
these things because I'm a friend of the family. A real
friend. I've concerned myself with all its worries and all
its problems. Take Amedeo, for example. Well, I've tried

to give him bits of fatherly advice from time to time. You weren't here, so I felt it was my duty.

(*Silence.* ERRICO *is now thoroughly discomfited*)

A woman on her own. No man in the house. Well, you know how it is. People are coming and going all the time so they put two and two together. But I can give you my word of honour, I can swear on my mother's grave, that Donna Amalia has always respected you and still respects you. Unreservedly. Passionately. (*Pause*) You've been treating me coldly since this morning. I've noticed it. Oh yes, it's been patently obvious. And that's why I've come back – to see you and have it out. For God's sake, Don Gennaro, are we men or are we children? If it's anyone who should be making excuses it's me. Not Donna Amalia. Not her. As far as she's concerned, you can be absolutely easy in your mind. Her conscience is snow white. (*Pause*) I'm leaving tonight for Calabria. Well, when you travel at night you never know whether you're going to arrive in one piece. Many people never arrive at all. And that is why I wanted to make my peace with you and . . . and . . .

(GENNARO *still ignores him. He gets up to go*)

If there's anything I can do at any time. (*He goes to the street door*) I hope the little girl gets better.

(*No response*)

Right then. I bid you good night, Don Gennaro. Good night. (*He exits.* GENNARO *does not move. A moment later* FRANCO *returns and makes his way to* RITUCCIA'*s room*)
FRANCO   Nothing. Sweet Fanny Adams. All I've found is this box of pills. I'll take them in to the quack now. (*He*

goes into RITUCCIA's *room.* AMALIA *comes in from the street.*
She is a changed woman, defeated, exhausted and looking years
older. She is no longer capable of pretending or putting on a front.
Her old accent has returned. She slumps into a chair by the table)

AMALIA   Nothing. I've been everywhere. I've knocked on
every door in Naples. Not a sniff. Somebody must have
it. But they won't part with it. They'd rather see a child
die. How the hell can they live with themselves? Profiteering on medicine! Holding back on it so they can push
up the price! I think it's downright criminal. It is. It is.
Downright criminal. (*She goes into* RITUCCIA's *room.*
GENNARO *follows her with his eyes.* RICCARDO *enters from
the street. He has a dark shabby raincoat over his pyjamas*)

RICCARDO   Excuse me. Not intruding, am I?

GENNARO   No. Come in.

RICCARDO   Good evening, Don Gennaro. I don't want to
make a nuisance of myself, but I hear you're in need of
some medicine for your poor little girl. (*Takes out a small
box from his raincoat pocket*) Would this be it?

GENNARO   Sit yourself down, Don Riccardo. (*Calls*)
Doctor! Doctor, have you got a moment?

DOCTOR   (*offstage*) Coming. (*Enters*) Yes? What is it?

GENNARO   This gentleman says he may have what we're
looking for.

DOCTOR   Where? Let me see. (*He examines the box*) Yes.
Yes, this is just what I'm looking for.

RICCARDO   Good. It's the merest coincidence, but six
months ago I had my second daughter down with the
same thing.

DOCTOR   Well, what a stroke of luck, eh? If you'll just
hand it to me I'll . . .

RICCARDO   Well, as a matter of fact, no, doctor I'd prefer
to give it to Donna Amalia myself, if you don't mind.

GENNARO   (*calling*) Amalia! Come out here a moment.

It's Don Riccardo to see you. (AMALIA *comes out of* RITUCCIA's *bedroom followed by* FRANCO)

RICCARDO Ah, Donna Amalia, good evening to you.

AMALIA (*sharply*) What do you want?

RICCARDO Well, as it so happens by a fortunate chance I happen to have the medicine the doctor prescribed for your little girl. I've taken the liberty of bringing it with me.

AMALIA (*going for her purse*) How much?

RICCARDO Well now, let me see. What would you like to give me back, eh? Everything I ever had is yours now. You've taken the lot – my house, my apartments, my wife's trinkets, our linen, family mementoes, everything. I had to come to you cap in hand, begging, grovelling, for a handful of rice for my youngest daughter. Well then, Donna Amalia, now it's your daughter we're talking about.

AMALIA But this is medicine. This is a matter of life and death.

(GENNARO *moves away and leaves them to it. So does* FRANCO, *not sure what is going on*)

RICCARDO Of course. And you're quite right to imply that without the medicine your daughter will die. But, Donna Amalia, if I hadn't let you strip me of the very shirt off my back, wouldn't my children have died also? Of hunger? Of disease? You see, my dear lady, sooner or later we all come to the point where we have no choice but to knock on a neighbour's door. At this very moment I know you'd give me anything I cared to ask for. Well, suppose it came into my head to have you running all round Naples as I had to in order to find a bit of semolina when one of my little ones was ill? Supposing I said to you: 'Go on, Donna Amalia, enjoy yourself. Start running round from house to house in a panic, hammering on doors and rattling on shutters and pleading and begging. You'll love it. It's the most tremendous fun. It's wonderful.' But I won't. No, I won't do that. I just want you to realise that there comes a time when we are called upon to hold out a helping hand to one another. That's all I've got to say. Nothing more. (*Hands the box to the* DOCTOR) There you are, doctor. I think Donna Amalia understands my point now. Well then, I'd best be going. Good night to you all. Best wishes to the little one. (*He goes out.* AMALIA *motions the* DOCTOR *impatiently towards* RITUCCIA's *room and follows him inside*)

FRANCO   What a carry-on, eh?

GENNARO   (*shrugs*) So how have you been making out, my old chum? How many millions have you got stashed away.

FRANCO   Me? You've got to be joking. I'm so broke every time I eat a tomato sandwich I feel like bleeding royalty. I did have a go at one or two little projects, but none of them came to anything. I gave up in the end. I went in with Pascalino, the painter, one time. We managed to get hold of fifty kilos of dried figs. I said to him: 'Tell you what we'll do – we'll hold onto them for a bit and wait for the price to go up.' You can guess what happened, can't you? We buried the figs, and when we came to dig them up, they were full of maggots. So we washed them and left them to dry off. Guess what happened. Terrific. Half of them were eaten by mice the rest had gone bad. Ach, there's plenty I could do, I guess, if I wanted to, but what's the point? The missus was killed in an air-raid. Typical cock-up, that was, too. We were in the shelter. We were standing as close together as you and me are now. And there were bombs falling right, left and centre,

and there were the two of us arguing. I ask you – at a
time like that and we were arguing. 'For Christ's sake,
keep your voice down,' I said. 'People are looking at us.'
But no. On and on she went. Yak, yak, yak. And then
down came this bloody great bomb. Bang! Right where
we were standing. A direct hit. One minute she was
there. Next minute she wasn't. She'd just had time
enough to say to me: 'When we get out of here, I'll beat
the living shits out of you.' And then – bang! She died
instantly without knowing what hit her. The best way to
go, if you ask me. So, as I say, I've got no one to worry
about but myself. So why should I want to go into
business?

GENNARO   I'd like you to do me a small favour tomorrow.

FRANCO   Sure.

GENNARO   I'd like my cubicle put back where it was.

FRANCO   No problem.

GENNARO   What happened to the wood? Did it get turfed
out or burnt?

FRANCO   No. It's all in one piece. I took it down myself
and stacked it in Pascalino's shed. It's still there.

GENNARO   Splendid. And you can put it back exactly
where it was?

FRANCO   Dead easy. I'll show you. (*As he leads* GEN-
NARO *to show him where he'll put the cubicle the* DOCTOR
comes in from RITUCCIA's *room followed by* AMALIA,
ADELAIDE *and* ASSUNTA)

DOCTOR   Right then, I'll be off. There's no need to worry
too much. She just has to get through the night. Once
she's over the worst, she'll soon be on the mend. I'll be
back early tomorrow and I'm sure I'll be able to give you
good news. Goodnight, then.

ADELAIDE AND ASSUNTA   Good night, doctor. (*He exits into street.* AMALIA *slowly sits down, tired and defeated*)

ADELAIDE   Now then, Donna Amalia, love, everything's going to be all right. You've got to keep your pecker up. The doctor was only worried because he hadn't got the right medicine. But now he's got it, you can see he's like a pig in do-dah. He's told you, hasn't he – she's just got to get through the night. You'll see – come tomorrow and she'll be jumping over five-barred gates. Well, I mustn't stop here megging like this. We'd best be going to see to the carrots. Give us a shout if you want anything. You know where to find me.

ASSUNTA   Good night, Donna Amalia. And don't worry.

(ADELAIDE *and* ASSUNTA *go out into the street.* FRANCO *sits in the chair by the front door.* GENNARO *stands there, looking fixedly at* AMALIA. *She looks uncomfortable and finally breaks the silence between them*)

AMALIA   Why do you keep staring at me like that? I only did what everyone else was doing. I had to look after myself. There was no one to turn to. No one. (*Pause*) Why do you keep staring at me and not saying anything? You've been staring at me and not saying a word ever since the morning. What am I supposed to have done? What are people saying about me?

GENNARO   You really want me to tell you? (*Pause*) All right then, I will. (*To* FRANCO) Do you mind? I'll see you in the morning, eh?

FRANCO   Sure. I'll be here first thing. See you.

GENNARO   You're sure you can fix it?

FRANCO   Like a dream, old mate. Like a dream. Tarra then. (*Exits*)

GENNARO   (*closing the door softly behind him*) I suppose in a

way that child in there is one of the casualties of the war,
too. What happened to her is just like what's been
happening to our country. You know, Ama, when I got
back here, I was expecting to find my family either wiped
out or carrying on with their lives as honestly as we
always had in the past. And I came back. And nobody
wanted to know. Last time, the last war, everyone was
clamouring to hear about it. They wanted to know
everything that had happened. Every scrap. Every
morsel. There was no satisfying them. When I ran out of
things to tell them, I had to make up stories. I was
bombarded with questions. Everywhere I went I was
mobbed by kids. 'Cor, a real life soldier.' 'Tell us about
the war.' 'Have a drink, soldier. Have a fag.' Why the
difference this time, Ama? I'll tell you – because no one's
heart was in it this time. It was forced on us. It wasn't
something we believed in. And then quite suddenly along
came money. All those thousand lire notes raining down
on you. You completely lost your heads, didn't you? At
first it started to come in a little bit at a time. Then it
built up. More and more came along. A hundred thousand. And then a million. And then figures didn't mean
anything to you. Millions, billions, trillions – just figures.
(*He takes two or three bundles of occupation notes from the dresser
drawer and shows them to* AMALIA) Look at all this lot.
Millions and millions of lire. And you don't see the
absurdity of it all, do you? To you there's nothing more
important in the whole world than this mass of paper.
Not to me. I've been away. I didn't see it come in bit by
bit. I saw it all when I came back in one fell swoop. All of
it. And I look at these pathetic scraps of paper and I just
can't take them seriously. Scraps of paper. Madness. (*He
hurls the notes in the air in front of* AMALIA'*s face*) Think

about it, Ama. I touch all this and I don't feel a thing. I thought you were supposed to feel shock waves of thrill racing through you when you touched thousand lire notes. I thought the heart was supposed to throb and the blood go racing through your veins. Maybe if I'd been here all the time, it would have gone to my head as well. Who knows? (*Pause*) Last night, in there with Rituccia, Maria told me everything. Every single thing, Ama. So what should I do? Throw her out on the streets? Most fathers would. And not only here in Naples. All over the world. Oh yes, they'd throw her out like a shot. And you, Ama? What about you who didn't know how to be a mother to her daughter? What am I supposed to do with you? Kill you? Christ, as if there weren't enough tragedy in the world. As if there weren't enough killing and mourning. And what about Amedeo? Amedeo, the thief. Oh yes, Ama, your son is a thief. He steals. He's a thief. But then maybe he's the only one I don't have to worry about, because it's out of my hands now. It's for other people to decide his fate. Ah yes, I think it's beginning to come home to you now, Ama. What it's brought home to me is this – my place is here. When a family goes to pieces, it's for the father to shoulder the responsibilities as best he can. (*Points to* RITUCCIA's *room*) If everyone were to take a look in there, they'd all see they had to take some responsibility for the mess we're in. Every single person in the world. (*Pause*) Well then, Ama, all we can do now is wait. You heard what the doctor said – we must see the night through. (*He goes to the street door and opens it. Noises of city bustle*)

AMALIA   What happened to us, Genna? What happened?
GENNARO   The war, Ama.
AMALIA   I just don't know. I just don't know. (MARIA

comes out from RITUCCIA's *room, carrying a small bowl and makes her way to the scullery*)

GENNARO Maria, would you mind heating me up some coffee?

(*Without replying* MARIA *crosses to a little table in the corner, lights a spirit lamp and puts a small coffee pot on it*)

AMALIA I used to go out in the morning and do my shopping. Amedeo would take Rituccia to school on his way to work. I'd come back and do the cooking. What's happened? In the evening we'd all sit round the table and say grace before eating. What's happened? (*Enter* AMEDEO *from street*)

AMEDEO How is she?

GENNARO We got the medicine. The doctor's done all he can. Now we just have to wait to see what the morning brings. You didn't keep your appointment then?

AMEDEO No. I changed my mind. It didn't seem right somehow with Rituccia ill.

GENNARO No, it wasn't right. I'm glad you came back. (*He gives* AMEDEO *a warm hug*) Go in and sit with your sister a little while, eh? She's still a bit fretful.

AMEDEO Right. I will.

GENNARO If she's better tomorrow, I'll come with you and we'll see about getting your old job back at the Gas Company.

AMEDEO Oh, that'd be wonderful, papa. (*He hugs him again and goes off into* RITUCCIA's *room.* MARIA *has heated the coffee and takes a cup to* GENNARO. *He gives her a kiss of forgiveness.*)

MARIA Papa! (*Somehow she seems liberated by the kiss and goes almost gaily into* RITUCCIA's *room.* GENNARO *is about to drink his coffee, when he sees* AMALIA *sitting tired, defeated and dejected. He goes to her*)

GENNARO Have a cup of coffee, Ama. All we can do now is wait. We must see the night through.

CURTAIN

METHUEN CLASSICAL GREEK DRAMATISTS